ILLUMINATIONS
FOR A NEW ERA

Understanding These Turbulent Times

A Matthew Book with Suzanne Ward

ISBN 0-9717875-3-0

Library of Congress
2003105560

This book was printed in the United States of America
Cover photograph by Michael Ward

MATTHEW BOOKS
P.O. Box 1043
Camas, Washington 98607

www.matthewbooks.com
suzy@matthewbooks.com

ACKNOWLEDGEMENTS

Although I have prepared the material and dealt with the publishing issues of the three MATTHEW BOOKS – *Matthew, Tell Me About Heaven, Revelations For A New Era* and this one – I am not their author. The various authors are not on Earth, so as the book's editor, I acknowledge with heartfelt thanks (however belatedly by this formal means) the people whose enthusiasm, encouragement and assistance have helped bring these books to life.

Jean Hudon introduced the books and has continued publicizing them and Matthew's messages on his worldwide network.

Russ Michael, whose global network has publicized the books too, also urged foreign publishers to review them.

Panos Aximakaros is publishing Greek, German, Spanish, Italian, Dutch and French editions.

Monica Visan published the books in Romanian, the first editions in any language to reach bookstores.

Ho-Chi Book Publishing Company, Taiwan publishers of medical texts, published *Matthew, Tell Me About Heaven* in Chinese as a spiritual complement to their clinical line.

Many individuals without global networks or publishing companies have been unconditionally supportive of the books:

My husband, Robert Chapman, whose understanding of my commitment to this greater purpose of my life has enabled me to devote most of my time since February 1994 to recording transmissions, working with the material, and persevering in getting it published;

My son Eric, whose generosity made possible MATTHEW BOOKS publishing company;

My daughter Betsy and my son Michael, who like Eric, have never doubted their brother Matthew's messages or thought their mother mad;

Iris Freelander, whose belief in my mission throughout the years of efforts to get the books published has been unflagging;

Betsy Jones-Moreland, an animal rescuer for over 30 years, and Gila Cohen, a hospice worker in Israel who helps all in need – their lives are an inspiration to me;

Nancy Leggett, who has directed her powerful energetic influence toward the books and the wellbeing of our family;

Taylore Vance and Roi Halsey, who have done the same and also bolstered my confidence through their spiritual healing classes;

Wilma Laan, whose interest in having Dutch editions led to the translation arrangement with Jeanne Mets and Ems Treves;

Michael Joseph, Eve Howard, Randy Mitchell, Antares, Bobbie Sandoz, Chooi-Chin Goh and Jean Hudon, whose book reviews are posted on www.matthewbooks.com; and

William Zach, webmaster and designer of that web site.

My gratitude also goes out to the hundreds of people who have written their appreciation for the books and have recommended and shared them far and wide. You know from my replies to your messages that your sentiments have been invaluable in assuring me that the purpose of these books is being fulfilled.

To all of you named and unnamed benefactors of the MATTHEW BOOKS, my boundless thankfulness to you for adding light to them and to the world.

ILLUMINATIONS
FOR A NEW ERA

CONTENTS

PART I   OF TIMELY IMPORTANCE

PART II   OTHER ILLUMINATIONS

PART III   TALKING WITH GOD

PART IV   MORE FROM OTHER WORLDS

PART V   MATTHEW: AN UPDATE

PART VI   WAR

FOREWORD

For readers whose first acquaintance with the MATTHEW BOOKS is this one, I shall mention that I am a channel for Matthew, my son who left Earth life in 1980, at age 17, and for many other off-planet souls who telepathically transmit information to me. Their messages here, just as in the series' two previous books, are meant to enlighten, guide and comfort us during this unprecedented time in Earth's history.

A recap of other signposts for first-time MB readers: Just as in the first two books, the selection of material for this one comes under the guidance of the Council of Nirvana (Nirvana is the proper name of the realm we call Heaven). While each book does stand alone, material in the first, *Matthew, Tell Me About Heaven,* aids in a thorough comprehension of the second, *Revelations For A New Era.* Likewise, those books provide background information for this one. Sprinkled throughout are references to one or the other of those books and its pertinent chapter with detailed explanations of topics only touched upon in this book, where there just is no way to adequately summarize that spectrum of information.

When I am "open," my energy registration automatically invites Matthew and any other light being into my thoughts and feelings. That's why you'll notice on occasion that my mental questions or reactions are addressed by whoever is transmitting during the "sittings," my term for recording the sessions at the computer as differentiated from telepathic conversations wherever I may be.

During several months in 1996 and 1997 the dark forces were seriously disrupting energetic connections, and Matthew's and my communication line was stabilized by about 100 souls.

Sometimes Matthew spoke alone and the group strengthened his connection with me, and other times the message was from all of them – a synthesis of their collective knowledge transmitted by one voice. When that reinforcement of souls no longer was necessary, occasionally a group came with Matthew just because they enjoyed doing so.

To explain my editing of the material I receive from Matthew, I preserve his phraseology and the integrity of all the information, but to the extent possible I reduce redundancy. One way is combining parts of different transmissions (including those circulated intact on the Internet), retaining the essence that serves the entire chapter and eliminating the passages that would be repetitious in their new context. Another is by cutting those same kinds of explanations in later chapters; the information was necessary in the individual messages, but it isn't in this book format. Still, a fair amount of repetition is unavoidable because the subjects are so widely relevant: The negativity that fear creates; love, the greatest power in the universe, and light, love's scientific expression; and the dark forces, that power battling the light for dominance on Earth.

Usually Matthew uses male pronouns to indicate both male and female. He asks the same of readers that he asked of me when our telepathic connection opened: *"Please accept this as intended, only for ease of my speaking and your hearing and NEVER as a suggestion of male priority in any respect."*

For all readers: The messages are not necessarily in chronological order, but rather what I hope is the most logical order of explanation – if such is even possible with this variety of information – and I recommend reading from start to finish. Some long sittings are divided into chapters, which accounts for the same dates in a few places. When parts of related material in different sittings are combined into a chapter, it is dated according to the information most recently received.

If you wonder (understandably!) why transmissions received in 1996-1999 are included here instead of one of this book's predecessors, in a few cases I'm claiming "technological error." Files were damaged during computer repair a few years ago and I missed some in the one-by-one conversion process. In my recent review of the old print-outs of those files, some sections prompted the Yes "nudge." However, except for those few cases, it was intended that this material not be released before "its season."

Especially during the past two years, decisions of the United States presidential administration have been on global center stage, and although some material herein deals with these, this book is not a political forum. Simply, the US government's activities are pivotal to stirring soul-level awareness on a worldwide basis. The current polarity – war and violence vs. peace and harmony – showcases our planet's evolution in the much vaster universal happenings.

In the previous books I cut many of my parts of conversations with Matthew and created a natural transition for his continuing. The Council's guidance here was to leave more of my contributions intact. While I'm not really comfortable about my larger role here, I do understand the reason, which also applies to the selection of messages for this book.

I am not alone in having alternating feelings of optimism and discouragement about what's happening in our world. We are here where it's all going on, the events that evoke fright, sorrow and rage as well as encouragement at the signs of heartening changes, and we are affected by all. Matthew and the others are "up there" where they see everything evolving and know we are moving steadily into the era of peace and love on Earth. By including my questions and comments, this book can reflect both the emotional seesaw here and the higher purpose in which world events are playing out our evolutionary role.

Matthew's sister Betsy, who was almost three when he was born, told the neighbor who came to greet our new baby that his name was Mashew. Although the nickname "Mash" that came from that eventually was discarded by the rest of the family, I continued to use that special endearment on occasion. I still do, so I left it in our talks that were chosen for this book.

Matthew's life has changed considerably since we first talked nine years ago, when he was a medical assister for souls making transition. *(NOTE: The personal welcome and customized treatment of each soul is described in detail in "Transitioning Souls," in* Matthew, Tell Me About Heaven.*)* You'll read about his current service and a unique celebration in that wondrous realm we call Heaven.

Just as in the second book, Matthew is not the only source of information. There also are presentations by representatives of extraterrestrial realms and God.

Just as this is not a political forum, it is not a religious forum, either. If there can be such a term as *"a religious"* in the same way that there is atonal music, that could be ascribed here. However, *spiritual* is the best – it describes the tenor of *everything* in this book.

That said, God is what I call the supreme being of our universe because of my Christian religious indoctrination. But the other names by which He is known equally serve, and if applicable, please consider your own designation for the supreme being in place of mine. *(NOTE: Formal presentations in* Revelations For A New Era *chapters "Hierarchy of Creator" and "God" explain the differences between Creator and God, the ultimate powers in the cosmos and our universe, respectively.)*

God chose the parts of our conversations He wants included here: *"I am not understood there. You know now who I am and you must tell others."* Many of our talks were about family and friends, thus the messages were private and in that confidence were passed on to the requesters. In the excerpts selected for this book, I correctly identified only my son Eric, whose permission I asked.

PART I

OF TIMELY
IMPORTANCE

THE HEALING POWER OF LOVE

October 1, 2002

MATTHEW: Mother, good morning! I've been nudging you to come to the computer because you are having many conflicting thoughts: *What's happening? I don't know what to believe anymore.*

To you, what is happening in your world is unacceptable, and you see that reported events are being greeted with reactions ranging from information overload and burnout to fear and helplessness. You're wishing the information you have been given could be widely known for encouragement and enlightened response, yet you realize that you also are falling alternately into one or the other extremes because what is happening is *repeatedly* happening. Or so you are thinking.

S: Matthew, that IS what's happening!

MATTHEW: Mother, the FULL truth of happenings exists within the godself, and you are rummaging in your head rather than listening to your soul connection. You want *dramatic* steps toward peace and love throughout the world so everyone will recognize this surge in light energy and embrace it with the ecstasy that will bring Heaven on Earth ever more swiftly.

You have been told time and time again that dramatic results of the light forces' efforts *are* underway, but in your impatience, you want *proof* of this truth to be so apparent and widespread that not even one soul on Earth can miss it. As my mother, you want this because you want my word that harmony and peacefulness, kindness and fairness, justice and love *will* reign on Earth to be proven true. As the total you, you want to see during your Earth lifetime people living in that glory.

S: Matthew, yes, I DO want to see that, and naturally I want you to be known as giving truthful information! Unless someone actually experiences telepathic contact, believing ANY informa-tion via that means requires a considerable stretch of faith. But all of the universal laws do – believing they even exist requires some assurance that our belief isn't misplaced, so I don't under-stand why their effects aren't more evident!

MATTHEW: Mother dear, you are not alone in this, and that is exactly why I want to have this discussion. What is hap-pening is like the eye of a hurricane but in reverse. The revela-tions of the widespread corruption and deception on Earth require a commensurate need for assurance that these disclosures are evi-dence of HEALING, not of ever and ever greater "evil."

A monumental amount of light is being beamed to Earth to reveal these wounds, but their extent is almost too much to assim-ilate. So people are tuning out the *positive* frequency – that only if these situations are known, "come to light," can they be fixed – and instead they're in suspension waiting for someone honest to do the fixing. Those who are hurting financially due to the dis-closures are tuning into the *negative* frequency of despair, fear or vengeance. We must get all of these souls to tune into the *right* frequency, the LIGHT frequency!

It may sound simplistic, but it is true: The pain of Earth *HAS* to come to light so it can be healed. As long as it remains in the dark-ness that spawned it, it never can be healed. LOVE is the only essence in the universe that can heal pain, whether in a single soul or in a force field of such power that you cannot begin to imagine it.

Light, the visible and inseparable component of love, is being infused into Earth herself and her collective life forms to accomplish the healing. While your world may seem hopelessly out of control, it is *NOT!* It is within each individual where the control lies, each soul's unlimited capacity for LOVE.

LIGHT AND LOVE IN ACTION

September 22, 2002

MATTHEW: Light is light, Mother, just as truth is truth, so it's not as if your tacking "divine" onto light promotes it into "lightest." Simply, light *IS* divine! The light attributed to the sun actually is from God through the Christed realm that was made by Creator, ruler of the cosmos, so regardless of how light is manifested within each person or how it is directed scientifically, it all comes from Creator. This self-generation of energy in light form is from that top technical expertise, you might say, so scientists who think they have gotten around the need for a supreme being are not as savvy as they think.

Light is the composition, or ingredient, of the soul, and it is the light streamers that identify each one regardless of its spiritual station, physical body or discarnate state, or location in our universe. Those souls referred to as "light beings" reflect it in their spirituality and morality, but even those who are referred to as "dark" retain a spark, otherwise they could have no life at all. The force of what we call "the dark forces" is the negative attachments to energy that cause fractures in their light streamers and eventually extinguish all light except that connective spark to Creator.

Light is within your spirit, the sensation you describe as feeling *light*-hearted because something joyful is happening or you're remembering it. That sensation is the light coming from your soul, connecting with your mind and flowing through your body to produce joyful feelings or an *Aha!* inspiration.

Reception of light is the province of the soul, *absorption* of light is the province of the body. The body directs the light into the cells, which have been programmed by the DNA to accept it, but the soul may deny its entry. This is how the topmost dark forces are able to make puppets of the people who make free will choices with dark proclivity. Their souls voluntarily deny the light entry, which precludes absorption by the cells and thus adversely influences the souls' DNA. Since DNA is the knowledge handed down from one soul generation to the next, the inclination toward darkness becomes more and more inculcated in that DNA until the affected souls arrive at lost soul status. *(NOTE:* Revelations For A New Era *"Lost Souls" chapter explains how souls reach that status and can be redeemed or reabsorbed by Creator.)*

S: *When you have talked about sending light, I've interpreted it to mean that we automatically do that simply by loving people, but now I'm not sure that's all there is to it. If not, then exactly how do we send light to someone?*

MATTHEW: You're certainly right about feelings of love for someone carrying light to that person, as love and light can't be separated any more than two sides of a coin can be. Light is the visual, or external, proof of its conjoining love, which has its own evidence in your world. But there is no division of this homogenized energy into a light compartment and a love compartment. Oh, you could say that light is the *makeup* of a soul and love is a *capacity* of the soul, but how can one separate those any more than one can separate the soul's linkage with Creator, the maker of no less than the cosmos?

But you're also right in thinking there may be more to it than that, and even though you don't have to understand the process of light-sending for it to be effective, you may want to know how it goes.

Think how you react when one of your dogs comes to nuzzle you or you hear one of your favorite symphonies or see a lovely flower, feeling as if your whole self is lighting up. That *is* what is happening! You actually are being filled with the light your body cells are absorbing simply by the experience. You didn't have to do a thing to get that light feeling, and the cause that evoked it didn't have to make any special effort to create your feeling, either. Simply by your soul's being receptive to the light, you get it.

The light passing from one person to another is no different in cause and effect, but you may want to initiate it by directing your thoughts, which are aligned with your feelings, toward someone, and when you do, instantaneously that vibration is with that person. The energy flows from you along your thought form of intent and intensity and it goes directly to the "energy address" you want it to. The quality and quantity of light that is received is exactly that which you send. True, the receiver will not consciously know this, but the receiver's soul always is aware of the incoming energy.

People known as "energy healers" act as vehicles for pulling in energy from the neutral universal pool, letting it flow through their souls where the love aspect and the direction are attached, and flow on to the person of that attachment. There can be no "false addresses" because the feelings are totally clear.

This is why it is vitally important to send light to people whose attitudes or deeds you regard as detestable, to try to influence a "lighter" approach in their activities. Verbal or written pleas may or may not touch their conscience, as that layer of the soul atrophies when its messages are ignored time after time after time, and light reaching their "entire" souls is the only way to help them literally "get it."

While it is true that one to whom light is sent may choose not to receive it, it is just as true that *ONLY* light with its healing love energy can eliminate hatred, violence, oppression and warring in the hearts of humankind. Retaliation in kind *never* will do it! Think of Earth's history – did the first war on the planet end all fighting for control and result in peace, harmony and kindness? No war ever guarantees anything except more of itself until light enters the scenario.

The souls who are inclined toward darkness in their thinking and doing aren't able to produce light themselves, so they can neither uplift their own motives and deeds nor influence any others toward benevolence. That's why love must be generated elsewhere and sent to them. When it is sent in such abundance that you could almost term it a "love assault," it cannot be ignored because the energy of it is too powerful. As the most powerful energy in the universe, love IS Creation, and where there is light, darkness simply cannot exist.

All in existence is manifested and connected through the energy generated by the continuous flowing of light love being directed and received. There simply is no beginning and no ending, there just IS – the All That IS, the I AM, the Totality. And each soul is part of it. Each soul has the capability of holding light or darkness.

And that brings us back to why I've often told you it is imperative to send light – or love, if you will, as they're the same – to those whom you regard as evil or cruel or despotic. This is *not* condoning what they do or being indifferent to the suffering they cause, and it certainly is not supporting their activities! What it *is,* is understanding that darkness is not the enemy of light or the opposite of light, it is the *absence* of light, and only by having that void filled can the darkness be overcome.

Withdraw the fuel of the dark forces by sending to them what is missing from their souls, something they cannot create themselves: Light. The soul in darkly-perceived reality believes it has been abandoned by its Creator. That soul is suffering from fear, and in its frenzy to rid itself of fear, its dark nature consistently turns to the false gods of political power and money. The presence of light is frightening because a dark soul knows it cannot survive in the light frequencies, but it doesn't realize that it can *thrive* if only it will receive and absorb the light within its being.

That is why we ask that you send light to those beings. We also ask that you not judge any but feel compassion. We ask that you not feel negative emotions about their deeds, as those do not have any effect at all on those beings, but they do have adverse effects on those who harbor those sensations.

S: Matthew, you've mentioned this before, but it's hard for me to separate my thoughts about the people who are causing such terrible suffering from what they're doing, so I don't see how I can be sending them light. Can you please help me with this?

MATTHEW: Mother, you would turn on a flashlight to guide someone out of the darkness of uncertainty and anxiety onto a path where they are confident and secure, wouldn't you? Those souls have lost their way and are fearful and foundering. Do not think of them as their deeds, but rather *what you want for the world!* Think of kindness, helpfulness and justness and sharing, think about the world's people living in harmony, peacefulness and love and send *those* thoughts to those souls in darkness.

S: Yes, I see, dear. Will you please put light and love in the context of everyday life insofar as our being receptive to it and also how we can express it?

MATTHEW: I am happy to do this, Mother! Being receptive to the light brings spiritual growth beyond third density limitations. These limitations include feeling prejudice and hatred of differences, acting in greed, judging others for their choices, holding resentments or desiring vengeance, progressing by ruthlessness and cheating, controlling others and denying their free will, blindly following dogma or orders when instinct tells that they are not based in godliness. And the greatest of all prevalent third density limitations is *fear.*

Actually, all of those negatively-bound emotions and motives I mentioned arise from fear. Without understanding that, you could logically think that in changing directions in some of those areas while remaining fearful of personal or world situations, you are growing spiritually. That is progress indeed, but not in the measure you may think. Spiritual evolution is learning to live *without* fear. It is learning to live with full trust in the power of love, the most powerful force in the universe. The word "love" has been so commonly used that it is severely abused, as in "I love artichokes" or "I loved that movie," so first I say what love is *not.* Food and entertainment can indeed give pleasure, and I surely am not debasing enjoyments that can be uplifting, but those fleeting sensations are not love.

Neither is love the physical attraction of one party to another that leads to anxiety about the long-term security of the relationship. Love is not controlling a mate, it is not pitying or worrying about family or friends, it is not professional success, it is not possessions.

Love is not dependent upon fame or financial wealth or others' opinions of you. Love is not crusading for your beliefs or proselytizing. Love does not require understanding mystical spiritual teachings or all karmic components of experiencing or the continuum that you call time and space or the universal laws.

So, then, what *is* love? In simplest terms, love is God's sharing of Himself with all of His creations. Love is the healing force of the universe. Love is within the soul and needs only your allowance of those innate sensations of loving others and receiving their love for you. Love has no limitations, no boundaries to its capacity.

In expression, love is treating others with kindness, fairness, honesty, compassion, helpfulness, caring. If love can be said to have "ingredients," then those are some of the ingredients of godly expression in action.

Knowing that you and God and every other of God's creations are inseparable is love. Knowing that Earth is a sentient, conscious life herself and respecting all of her life forms is love. Realizing that no one can know others at soul level and therefore does not judge them but rather does not condone an action seen as injurious, is love.

Listening to one's godself is love. Living the kind of life that engenders loving self is love. Feeling joy yourself when you see it in others is love. Doing something that brings joy to another is love. Forgiveness of self and others is love. Sharing your resources with full heart is love. Doing good deeds without attaching expectations is love.

Feeling peace of heart and mind is love. The quiet thrill of seeing a sunset or hearing a songbird is love, and a smile is one of the simplest and most radiating expressions of love.

In any or all of these instances and many others that you may encounter that instinctively you know are love in action, you are manifesting your love for and of God.

Mother, I don't think I've told you anything at all surprising. But perhaps it is good to have some references as a guiding *light* in these times when darkness may seem to be overshadowing the magnificent abundance of love that is in your world.

HOW PRAYER WORKS

August 29, 2001

S: Matthew, what do you think about a group meditation focusing on China during the Fall equinox and also expressing gratitude for the ETs who have been helping to preserve and uplift Earth? Would you like to give some guidance on this?

MATTHEW: With eagerness, Mother! Strength of any sensation will be considerably heightened during that timeframe, so it's especially appropriate to offer special thanks to the extraterrestrials whose love for and efforts on behalf of Earth are helping you and your planet.

As for the proposed meditation focus, it is true that China is in very great need of the light in individual and group prayers. However, ALL of Earth is in powerful need of prayers, and focusing solely on China when such heightened energy steamers will be beaming intensely at Earth is not, in my view, the most prudent way to assist in this excellent opportunity to uplift your whole planet. So it is my suggestion – please, let me be more emphatic and call it my *recommendation* – that no place on Earth be excluded.

A simple but powerful meditation approach that expands the prevailing light is visualizing Earth glowing with the light of the universe. Anyone who is moved to participate in this kind of loving prayerful effort is a light-worker and probably knows the effectiveness of this method.

S: Are you saying that Earth would be better served if no specific place ever is the focus of group and individual prayers?

MATTHEW: Mother, specifying each place, circumstance or person on Earth who would benefit from increased light would leave time for nothing else, as no cubic inch of your world and not even one of the tiniest plant or animal lives is unworthy of being sent light. However, I think that the effects of focused prayer, such as in group meditations or prayer meetings or even individuals' prayers, are not well understood.

It is not that formal concentration on a certain area means it is being especially blessed because it is in some hearts and minds, but rather that the light brought forth and anchored on Earth by individual and group prayers goes to the areas where it is most needed. So, even though a large group of you may *"Think China,"* let us say, the light brought in by those focused thoughts and feelings is not disseminated only to China, and furthermore, it may not be received.

S: How could any place not receive light being beamed to it?

MATTHEW: A "place," although perceived as a geographic area, actually is the manifestation of all energy prevailing there, and its energy essence is its interacting life forms, each with the capacity to receive or reject the light being offered. A majority of souls in the "place" may indeed receive the light, but this may not be recognized widely because very little changes overall due to the few most powerful souls rejecting it and continuing their unen-*light*-ened ways.

S: Well then, since light goes where it's needed, why would it make any difference if that group chooses China for its equinox meditation?

MATTHEW: The free will choices in prayers must be honored by universal law, so the light of the meditation effort would be honored in total. However, by the universal law of All That Is seeking balance, only temporarily could the narrow focus of the light in the prayers be maintained. What happens with light directed to any specific area is not that the life forms there ideally would "use it all up" and thus only goodness and peace would result. What happens is that the bandwidth within which light can raise planetary frequencies would not operate as effectively as it potentially can.

Non-focused meditation has greater effectiveness because anything in balanced measure is more potent in energy "spread." You know how often I have stressed the imperative nature of balance, and sending out light in equal measure saves the effort to reallocate imbalanced provisions. Light is the love of God being expressed in a tangible, maneuverable, influencing energetic form. Energy itself is neutral, of course, but its "instructions," so to speak, come from every thought and intent of every life. In the meditative use of light, *love* is really what you are talking about, so you can see why it is God's prerogative to smooth out the bunched-up light, or love.

People are verifying their own beliefs and often expressing their personal emotional needs by praying for their choice of place or person. However, the overall effects of their prayers become the province of God, who knows more than you do which souls are most in need of the divine love that we're speaking of as light. If this were not so, your world would be in far worse shape than it is!

The matrix of light allocation must be in keeping with the ultimate goal of balance. Therefore, the leveling, or balancing, motion of light is constant, like water making its way from heights into low-lying elevations and eventually smoothing out all the tumultuous peaks and valleys so as to create flourishing everywhere. If light were emitted in balance from every soul on Earth, the flourishing of an Eden paradise would be *NOW*.

S: I see. What about the healing of a sick or injured person in a mass invocation – is that energy also dispersed so that only enough for healing goes to that person and the rest goes to others?

MATTHEW: This involves the soul's pre-birth agreement longevity clause. Maybe the person's chosen physical lifetime is completed, but the crowd directing enormous energy toward his healing can't know that and may regard his death as unanswered prayers or their failure to pray sufficiently to save him. If the person's physical life is not meant to end imminently, a healing can indeed happen through the concerted prayers. If living with infirmities or debilitating pain is not part of the person's agreement, then the mass energy directed toward relieving those conditions also can be effective.

In that same situation, the prayer of the affected person alone can accomplish healing if it is not compromised by his fear that he'll never be better. Fear will generate *more* of what he's afraid he'll always have – and therefore he will.

All of this applies equally to the patients of people in the various medical treatment fields. The practitioners feel a great responsibility toward fruitful therapy or preventing the death of patients, and when those intended outcomes do not occur, they may feel that they failed. While there are indeed cases of ignorance, negligence or outright error, it is possible that nothing within the practitioners' power could have prevented their patients' lack of positive response to appropriate treatment.

But in reply to your question regarding dispersion of energy generated by mass prayers, that which is not required for the individual healing ripples outward into a leveling pattern and raises the soul-light level of others who are receptive. This is true whether or not the healing occurs, which is a matter of the person's soul-level agreement, as I said.

Since no one knows another's soul contract, praying for "the highest good" of the person – or of self! – is recommended rather directing a prayer toward a specific outcome regarding health or length of physical lifetime. Further, prayers offered with such fervency or desperation that the energy put forth is fractured rather than flowing in balance are not helpful. Thus praying for one's highest good, with loving thoughts flowing evenly, is the most effective way to proceed.

S: OK, thank you Back to group meditation if 100 people are focusing on the same prayer, would that be 100 times more effective than one person's prayer?

MATTHEW: Universal mathematics works here, Mother. The light emanating from the 100 would mingle and rise to exponential heights of effectiveness, with results almost immeasurably greater than one because of the ripple effect. It is not that a single prayer is less valid in intent than the composite prayer, but rather that when the universal law of exponential growth and the balancing motion are recognized, the difference is incalculable. So, even with a focused rather than a global approach, the prayerful thoughts and feelings cannot be acclaimed too highly for their benefits to Earth.

I would like to clarify here what prayer really is. It is not repeating some formal petition with a multitude of others and it is not a single plea that must be expressed in a special manner or only when kneeling. Prayer is what is in one's heart and mind, in every moment, in any place or circumstance. *Prayer is your very life!*

In your concept of prayer, it is only for something good to happen to self or others. However, within the universal law, every single moment of every life is a prayer, because not a single moment is exempt from the universe registering every thought, feeling, motive and action as the basis for self-judgment in the next world. And that includes all the people whom you consider to be doing "ungodly" things.

You say, "Be careful what you pray for, you may get it!" Indeed you *WILL!*

S: I see! Matthew, what do you think about the residents of Nirvana joining in a special meditation service, or isn't meditation part of life there?

MATTHEW: Nirvana is a *continuous* meditation scene, Mother! There are monitors by the hundreds of thousands keeping the entire realm abreast of all happenings on Earth, and through them we are aware of the many areas wherein there is a need for prayers. However, we do not direct our light to specific areas for the reason I explained before about the benefits of prayer energy being spread over the globe and not bunched up at a point of geography.

At any rate, that is a beautiful idea and on the basis I have just mentioned, you can consider it a "done deal." Actually, by your thought alone this was posted on our bulletin board. Oh, indeed we do have a bulletin board, just not exactly like the ones there.

As for something other than what I have just described of our ongoing prayerful state, I'd have to say that full participation from here is highly unlikely. Getting everyone in Nirvana in any one moment to focus on one thing would be as improbable as getting everyone in Chicago to have the identical thought simultaneously. Our population changes by the nanosecond, with arrivals transitioning from Earth physical lifetimes and all the others coming and going.

Some high souls come to teach and others come to learn from them, and there is such frequent rotation in just this respect of our population that you could think of Nirvana as having swinging doors. Then there are the millions who are leaving in any one moment to visit family on Earth or in other realms, to reincarnate on Earth or in other realms, or to return to their far distant homelands and take up their normal activities once again. Some come here after very difficult lifetimes in other civilizations specifically to rest in this inspirational atmosphere. Many souls come virtually as tourists, because this sanctuary realm is the most beautiful in this part of the galaxy – from my travels, I'd say it is the most beautiful in the *entire* galaxy.

It's not very likely that anyone who hasn't read and believed the first two books can imagine such hustle-bustle in this place that's religiously associated with clouds and harpists. You have no idea what being "in the fast lane" really is until you get here!

REALITY

April 23, 2001

S: Well, Matthew, where is the evidence that the light being beamed to Earth really is diminishing the effects of the darkness? I don't think this is a matter of discernment. Either the progress of the light is a reality or it's not – and I can't see that it is because there still is so much suffering all over the world!

MATTHEW: Mother, there is indeed evidence of the light's progress, but first let me address "reality." In the universal sense, it is the harmonious coexistence of spiritual clarity and scientific principles that what you see as solid is not solid and what you see as reality is not real. What is within each light-filled soul – love, joy, trust, worthiness, honor – is *solid*, and reality is what the soul knows of the eternal inseparability of all creation.

More to the point in third density grasp of reality, it is what each person accepts into his consciousness as real. If someone has no knowledge of something, for him there cannot be any reality to it. If he has the knowledge but does not believe it, then it is not real, either. And, if an individual fears something that does not exist outside of his fear of it, nevertheless, for that individual the feared object or situation is absolutely a reality.

In this sense of the light diminishing the darkness, that is the reality of individuals who believe this truth, but it is not to those who also have heard of it but who deny its credibility. To most people there is no reality to it at all because they don't know this is happening. You do believe what you have been told, that light is being spread throughout Earth, so this *is* your reality – you just can't understand why there still is so much darkness that keeps the suffering going on.

The universal law of like attracts like is what is in effect. The light pockets are meeting other light pockets and in their uniting are beaming ever more confidently. The pockets of darkness are doing the very same, but they have less power than the light. Every new spark of light in any soul is increasing the light's effectiveness and decreasing the power of the darkness. When there is a preponderance of light being sustained so that by natural law the darkness is diminished, then vanquished, the reality of *only* light prevailing on Earth will be evident to everyone. But until then there will be the ongoing conflicts between the opposing forces and so those will continue in your reality.

S: Matthew, are wars, famines, oppression and such and the suffering these cause a reality only because we believe they exist? Can we turn that around by focusing light on their nonexistence?

MATTHEW: Dear one, focusing light is essential, yes, but you are wishing for a situation that is not "do-able," that all suffering could stop with denial of its existence. This is an oversimplification of manifesting reality. Even though part of your world population – say tribes living in deepest jungles – might have no knowledge of those situations that cause suffering and thus cannot give them any reality, that doesn't affect their recognition by the rest of the world. And even if all people not directly affected by those conditions were able to withdraw all sense of their existence, the people being directly affected surely could not.

S: So then to change those situations, we need to create a positive new reality, is that it? If so, exactly how would we do that?

MATTHEW: The basis of the manifestation process is, whatever can be visualized, or imagined, can be created. First the concept, or the idea of what you want, is created by your thought of it. When there is sufficient mind energy directed at the concept, it is given life, or reality, by the numbers of people who consider it so. This works equally for manifesting what you think of as goodness and what you think of as evil.

But Mother dear, understanding this process isn't going to accomplish what you want – the end of all suffering *now*. Although this is what you feel is for the good of all, you are not considering the need for the karmic influences and the resultant balancing to run its course, the free will element in all of this, or that energy set in motion cannot be stopped midstream. But that doesn't mean it is not fervently desired that the light of every soul would focus on the peace and harmony that would end the suffering!

The value of directing creative energy toward a concept *within* the light from the onset cannot be overstated! Imagine – *envision* – a world glowing in the golden dawn of people caring for and about each other, a world with equality in the distribution of its gifts, a world of health and abundance for all. Imagine Earth restored to the paradise she once was, and make *this* a reality!

It is easier to create beauty and harmony than to create hatred, greed, terror and dis-ease. From the beginning only love and light have been building materials for everything from a tadpole to a star, and to distort these into making products of darkness, one must seriously digress consciously from the soul-level urging to co-create within the godly provisions. Conscience, your inner voice, is the route, and listening and heeding is the journey to the destination of remembering who we are and our beginnings. That is the wondrous promise of the light.

There is no other way. There can be no changing from the

universal laws of energy alignment and the conflict between the positive and negative forces. We can call upon God to be merciful to one or to billions, but in the end, the laws of the universe set in motion must be played out in this entire Earth scenario. All the strength of any force is aligned in the direction of joining with or resisting the light. This is the most basic law of this universe. This is the zenith of reality.

S: Matthew, all of this seems devoid of feelings, as if everything is impersonal and nothing counts except the universal laws and the energetic force of light.

MATTHEW: Then I have done a great injustice to my explanation, Mother. The light is total LOVE, the essence of God manifested in a visible and tangential form that includes the make-up of every soul. It is *totally, intensely personal!*

EARTH'S ASCENSION

August 10, 2001

S: The next two questions are about this ascension process. What percentage of the population has to achieve light status before the planet can ascend into the dimension of fourth density?

MATTHEW: *NO* percentage of Earth's population is required for the planet's ascension into fourth density – *that she is doing!* Of course, every soul who leaves negativity and emerges into the light will make this journey with her, but there is no special number or percentage of souls there who must attain a certain level of benevolence or spiritual clarity before Earth *herself* is capable of rising.

As well as being the synthesis of all her human and other conscious life forms, Earth has her own soul and consciousness. She was her own essence long before life forms were introduced on the planet, and like every other soul, Earth's own soul is inviolate. So is her free will, and she has chosen to ascend into lighter density. The alternative was to die from the devastation that has been caused by the negativity resulting from all the sources of monstrous damage to her physically and emotionally. So, with or without anyone or everyone there, Earth is on her way!

S: OK! The next question is almost a reverse of that. Someone who read that Earth's ascension into fourth density is almost complete and then there will be rapid movement into the fifth said that's a lot further along than you've indicated—she wants to know what you have to say about this.

MATTHEW: I say that someone is more optimistic than real-istic. If Earth were almost entirely within fourth density, the travails would not be happening in the intensity they are. At the point of near completion into fourth density, there would be some residue of the dark forces' handiwork and some need for more cleansing, but there's no way that at the scale both are active, that level of spiritual evolvement is almost achieved.

S: That does sound more logical. But Matthew, you keep saying that the light forces are progressing, yet it seems to me that the world is getting crazier, not better. Why?

MATTHEW: Mother, free will reigns! And in short, a balancing act is in process. The acceleration of light energy movement that is intensifying emotions and making the sensation of time passing more and more rapidly is bringing out the best and the worst in each soul. What's more apparent there is the *worst*.

This is a critical time, the moment of everyone's accounting for all choices throughout the lifetime. It is the moment of completing chosen karmic experiencing, of deciding to accept or deny the light and the consequences of the latter. Each soul must decide to go along with Earth into the higher light frequencies or start back at the beginning of consciousness. But regardless of individual choices, the progress of the light that is enabling Earth's ascension *is* steadily increasing. That is *why* you are seeing more and more evidence of the darkness at work – the increasing light is revealing it – and still more of the dark intentions will be "brought to light" before the planetary ascension is completed.

Mother, please know that I do understand your discouraged feelings despite what I often have told you. Of course it is difficult for you to see this as we do! You are on Earth where all of the "craziness" is taking place. We are *literally* able to see the progress of the light forces, and I can assure you they *are* steadily making headway! If you need more reassurance of this, you have it within your godself. Therein is all the assurance, comfort and guidance you need to sustain your spirit during these profound times on Earth.

TIMELINES

January 7, 2002

*S: So, did you absorb as much as you need of that material
to comment on it?*

MATTHEW: Yes, Mother, thank you. The idea that simultaneous happenings affecting a mass of souls can be confined in any
manner at all is erroneous. Even when the energy streamers of
each and every soul are in the light and the body of souls moves
at the accelerated pace of the universal flow, the consciousness of
each individual will register the newest experience in the context
of all preceding experiences. Just as perceptions of the same happenings are unique to each soul, a timeline – experiencing within
a defined time framework – is also.

Earth's population is more billions of souls than the census-
takers can count, and no two are identical. Although the vast
majority is third density in spiritual and intellectual attainment, a
few souls embodied there are as advanced as seventh density and
others in are densities in between, and each one arrived at his
energy niche individually. Even more to the point, each will continue to grow or regress in all aspects of being wherever in the
universe the next stage of learning is presented. The next lifetime's growth or regression, respectively, is by the soul's choice
of higher frequency placements or its self-consignment to a lower
energy level, and in both cases, the next experiencing is in accordance with this lifetime's free will choices.

Not only is time regarded by each individual in the context of
what is transpiring in the moment put into the context of everything that has happened previously and what is planned for the

future, but you also perceive time outside of your linear defining. The months a woman is awaiting the birth of her baby may seem endless, while that same calendar period after the birth is so filled with joy and amazement at the baby's rapid changes that the months seem to fly by. Both periods of experiencing are identical in your timeframe, but quite different in the mother's perception, and her perception is her reality.

There are as many individual realities – or timelines — as there are souls who experience in any form anywhere in the universe, and that number is numberless, we could say. It's like snowflakes, each with its complete value, no two identical, and just as there are no "mass realities," there are no "mass transiting timelines."

That is all to your benefit, you should know! Setting timelines even with broad parameters is trying to define something that's indefinable with any accuracy whatsoever. There are no pre-cast destinies and no limiting capacities for change in any of a soul's attributes, attitudes, decisions and activities that form the lifelong journey. That is, there still is "time" for improvement or backsliding!

There are measuring sticks, or milestones, that will become more evident as the days pass and will make the truly numberless timelines more understandable to soul-searchers. What already is evident and will become much more so, is that souls are aligning within the same major fields of potential. And this is where the point of that material is applicable: Categorizing the souls whose spiritual evolution zooms, those who embrace the light a little less and a little later, and those who stubbornly refuse the light.

It is understandable that no one on Earth can envision even a minute portion of "future" or "past" in the continuum because the third density still primarily prevailing there blocks this awareness. Even in the fourth density that some individuals are experiencing in soul-discovery, there is an eagerness to accept mentally but not yet a corresponding capacity to assimilate this completely. And it's not expected of you.

It's the difference between *living* in that higher light where the human brain is not constricted as it is in the third density of Earth, and *having faith* that there even is a higher place. Searching for understanding beyond that which you know is the best evidence that the "beyond" *does* exist and is without the current limitations the planet's density imposes upon you.

These limitations are diminishing even as I am speaking to you. Lazarus and his engineers are paving the celestial roadway for other beings to direct their light to Earth without disruption from the dark forces. Lazarus' troops have the technology to thwart the intrusive efforts of base energy at this level and as high as there may be any need during this period of planetary cleansing. Other civilizations are serving in their respective fields of technological expertise, and myriad sources are beaming light in aid of Earth.

Of course souls still have the choice of accepting or rejecting the light, but Earth as her individual soul has chosen the light. In her prayer for assistance to receive the light in a sustained manner to rid herself of millennia of accumulating negativity, those civilizations that have been connected with Earth populations since the first habitation of the planet are heeding her call, and other civilizations are doing so as well.

The cleansing is not separate from the ascension process that material has squeezed into three timelines, and the timelines are not separate from each other. *Nothing* is separate from anything else! All causes and effects are jointly created and experienced at the zenith of consciousness, but the make-up of that consciousness is the input of *each and every* soul's experiencing, like the formation and drifting of each single snowflake is part of the snowfall.

Mother, I have told you that even family members who die simultaneously cannot make transition together because each individual soul arrives at its energy registration point. That same universal law is at work here. Each soul is eternally independent, unique and inviolate, and at the same time is inseparable from every other soul and aspect of Creation. *That* is why there are countless timelines—there is one for each of the innumerable souls journeying back to God and Creator.

DO NOT FEAR!

August 28, 2002

MATTHEW: Mother, regarding that "doomsday" letter swirling around the Internet, first I say: **Fear NOT!** That dire prediction of a massive earthquake and loss of billions of lives on September 7 is NOT going to happen!

Is this "message from God" via that person who is intending to alert the world to this imminent event not the same End-of-the-world idea that has been considered inevitable for centuries by doom-sayers? It *IS!* The dark forces originated this concept so long ago that current Earth history has no record of its initiation into belief systems. It is not its origin in antiquity that DISempowers this concept, it is its origin within the darkness that literally dooms it!

Manifesting any date for planetary destruction so severe that Earth could not survive is no different from manifesting anything else at all – it is a matter only of sustained belief and intent that brings about happenings. This would be the manifesting capability of the soul at work co-creating with God, implementing that law of Creator that exists inseparably with free will.

This works with one consciously-focused mind or with billions, and when the latter, the term "mass consciousness" comes into it. I reluctantly use that term because of its application to "ascension," which is another term often improperly applied, as if bodies will be lifted off the planet into the heavens. Moving into the lighter density of the universe, which is by the opening of hearts and minds unto the light of love that enables Heaven on Earth, is ascension.

So I ask that "mass consciousness" be understood as *the majority of energetic interaction on Earth choosing to anchor and sustain the light on and within and throughout the planet.* This is not the same as a specific number or a defined percentage of souls consciously sharing the same belief or focus, which is the prerequisite of a different interpretation of mass consciousness and is not the correct understanding of the actual physics operating.

Now then, there are two essential considerations about this "inevitable doomsday idea." First, this could happen *ONLY* if this concept were to sweep over the world and mold more than half the mind power – not half of the souls, but half of the *mind power* – into the rigid belief form that Earth actually is hopelessly doomed. Please note that it is not "would" happen, but *"could"* happen, and that brings us to the second of the two overriding factors here.

Even if that degree of doomsday conviction could be mustered, "doom" could affect only the energy *embodied* on the planet. With only physical life at stake, which in your current belief system is meant to be only short-term anyway, an arbitrary, identically-timed ending to everyone's *eternal life* really is ludicrous when you think about it. Just Zap! – totally discounting the stage of spiritual awareness and intelligence advancement and soul evolvement, not to mention the plans of God and Creator? I don't think so!

So then, "doomsday" is only an idea, a concept, a topic of discussion, a nonexistent event that got talked about way beyond the originating circle. So what is to be feared? To actually create that fearful-sounding scenario would require the power of focused minds without any great opposition in belief, in feelings, in intent of energy direction. And therein lies the doom of the doomsday *idea!*

There *IS* massive disbelief, disagreement and opposition to it! There *IS* a massive abundance of light firmly anchored on Earth that is in complete energetic opposition to the darkness, within which the doomsday concept was developed, and there *IS* massive soul-level knowingness and emerging conscious awareness of whence this doomsday fallacy came and why!

It came from the dark forces specifically to create fear. There is no issue of greater importance today than clearly understanding how the darkness uses fear as its ultimate weapon against individuals, nations, your whole world. Fear of an idea, of what *might be*, is as much a captive state of consciousness as the fear of what you consider concrete actuality.

When information about merely conceptual fearsome situations is passed on as foregone conclusion by sincerely well-meaning individuals, they may be doing so in concerned innocence, but the fear that's created nevertheless is as virulent as if the peak of darkness itself had pronounced it. This is what happens:

The energy of fear forms a barrier between the feared object or circumstances and the energy of light. Because of the barrier, the light in the souls of fear-full people cannot reach their consciousness to dispel the power of those fears over their lives, and the light being sent to them by light workers cannot penetrate. The barrier feels like a real wall, isolating the person with the consuming fear and leaving no way out. This energy blockage of the light intensifies the power of whatever is feared, thus enabling it to draw to itself more manifestations to be feared.

Fear is wildly contagious, and due to its magnification in power, fear sensation streamers have sticky edges that attract the kinds of energetic interactions that omit common sense, sound judgment, and wise decisions. Fear is so insidious that it can convince a person that the only way to escape is through portals leading deeper and deeper into darkness. Fear is the forebear of such actions or characteristics deemed prejudice, tyranny, greed, cru-

*elty, belligerence, deception, dishonor and hatred, and even those
seemingly senseless tortures or deaths of innocents arise through
psyches that have been twisted and tormented by fears.*

The light, in which love and universal knowledge and spiritual clarity abide, cannot reach those souls to let them know their
spiritual powers are far stronger than anything the dark powers
can conjure to frighten them. *Nothing* is stronger than the light,
which is the gift to every soul of the love and power of God.

Because the dark forces cannot create light or capture it and
they cannot coexist with it, they can only try to create fear and try
to capture souls through fear. The magnified energy of fear draws
to the people like thought forms from the universal soup, and the
power of natural laws then brings into reality the fearsome ideas
manifested into form through sustained conscious belief in their
existence. Then there is indeed something to fear – *it's what fear
itself created!*

The viciousness of the cycle permits people to be held captive
by the darkness whose stronghold is simple: It doesn't permit
them to "see the light" because that light would reveal that what
they have been told to fear is only an *idea. Belief* in the fear-filled
idea's *reality* is what makes it so. Literally "seeing the light"
exposes the fabric of lies and desperate measures of the dark
forces and destroys their grasp on awakening minds. Now fearing
for their own continuation, these forces are creating fear through
any possible means, no matter how transparent or arrogant the
falseness of their claims in their last gasp to maintain control of
their darkly-inclined helpers on Earth.

What you are seeing in every avenue of what you may call
evil, from kidnappings to killings by children to greed and corruption of global degree to hopelessness of entire nations to talk of

deterring a nuclear invasion by preemptive war declaration—
KNOW that these are abounding because the receding of the darkness is underway! These forces that steadily have chosen to harm
others rather than allow love to motivate them will not much
longer be on your planet to create havoc and despair.

The light is increasing in abundance and power in consonance
with Earth's own chosen pathway, and the bodies of people who
continue treading in darkness simply would be destroyed if they
were forced into the light, like crystal shattering at certain frequencies. The souls of these people will be transferred to a density station compatible with their energy registration, which is
determined by the lifetime free will choices.

No, Mother, I don't know if the promise of beauty and peace in
Earth's new world will persuade these souls to let the light fill their
voids with love. We pray that they will desire this, but we cannot
influence the free will courses they choose. And no, I don't know
whether in body or only spirit they will experience their next opportunity to follow the light, nor do I know where they will go, because
in this unique time universally, those dark souls cannot come here.
There are placements in the universe where life starts in very primitive form and progresses as light guidance is given for remedial lessons. *"In my father's house are many mansions"* means that the universe contains many varieties of living arrangements so that all stages
of souls' evolvement can be accommodated.

Let me return for a moment to the manifestation process, the
effects of intent. Let us turn around that prediction of the end of
the world through destruction into oblivion and let us intend that
there be a world-ending to Earth's agonies, an ending to the violence, corruption, deception, injustices, diseases, starvation, brutality. Let us intend that there be an ending to the warring, killing,
terror, to the destruction of bodies and land and hope.

Focusing on a replacement for all of that – focusing on love, peace, justness, decency and sharing in the world – can have mammoth uplifting effects on what already has been long in process, the return to the paradise your planet once was! The progress would have been much faster if more of you had affirmed that a kinder, more loving and more harmonious world *already* had risen out of the ashes of the futile last stand of the darkness. *If not before, then now add your light to this!*

When the struggle is over, there will be a return to the true Eden that once existed there. There will be peace and harmony and respect between and among all life forms, the animals and the plants and the currently unrecognized Devic kingdom whose efforts are so essential to Earth's preservation. So, let's not have a benediction because the world is ending. Let's hear a clarion call for renewed awareness of the cosmic Oneness and the Christed spirit within every soul!

PEACE IN SPACE

February 6, 2002

S: Matthew, good morning! A leader of the global Peace in Space movement requested a message from you for their opening presentation. Are you aware of this effort to create peace in space?

MATTHEW: Good morning, Mother. Indeed, this effort is well known in this realm. The inspiration for this initiative idea was created here and filtered to the persons who have become active in this God-blessed spiritual endeavor. Banishing the fear of war in space with weapons of greater mass destruction than ever before in your recorded history is a paramount undertaking in the salvation of your planet.

Although fear can be manifested with any object as its focus, fear of dying still holds the most sway on Earth, and war is one of the greatest causes of death. In war, death may come by an implement unseen and thus no defense, and most likely, with no beloved soul to tend one's last moments of life on Earth. War promotes fear in the hearts of those waiting at home that perhaps their dear ones will never return but will die without comfort, without good-byes. Fear flourishes in the *anticipation* of physical death by those in combat or in surrounding areas as well as the loss of loved ones, thus in space weaponry with unsurpassed capability for mass death and maybe even worse, the plight of survivors, you have fear without peer.

Because the energy of fear prevents light from entering souls, creating fear on the planet is a foremost aim of the darkness. This includes but goes beyond war. The ultimate aim is to prevent the space brotherhood's light-bearing service on behalf of Earth's preservation. While this dark effort cannot be successful by decree of Creator and God, working for peace in space is the avenue whereby people's free will choices can assist in upholding that decree.

To all in the ranks of this peace effort, know that light beings within, on, and above the planet are in force with you and adding to your efforts. Those in the vanguard, know that you have been inspired to take the reins because you yourselves selected this in pre-birth agreements. All of you, know that being fearless in your thrust forges the energy direction for the ultimate success of your goal: *Peace in space.*

VACCINATIONS:
THE GREATER SIGNIFICANCE

September 19, 2002

S: Do you have anything to say about smallpox vaccinations, with the threat of biological warfare being the justification even though the disease hasn't been around for many years?

MATTHEW: You can bet I do have something to say about this! Mother, you know that anger isn't a sensation that lingers in Nirvana and neither are resentment or heavy sorrow or any of the other common negative feelings on Earth that arrivals bring with them and are quickly dispelled. This is different. This is feelings anew, with unusual intensity at discovering that masses of people have been deliberately misled, gravely deceived.

Not only is the disease being misrepresented, but this new ploy is designed specifically to create *mass fear*. This is *betrayal!* Once again you are being told huge untruths so you will be pliant and go along with the introduction of this plan designed specifically to create additional fear if such were needed in 11th hour moves for the darkness to fend off the light's steady advancement. And that is what this is all about, because it *is* the 11th hour for the dark forces!

Some new arrivals suspected they were being told lies by their leaders, but they didn't know for certain until they came here. Their very recent Earth lifetimes and especially knowing their beloved people are being victimized makes their reactions natural and understandable. Still, emotions with such heavy negativity cannot remain long here, and the initial feelings that range from outrage to deep sadness are being released by being blended into disappointment.

These feelings are shared by many other civilizations because of the severity of the situation that includes this smallpox issue, but with a profound significance that goes far beyond that. As you know, the actions of the apparent "evildoers" have been of major importance relative to karmic lesson completion in the essential nature of bringing balance to all souls. But it is past the time for them to give this up, and they are not moving into the light as they had *AGREED!*

Physical density denied them the remembrance they thought they would have at the appointed time for spiritual awakening, but that is not sufficient reason for them to continue their course. With this late hour upon them, the light forces have been urgently reminding them, so their habit of working in darkness notwithstanding, these souls are intellectually aware that no longer are they serving within their agreements. Even with doubled and redoubled light offerings constantly offered, these dark souls are so intent upon achieving their objective of world domination that they are refusing to respond even an iota for what could offer them enlightenment, solace and rejuvenated spirit.

More so, their responding to the light would reduce and eventually eliminate the suffering they cause. That still *WILL* happen, but needless deaths and devastation are being caused and will continue to be caused as long as these souls in darkness are determined to hold onto their remaining power. Their doing so is *NOT* the original design of this tiny part of the universal tapestry!

I must clarify that I am speaking of the Earth souls who have been operating in dark endeavors by soul level agreements to serve specifically for karmic balancing. I am *not* speaking of the universal force of darkness. Its identity is not an individual soul or even collective souls, but rather a force field that moves stealthily and without a placement so that, unlike on Earth where light can be steadily directed to individual souls, light cannot be directed steadily to the ever-moving dark force field. This is the great difficulty with the light overcoming the darkness in every speck of universal space.

The civilization in our universe that has been especially intrigued by the darkness is the reptilian. Certainly not all in that civilization are, but those who preferred the power of the dark over the greater power of the light have been in the forefront of the negativity-creating on your planet. They do not need to be obvious or even present for their controlling influence on their willing human puppets anywhere to be evident, and it is their puppets on Earth to whom I referred as causing such havoc and misery there way beyond their karmic agreements.

I'm sorry, Mother. I know I got carried away and digressed almost immediately from your question about vaccinations, but what I've just said really is pertinent. The threat of a smallpox germ release being planned by any country is a ruse of the cruelest kind. It is one thing to threaten a world with talk of war. War is familiar to you, and as much as this is a lamentable commentary on your world, it is an accurate one. War has become almost an accepted routine because somewhere on the globe war has been in motion for untold centuries.

It is quite another thing to put immeasurable fear into a world by such great deception as the threat of the reemergence of a disease being touted as so virulent that it can wipe out your global population unless precautions are taken prior to even one case occurring. This, and proclaiming the "threat of germ warfare" along with announcing that vaccines are not available for all, that vaccinations can have dire side effects and even cause death, and the intent that military and medical people will be inoculated first, are designed with diabolical cunning – it leaves no one feeling safe and secure.

In some cases types of vaccines have been deliberately contami-
nated and their usage mandated with severe, just different, consequences for those who get the inoculations and those who refuse
them. It is this: *Be fearful that you* won't *get a vaccination; be fearful that you* will. THIS **FEAR** IS EXACTLY WHAT IS INTENDED!

The fear being created by the dark forces is due to the fear they
themselves are feeling. They see the sustained light prevailing and
increasing, and they are in combat for their very existence on the
planet. It had been anticipated – maybe "hoped" is more accurate –
that the perpetrators and perpetuators of fear-filled tactics would see
the light and embrace it and move as One with the rest of the light
workers. This was their soul contract. By refusing consciously to
abide by their agreements, the betrayal is to themselves and to the
people they rule, who didn't agree to experience this.

You are thinking that betrayal is nothing new. Mother, *this is
new* and it is a sadness for us, but it will not affect Earth's ascension progress or individual souls' evolution. What it *does* affect is
the larger picture, and that is why other civilizations also are seeing this as such a serious situation. The intent was that humankind
and the full reptilian civilization in this galaxy once again would
unite in the light and exemplify what you sing, "A mighty fortress
is our God." Unity of the two groups would be a light fortress for
this part of the universe, and now it seems clear that the darkly-
enchanted reptilian members are determined to thwart this intended and sacred light protection.

*S: Of course I had no idea how extensive this issue is! Do you
know if smallpox germs will be released simply to prove that the
government's warnings were in fact valid, and will the mandated
vaccinations at least be with pure vaccines?*

MATTHEW: We do not believe that any smallpox germ warfare or deliberate biological release labeled "warfare" will happen because protection cannot be guaranteed lifelong to the families and others close to the few people who have the power to direct such an action. That is what we see in the field of potential at this time.

Contaminating the vaccine is not necessary for creating the dreadful upheaval and fear that the dark minds in power want. The vaccine itself is dangerous because even though in mild form, it *is* the disease and can seriously affect or even kill bodies not equal to the task of warding off its effects, including the very young and the very old.

Due to unhealthful life styles of many residents there, especially bodies addicted to drugs of any sort, they would be more susceptible to the mild disease effects than if they were physically fit. If vaccinations get as far as the areas where starvation is rampant and the African nations where AIDS already has weakened many of the population, there would be genocide faster than is occurring now.

There is another, equally dark aspect of this matter beyond the strategy to create fear: mind control. Inoculations offer the perfect opportunity for individuals to unwittingly receive microchips that can be triggered into the programmed reactions of anything from "Feel depressed" to "Kill." It is not by accident that so many in your country are afflicted with depression or that shocking and inexplicable killings are taking place.

S: Is this part of what has to "come to light" before the darkness can be totally vanquished or can collective opposition prevent it?

MATTHEW: In the field of potential there is the same kind of accelerated activity as is happening universally, where *nothing* in this moment is so firmly fixed in its momentum that collective consciousness cannot affect it. However, the consciousness on Earth is scattered because there are so many fronts on which to focus.

I hesitate to say that you're in a frenzy there, because many souls are holding steadfastly in the light and many others are discovering their godselves. But there is more mental, emotional, spiritual and physical activity, much of it in turmoil, than at any time before on Earth even during the wild last years on Atlantis.

As you have been told by me and many other sources, it is the "last gasp" for every soul to consciously determine its ultimate pathway in this unprecedented era of your planet. Everything is in acceleration. If those on a dark path can be touched by light and wish to turn into the light, that can be done with universal rejoicing until the last nanosecond before "time's up." That moment will be when the light is so strong that the vibrations of a soul in the lower density of darkness will cause the body's cells to short circuit, you could say. The body will die and the energy of the soul will take it to a placement of corresponding energy vibration.

REPTILIAN INFLUENCE

April 6, 1999

S: Good morning, sweetheart! Isn't it a glorious spring morning here!

MATTHEW: Good morning and good *life,* Mother! It is a glorious morning indeed! I have been following your thoughts and am ready to answer your questions to the best of my knowledge.

S: OK, dear! Then you know that I've just read that 12 million aliens will be settled in Kosovo and that's why the area is being "cleansed," and that shape-shifting reptilians in disguise here have been systematically destroying the planet so human survival won't be possible much longer. I think all of this is crazy – but I want you to tell me it is!

MATTHEW: It is *totally* crazy, Mother! That "settlement" in Kosovo is nothing but an absurd concoction. The ethnic hatred and conflicts that have flourished so sadly in that whole area for many centuries have been inflamed by outsiders, that is so, but it is within the populations themselves that the continuing wars for domination have been fought.

It isn't necessary for "alien" civilizations to do anything to encourage the atrocities there, so, as much as you still find those unconscionable, at least I can assure you that "12 million aliens" are *not* going to be living in Kosovo. Or anywhere else on Earth.

As for the "shape-shifting" beings on Earth, yes, some reptilians in human disguise are at work on your planet and they have that capability to alter their appearance, but they do not draw attention to themselves – secrecy is the way in which they operate. The vilest of all reptilians are not acting openly, but rather are behind the happenings, pulling the strings of their puppets. Why would the "shape-shifters" disclose themselves publicly – who on Earth would believe they were seeing correctly?

Reptilian influence on your planet has been in evidence from their first landing, some 200,000 years back in your time, and this has been the cause of all the brutality in any form that has occurred there. Even though none of this is attributable to them, from this vantage point it can be seen how they manipulate humans to create wars, famines, poverty, disease and other situations that accomplish the reptilian purpose.

The darkness that has been on Earth since the beginning of her human seeding program has been influencing those who choose to leave their spiritual beginnings and birthright. They fall into the darkness of greed, power and control and deliberately create fear among the people. *(NOTE: The human seeding program is explained in "Origin of Earth Humankind" in* Revelations For A New Era.*)*

But the fact that reptilians rather than humans started this makes no difference at all in the *effects*, so there is no more reason to fear them than if some Earth human had started it. Other beings also "alien" to Earth – the light beings of advanced civilizations – are in combat with those reptilian representatives. Furthermore, not all reptilians are in the dark forces, and those in the light also are in combat with their dark members.

Remember my telling you about meeting two reptilian military commanders who came to Nirvana to discuss means of preventing an invasion of this galaxy by hostile forces? I was favorably impressed with their ideas and their interest in wanting to improve their sanctuary realm, which is why I met with them after their conference with the Council.

S: Yes, I remember that. So, do you think the authors of this kind of crazy information are doing it because they're mind-controlled?

MATTHEW: They may be, but a great deal published there is through just plain control, and it is likely that all information that evokes unnecessary fear is by that intent.

MEDIA REPORTING

August 9, 2001

S: But Matthew, there's still so much suffering and violence, sometimes it's hard to believe things really are getting better even though you keep assuring me they are.

MATTHEW: Mother, you see much more evidence of "worse" than "better" because that is what your main media sources are publicizing. The "better" are the many individuals who now are more spiritually enlightened than previously, and they are not publicized at all. Many are having light influence way beyond their own uplifted lives, and that, too, is usually unknown except where it is personally noticed. Large groups are working for peace and justice throughout the world, and although the media give occasional glimpses of that, it is a paltry amount compared to their focus on the negative news.

It is by intention that you are pummeled with detailed stories and films of brutalities or tragedies of one kind or another rather than the goodness that is increasingly emerging. You may be tired of my tying things to the influence of the darkness, but there is so much of this that I can't refrain, and controlling what your media report is another aspect of it. The point is, negative emotions – primarily fear due to the plethora of violence – are aroused by what is *selected* for publicizing, which is precisely the dark purpose in doing this.

S: Well, there is some publicity on positive things, but I compare this with the many news stories and even documentary films on the millions of wretched lives. You stress the importance of balance, and I can't see any balance in the numbers.

MATTHEW: There isn't any in the numbers, Mother. The balance is in the abundance of sustained light on Earth. It cannot enter the hearts and minds of those who are so captive of darkness that the light cannot penetrate, and this still is causing widespread suffering. The light cannot penetrate the minds of those who are fearful, either. So, while it is true that the numbers are terribly disproportionate, there is little that can be done about this until the leaders who are initiating and controlling the sources of fear and other negativity stop. And this includes your media saturating you with both horror stories and untrue news "fed" to them.

Anything reported by your media that is fear-based may or may not be factually true. It isn't necessary to report only non-truths when the *selection* of truths being headlined, especially those done repeatedly, are about disturbing happenings. Think of your local newscasts and headlines that feature prolonged publicity of an act of terrorism, a murder or murder trial, kidnappings, deaths in a train wreck or fires or plane crashes, any or all of which may be half a continent or half a world away.

By intent, violence and tragedies all over the globe are standard fare.

The purpose of these selected "news" stories and other programming of minds that far more emphasize the "bad" than the "good" is to create the negativity that prevents light from reaching souls. Always you are encouraged to use your discernment about what is publicized and why, about what is the truth and what is deception of any situation.

S: Matthew, from your vantage point, it's far easier for you to know the purpose and truth! We are captive of what we're told, whether we believe it or not, because the deception impacts us just as surely and severely as if it weren't self-serving manipulation!

MATTHEW: I deserve that chastisement, Mother, and I apologize for my lack of sensitivity. I do not like that trait of being so insensitive that I demand of *myself* an apology, and I shall be more diligent about never succumbing to that tendency. While individual discernment *is* important, I do realize the situation within which you are bound to function. Your hearts and minds are free to be soaring in the light, but you are indeed captives of the unjust laws, corruption and deception of your governments.

S: Thank you for saying that, Matthew. I still feel hurt by unfair criticism, even though I know you would never intend that.

MATTHEW: Mother, dearest soul to me, *never* would I intend to hurt you! *Never* would I wish to cause you even a momentary sense of hurt! Although I lapsed into a trait I do not admire in myself, either as Matthew's personage or his cumulative soul who is speaking, it certainly does identify your teenager who often felt that his opinions were superior to yours, doesn't it? *(NOTE: "Communion with Matthew" in* Matthew, Tell Me About Heaven *and "The Cumulative Soul" in* Revelations For A New Era *discuss in depth the personage and cumulative facets of the soul.)*

Mother, now it's *just* me. Remember that trip back from Betsy's college when finally you admitted that I was right about the directions and you were wrong? After all your wrong decisions, I was feeling so smug when you turned around and drove in the direction I told you was the right one. I'm grateful that we can share enjoyment at recalling that – you sure didn't feel that way at the time! Now then, shall we press forward with our lighter hearts?

S: I love you, sweetheart, and especially when you sound like my Mash, I feel so much more like your mother than I do when you sound like a professor.

MATTHEW: I know that, dear soul, and I don't *ever* want to sound like a professor! I only want to answer your questions as comprehensively as I can, and now more needs to be said about the results of your media control.

On one hand you are bombarded with all those actual accounts of murders, rapes and other violent crimes, tragedies and wars, with pictures and films to further emphasize your vulnerability to becoming a victim yourselves. On the other hand you are inundated with TV programs, movies and computer games with the very same kinds of happenings. So your psyches are being maneuvered into both personal fear of violence and killings and the "entertainment" ingredient of all of that. The most vulnerable minds veer from that latter aspect to committing the actual deeds, which feed the "news" reports.

Eventually you have a population focused on killing and death, a population that is not thinking about what is *not* being reported. You are being strategically offered all those diversion options so you can immediately switch to them from the "news" without questioning what has been reported or noticing the lack of substantiation for their "facts."

But not all media can be controlled nor are all minds too narrowly focused to look beyond the major news sources and their selection of reported information. Many truth-filled Internet offerings are being given more attention and credence, and many people are beginning to doubt the truth of mainstream reporting. You will see more and more evidence of this.

Eventually this will include the reporters themselves, who no longer will comply with directives to squelch the truth, report lies, or emphasize over and over stories and films that evoke negative emotions. Not only will those kinds of events *not* be happening, but also your powers of discernment will be far greater than now even though you won't need to use them to decide whether what you read, hear on radio or see on TV is the truth. By then, *it will be!*

BELIEF MAKES IT SO

August 30, 2002

S: I've been reading warnings about microwaved food – is there anything to this?

MATTHEW: Mother, if you now feel hesitant about eating food cooked that way, you will be better off to forego that form of cooking. If you can wholeheartedly believe that it is not harmful to your body, it won't be. However, if fear enters any situation *across the board*, then that becomes the collective perception of it. If it becomes totally accepted that microwaving is harmful, it will be for people collectively, and conversely, if no collective fear is connected with it, it will not be harmful to anyone. In the unlikely case that an individual's fear of food cooked that way is overwhelming but he eats it anyway, that food will do him no good because his strong thoughts about it will diminish his body's capacity to absorb its nutrients.

S: Well, when the genetically engineered food controversy first started, you said not to be unduly concerned because the people who worked with that food were imparting light to it since they believed its development was beneficial. Now it seems that considerable harm can be done by these foods, so what about this?

MATTHEW: Mother, when you asked, the situation had not reached the condition that now exists. At the onset it was felt that the light infused into the grains by the workers would offset the dark intentions of the designers. Now that is not the case. We see that considerable upheavals are being caused as word of the harmfulness has sifted down to the working ranks and their previous focus on the goodness they felt was the truth of these crops' development has veered into the grave concerns that have arisen in the general public. Simply, the light formerly in those foods is gone. It was replaced, or more accurately, displaced, by fear.

The power of thought cannot be overstated! Despite that truth being told by many respected channels, it is not becoming widely known or believed, and even some of the believers do not apply it sufficiently. It is the *collective thoughts* about the dangers of this altered foodstuff for humans and animals that have brought about this new element of harm in consumption.

Think of all the hybrid fruits and vegetables that have been created by this same means, genetic alteration, that for many years have been greeted not only without anxiety, but with great eating enjoyment and no ill effects whatsoever. You have flowers and other fine plants and trees produced the same way, and they have caused no problems either, but suddenly there is "Danger!" in consuming the grains. *Why?*

Do you not think that the same darkness that devised this idea that "GE" grain foods *could* be harmful also initiated the spreading fear of them so they *would* become harmful? Mother, do not underestimate the cleverness of those dark minds!

S: Matthew, are you saying that if no one had ever felt there was any danger at all in the grains, that despite the dark intentions of the designers, these would be safe, and that it was believing the publicity about their harm that made it so?

MATTHEW: Exactly! BELIEF in *anything* is what makes it so! I don't mean that one person's anxiety about changing the DNA nature of food can turn a nourishing substance into a harmful one, but the power of collective thoughts focused on that *can*. And that's what happened here. The risk increased in prevalence and intensity through being widely publicized and thus you manifested exactly what you focused on – foodstuffs harmful to the physical body.

Mother, it cannot be repeated too often how essential it is that you realize the power of your thoughts, feelings, actions and even the words you choose to describe any thing, person, situation, hope, intent. Collectively these are your reality, and collectively you have created it.

S: If we all switch to believing these foods are good, will the harmfulness disappear?

MATTHEW: You pose a good point, and while reversing any situation never should be considered impossible, in this case, I have to say it is very unlikely because the collective belief is so well entrenched. Some circumstances that have been created are beyond your ability to alter, such as toxins in chemtrails or radiation from nuclear waste and other situations so heavily laden with poisons that reversing them requires belief systems beyond the third density still prevailing on Earth.

Another example is AIDS. Can your world start believing that the widespread devastation of AIDS can be stopped by your collective belief that it has? The collective belief in the opposite situation is so strongly entrenched that I don't think so.

S: All right, I do see that, but when I first asked you about GE foods, why didn't you tell me what was going to happen?

MATTHEW: I didn't know! Situations are set in motion and the energy that has been put into the process is registered in symbolic form in the field of potential. At the time you asked, the dark intentions that were firmly registered were being offset by the light-filled energy being registered from many souls involved in the laboratory and field work.

This is your "Monday morning quarterback" saying that perhaps I could have used better judgment in my reply back then. But I felt it wasn't wise to mention that thinking positively that these foods being altered from their natural states would keep them from being harmful to your bodies, and thinking negatively, that they're potential health hazards, would indeed bring those hazards on.

Once a thought is given words, it tends to spread far and wide, and in the case of a negative connotation given a plain statement of truth, an alert becomes *alarm*. I didn't want my comments to have that kind of outcome and so I didn't mention that. At least I have a clear conscience about not being responsible for starting that turnabout attitude regarding fussing around with grains' DNA.

S: OK, dear! Since our collective belief is that AIDS is a devastating lethal disease, how can it ever be stopped?

MATTHEW: There can be no cure as things stand now, but AIDS will not last much longer on Earth. As your planet moves into the higher frequency of fourth density, disease and events and conditions now bringing great harm to Earth and her life forms will diminish and then disappear entirely.

As you know, physical survival in that higher density requires cellular level changes and it is the light that enables these. As more individuals become receptive to the light, they add their light to that already being generated on and off-planet, which has surpassed the sustained amount required for Earth's assured ascension. During this evolutionary process, the collective belief will become that AIDS does *not* exist.

Once this has occurred, the people who have AIDS will be healed because the disease cannot continue to exist within their new cellular makeup. Obviously, there will be no new cases. AIDS patients who are not receptive to the light cannot physically survive Earth's ascension because their third density bodies cannot withstand the intensity of the lighter density and will die. Their souls, like those of all other people who refuse the light, will depart for placements compatible with their lifetime choices.

S: Will cancer, neurological and mental disorders, and contagious diseases all be eliminated?

MATTHEW: Yes. All of those are produced by third density cells, which are vulnerable to them. Those afflictions exist now because of stress that creates weakness in the various body parts – nerves, muscles, organs and brains – because Earth density belief systems incorporate those effects of stress. Although cures or at least relief are available now for these conditions, they are suppressed by the establishment that controls medical treatments and medications. Neither bodies' limitations nor those controls will exist once Earth is completely within fourth density.

CHEMTRAILS, *NO* NUCLEAR WAR

September 19, 2002

S: Were the chemtrails directly over our house almost two weeks ago really much lower than any I've seen before? Is the chest congestion I've had ever since a direct result of those or is my knowledge that this has happened to many people what "allowed" me to get the same?

MATTHEW: Interesting thinking, Mother. You are right that the chemtrails were extremely low, but as for your other question, I can tell you that whether or not you were thinking of being susceptible to their effects, you would have had them. These are Earth elements designed to be toxic to bodies, and their effects on you would have happened regardless of whether you had seen the trails or had even heard of them. So not always is it a person's state of mind that creates the physical effects of meeting up with an occurrence such as the chemtrails.

This is like the "GE" foods situation. At the outset of the chemtrails the harmful *intention* was in place, and the intentional *publicizing* of their risk to health grew like a forest fire after a long drought into the harmful effects of this collective belief that you have today. So despite one's not believing this is so, or ignorance of the very existence of this manmade source of physical harm, Earth bodies are vulnerable to it.

S: Yes, I see. You know I rarely read material channeled by others so I don't have information that might influence what I receive, but I did read something about ETs containing nuclear detonations "as much as they can." It sounded as if they may not be able to prevent all. Is this a change from what you've told me?

MATTHEW: Mother, your understanding could only be a misinterpretation of any accurately received message from extraterrestrial light forces or a misunderstanding by the receiver or the transmission was intentionally skewed by darkness to create more fear. *There will be NO nuclear destruction on Earth!*

S: Well, I know you've said that many times, but since you've explained that through fear we've created AIDS, harmful GE foods and chemtrails, I'm wondering if this same reversal of no-fear to fear could apply to war threats against Iraq. There must be millions of people who are afraid that nuclear weapons will be used, so could that collective fear-thought create their use? Or will their use be prevented because of the collective hope that they won't be?

MATTHEW: I'm not discounting the value of the collective hope-thoughts, but these are not comparable situations, Mother. The GE foods, AIDS and chemtrails affect only Earth bodies. The damage of nuclear detonations is not confined to your planet or to only physical bodies. It is universal in scope and the damage that has been caused to the DNA equivalent of the make-up of souls will never again be permitted by Creator. In this universe, God is in charge of prevention, and you definitely can count on God to handle this mission!

The arms of God, you could say, are the powerful extraterrestrial civilizations whose greatly advanced technology and spiritual evolvement are at the helm of the prevention force. Some of these beings have been living among you for some time, unrecognized because they look like any other handsome and intelligent human, and they are influencing against the use of nuclear weapons. Equally advanced beings are off-planet, poised to cause the malfunction of any nuclear missiles that may be launched. In fact, they *have* caused this in launched missiles with nuclear warheads, so you can ease your mind about whether those efforts would be successful, Mother.

EMOTIONS

May 23, 2002

S: I'm concerned about this new "detached" feeling I have regarding all the tragedies and pain everywhere. You've said being balanced is so important that I'm trying to achieve this, but I don't want to lose my emotions to do it.

MATTHEW: Mother, I assure you, you have *not* lost your emotions! They just come, and not *necessarily* because you have invited them, but the heavy negative emotions do you no good. They do NO one any good! They block your connection with wisdom and the ability to correctly assess a situation so you can know how best to help.

Compassion is not feeling the depth of pain the person is feeling, but rather the willingness to reach out and do whatever will most assist and comfort. That's all you need to do! You must keep peace within so the balance you need is not destroyed each time you become aware of others' suffering. You can feel compassion without allowing your emotional and spiritual balance to be drawn into personal or national traumas.

If you are overcome emotionally, how would you know whether you are feeling for the person you are reaching out to or whether you are remembering a similar experience and reliving *your* emotions? Empathy isn't reliving your own pain and sympathy doesn't require your feeling the depth of another's pain. Those whose professions are constantly in the midst of others' suffering would become basket cases if their emotions were as powerful as the ones they are there to help, and they would be completely ineffective.

It is natural to react with sympathy or empathy and compassion toward people who are suffering. And yes, sorrow, anger, fright, frustration, bitterness and helplessness are natural human responses, too. Earth lifetimes are precisely to *experience* these emotions! But that experiencing is for growing spiritually so that you can look beyond the events that cause the emotions and understand their *purpose* – the playing out of the last vestiges of karma that is required for Earth and all her light-receptive souls to move within higher densities.

Back to my stressing *necessarily*. Your thoughts precede emotions, an infinitesimal lapse that you may not recognize because you feel it as simultaneous. When you are thinking of devastating situations – perhaps the impending loss of a beloved person or money anxiety or fear for your very life – your thoughts turn into the emotions that are natural reactions to whatever you are *anticipating* and the energy draws that event or circumstance to you. Energy is neutral and doesn't know "good" from "bad" thoughts and feelings. It simply follows the universal law of like attracts like and brings to you whatever you were focusing on.

I don't mean that if you are "afraid" someone will die that your feelings hasten the death, but do realize that in effect, you are mourning for your anticipated loss rather than lightening that person's last days on Earth. In the case of circumstances you feel anxious about, you do indeed create those by your preoccupation with thoughts about them.

You know that grieving can be healthfully endured, that you manifest the very situations you fear may happen, and how essential balance is not only to each person, but its out-flowing from each has beneficial influence even on a universal scale. So please put into this context your "detachment" and feel blessed that you have reached this stage of spiritual clarity.

FOCUS *FOR,* NOT AGAINST

December 8, 2002

S: Matthew, hi, dear! I need to talk with you here at the computer so I can record your comments.

MATTHEW: Hello to you, Mother! I've been aware of your consternation and I agree that it's better for you to have a record of my reply rather than paraphrase it to answer that letter. So, please have your say.

S: Thank you. Actually, I've heard from three women whom I respect for their light service that they choose not to be involved in movements like stopping war build-up, erosion of civil freedoms, killing whales, etc. The one who wrote today reminded me that you said not to add fuel by taking sides, but instead ease intense feelings so the energy of the opposite side will subside, too – the balancing act you talk about.

But you've also said—and so have my sources in the ET civilizations that are helping Earth—that we must help ourselves, so this seems contradictory. Now that dark activities are being exposed, aren't we supposed to actively oppose them? Surely ignoring them isn't going to help anything!

MATTHEW: Mother, I know you are viewing this situation as contradictory and thinking that only one of the two sides you've mentioned can be right, but ignoring the darkness is not the only alternative to actively opposing it. Although I applaud the enlightened outlook of your correspondents, what they have shared with you is not the whole story of what is happening.

From dimensions of higher spiritual awareness, it is known that both sides of this seeming contradiction are within the universal laws of energetic interaction. Certainly the outpouring of letters, petitions, marches and global prayer or meditation gatherings is *necessary,* but that is not in itself enough to conquer the darkness that still is having its impact.

What you and millions of others are doing is indeed a necessary part of this transition, but too often it's without the most beneficial results. If the active participants stopped focusing mentally and emotionally on opposition to the activities of the darkness and instead focused on manifesting the love and light-filled traits in humankind that will displace the darkness, it would greatly aid in bringing that day sooner.

Although by now many there have heard of this universal principle of manifestation, not all accept it as a sufficient effort, and very, very few have the focusing intensity to produce the object or circumstance of their focus. However, those who are concentrating on *positive* results of others' "pro-light" activities but are not participating in them, are aiding this process just as directly as those who are signing petitions and marching, and often with more effectiveness as far as the abundance of light resulting. Those who focus on the heinous activities and feel guilty for not being able to actively oppose them are unwittingly diminishing the light produced by others.

S: Matthew, why haven't you made this clear to me before!

MATTHEW: Until you received that letter this morning, you *were* clear on this! No, not with that identical crystallization of words, but from the synthesis of all you have learned and your feelings, your *approach* was clear.

Mother, I know your heart and mind because your invitation to me is nearly constant, and your heartfelt emotions and your thoughts have been on the *positive* outcome! Your doubting, your sudden sense of having been given contradictory information, came into play just in the reading of that letter. That is when suddenly you felt in a quandary and saw this as your having to be on one side or the other and you didn't know which was the right one.

Dear soul, the WHOLE of everything has two sides. Do you remember Menta talking about this, saying that everyone chooses whether the positive or the negative side of the "coin" – and she meant either light or dark choices – will be the "upside"? *(NOTE: Menta, a vast entity of collective souls, gave a lengthy presentation in the chapter, "Menta," in* Revelations For A New Era.*)*

S: *Yes, but both "sides" here – being active or not – seem to be in the light So, is one just so-so as far as being effective and the other is better? Already some terrible situations have been turned around by the great amount of vocal and written opposition!*

OK, you're saying that continued active participation is necessary, but we all should focus on what we DO want and not on what we DON'T want. Well, most of the activity already is FOR peace, FOR saving the environment, FOR saving the whales, FOR preserving civil liberties. That's the wording on posters, petitions, letters to governments, signs people carry and individuals' comments on newscasts, so what should be different here?

MATTHEW: Mother, the coin of my illustration does have two light sides – I didn't have a chance to carry out my point on that because you jumped in with your comments. We are *greatly* heartened to see some dire situations being reversed by national or global outcries! But *words* FOR something are not enough.

Thoughts and emotions register far more intensive energy than words. Often words are meaningless because they are without conviction or are with misrepresentation – consider political speeches! – or they are spoken with unhelpful feelings.

There is genuine hope behind all of the "pro-light" activity, indeed, but too often it is over-laced with *fear* of the current and potential happenings, not *faith* that the light will overcome them, and *this* is the problem. It is the *collective thoughts and feelings* FOR peace, FOR love and light to prevail that are so greatly needed! This is the message that all of us in higher densities have been giving you all along!

S: You're right, I do know that. But how can this reach people who don't know it?

MATTHEW: That is the rest of the story. When the exposure of the deception, corruption, cruelty, greed and fear-causing tactics reaches its zenith, then the light that is being raised by opposition to what has been exposed – and still more darkness will be exposed – that light also will reach its pinnacle of polarity. That is when the clarity of the light will reach the consciousness of the receptive masses.

With it will come the realization that their focus no longer need be on opposition, but on the glories that can be manifested through the solidarity of hearts and minds in serenity, balance and godself-assurance of Oneness. Then you will know what you have been co-creating – the era of love, peace and harmony on your planet.

Mother, every soul came into this lifetime having chosen the role each would play in this unprecedented hour on Earth. Those who came to personally and publicly rebel against the efforts of the dark powers are forcing the exposure of those activities, otherwise those powers would continue as they have for eons. Souls who came in to be more meditative in their service, the ones who are quietly focusing on a loving, peaceful world, are perfectly fulfilling their chosen missions. These two sides of the "light" coin are one swing of the metronome, you could say, and the darkness is the opposite swing.

When the process reaches those two points of polarity I mentioned, the swinging will slow as the light reaches more and more souls, then it will reach the balance that is the world of light and love and spiritual clarity – the fulfillment of all light workers' chosen roles. But remember, you cannot know if a soul is fulfilling or defaulting in chosen karmic lessons to attain this balance, so you may be shocked when you discover which is which. We do know, and the purpose of all light sources within, on and surrounding your planet is to reach as many "defaulting" souls as we can.

MOTHER NATURE – *OR NOT?*

August 22, 2002

S: Are the fires in the Northwest and floods in other countries all due to Mother Nature or is weather control involved? I was shocked – that technology actually was mentioned in a local newscast last week! And is global warming going to continue – will it cause major changes in seacoast areas?

MATTHEW: Your planet is indeed experiencing a great deal of dramatic weather as well as overall climate changes. Although the wildfires, monsoon-type downpours, drought, earthquakes, volcanic eruptions and record-breaking temperatures can be attributed to the season, the area or global warming and thus nothing is greatly suspicious, has Mother Nature alone caused *all* of this? *Not on your life!*

Even what you think of as weather patterns, such as the alternating years of El Nino and La Nina currents, have been started or exacerbated by weather technology. At no time in almost the past 50 years has a major weather condition not been deliberately adversely influenced through specially designed processes or by the effects of other types of technologies.

These technologies were meant to be kept secret but could not be. In the beginning the efforts were few and feeble because the designs were new and testing was cautious. By now it is well known how to wreak extensive havoc weather-wise to purposely cause loss of life and property, severe deprivations and disease, and economic chaos anyplace on the planet.

This heavier bombardment of the atmosphere to cause increasingly violent effects is in keeping with other intended effects of climate-changing conditions. At this point we go off-planet for explanations and instigators, because a great deal is behind your "natural" weather or climate changes.

These are manifestations by the forces beyond Earth that are telepathically imparting their technology and influencing their willing puppets on the planet to cause the spectrum of destructive weather elements. The aim is the increased negativity that results from weather-related traumas like flooding, drought and the warming oceans that cause the agony of many millions of humans and countless animal lives in your seas and upon the land. That devastation is in addition to the anguish of the entire Devic kingdom about pollution in the atmosphere, which is Earth's major breathing system; the shrinking rain forests; the loss of her fertile soil; the drain on her blood supply, the oil that is being sucked out of her interior.

But back to weather, and this is the paradox: Even if weather technology were not a major factor in causing vast destruction, given the collective negativity from all of its sources, Earth still would be reeling in fires, storms, eruptions and quakes. They are the planetary cleansers, the reducers of negativity, the relievers of kinetic energy build-up, the leavening factor that aids Earth in rising into lighter density and emerging from domination of the darkness.

It is not easy to believe that some humans are being manipulated by non-human forces or to accept that those humans have intentionally caused massive weather damage and great loss of life to their fellowman. These are the same humans who have created the dismal environment by such as the chemtrails and other toxins that befoul air, land, water and bodies of all life forms. They are the ones who manipulate national and global economies with the intent to bankrupt while claiming it is financial aid. They are the ones who start and finance wars, all the while publicly stating that all they want is to bring lasting peace.

The blatant lies, the abuse of power – there is no end to the negativity the effects of these actions cause in each moment, and into this soup of deliberate pollution, toss that which is created by fear, thoughtlessness, uncaring, or ignorance. The total is an unimaginable measure of negativity that still must be removed from Earth, and what are called "natural disasters," whether truly natural or not, is Earth's removal process.

There is no difference between the *results* of the same kind of action – for example, the damage resulting from a fire caused by a sudden wind gust spreading a campfire's sparks is no different from the damage caused by the same size fire started by an arsonist – but there is an immense difference between the energy attachments created by each.

Intent, or *motive,* is its own energy form and is registered apart from the activity itself. For example, subsistence farmers unaware of the damage they are doing when they leave their small rough homes and ruined topsoil to move on, cut down and burn more trees, wear out more topsoil again and again, nevertheless are aiding in the destruction of the rain forest. Others cut the trees to sell rare woods even while knowing but not caring that preserving the forest is imperative environmentally. In both cases the trees are killed, reducing that vital element of Earth's well being, but only in the latter case, where greed handily wins out over awareness, does the action result in double-dose negativity.

Destruction through weather control technology and its aftermath is *intended*, so it also results in twice the negativity as a naturally occurring weather event. Although droughts and floods are the most easily achieved effects of weather manipulation, earthquakes and volcanic eruptions have been "improved" so that target effects often are partially attained. The caricature of the mad scientist with flowing hair and popping eyes is almost applicable, as the few people with the knowledge and the authority to *literally* "Make my day!" weather-wise on Earth are not rational. And their source of "inspiration" is not human but is the dark ones among the reptilian civilization. However, with thanks to the advanced technology of our space brotherhood light workers, the weather controllers' plans never have been fully successful and their most diabolical efforts have been almost entirely thwarted.

This is not to say that severe weather-related events will not continue with potentially serious consequences. That is the most likely scenario as the light *vs.* dark battle rages on. But due to our benevolent space warriors, nothing will be as bad as was anticipated before they came to the aid of Earth with doubled and redoubled light efforts.

As for global warming – and no respectable scientist on Earth will deny this is happening! – what has caused this? The hole in the ozone layer? No, that is another *result* of what has caused global warming: Negativity. The thinning of the ozone layer that eventually resulted in the hole was initiated some time ago by vehicle and heating fuel systems and other chemical reactions and emissions, which also are effects of negativity. No, that is not a surprise, but *this* may be – the ozone situation would have happened without any manmade efforts, solely as a natural and desirable result of the light increasing on Earth.

The thinning is helpful in purifying the atmosphere and lightening the density immediately surrounding the planet. If this were known to your scientists who could publicize it, there would be no grave concerns about the diminishing ozone. But so far this is known only to the few scientists who deliberately do *not* publicize it, a strategic reversal of the dark intent regarding publicity to create fear. In Earth's third density the protection of the ozone area has been necessary for her life forms, but the need for this is lessening rapidly as the planet is absorbing more and more light in tandem with all her life forms from human to algae.

You asked if global warming will continue. Yes, because whatever has been set in motion must run its course – energy doesn't get directed and then of its own volition, stop and hover or turn unless it reaches equally strong opposition. And that is *coming!* At this point enough souls have awakened and are seeking Truth so that there is a great rising, yet still subconscious, of requests for *assistance* to avoid planetary destruction. This has enabled the detrimental effects of the warming process to be brought within the guidance of the light brotherhood, whose advanced technology will lift and steer the energy streamers into positive outcomes.

This would be stabilizing temperature ranges to attain better distribution of heat and cold, and leavening the extremes in arid and humid, fertile and abused, lands. It would be getting rid of air pollution and neutralizing toxic wastes in water and soil and radioactive waste in leaking storage containers and in discarded weaponry. It would be the recovery of the most damaged parts of Earth, reclaiming a balanced ecological system and restoring the harmony that once existed within all of her animal and plant kingdoms.

Some there know of these off-planet sources of assistance. It is time for *ALL* there to recognize, welcome and thank our extraterrestrial family of diverse civilizations whose massive light-beaming and technology have been and will continue to be literally lifesaving for Earth and all her light-receptive beings. This assistance is more complex than you yourselves can manage, but it is not the responsibility of your space friends – your space **family!** – to manage all aspects of this salvation for you.

They answered Earth's own plea for help, and myriad others in light service are helping also, but assisting these sources to re-create Heaven on Earth is the mission and birthright of all you souls who *chose* to participate during this unprecedented era. Your positive thoughts and sentiments are required for the return to health, peace, love, harmony and remembrance of your relationship with each other, with God, with all life forms throughout the universe.

This is not merely a prayer or fervent hope. It is a reflection of the universe. The changes within each of you and the planetary changes are only the reflection of the most pervasive universal changes since the birth of the various worlds of the cosmos.

Mother, I know this goes way beyond your questions, but it all is related. As I have often said, everything happening anywhere on Earth is related to *everything everywhere!*

PART II

OTHER ILLUMINATIONS

SALVATION

May 18, 2002

MATTHEW: The "saving" of one's soul into godly realms instead of "losing" it into the depths of base energy registration is not generally understood on Earth. Salvation is up to each individual, but the means whereby it comes is incorrectly taught there. Salvation is not a single occurrence, it is not an automatic result of a declaration of belief. It is each person's lifelong conscious choices that forge the salvation pathway. It is a gift for the soul-seeker who asks what salvation is or a lifetime of delusion for the one who does not ask because he's so sure he knows.

Soul-seekers, exalt in your awakening spirit and remembrance of your spiritual heritage. Exalt in your inseparability with God and with every other soul on Earth and throughout the universe. Exalt in the knowledge that you and the life travelers by your side *chose* to be journeying into this New Era with the blessings of I AM Infinity! *This* is salvation!

DNA AND OTHER INSIGHTS

January 15, 1997

S: Can you tell me anything about 12-strand DNA?

MATTHEW/GROUP: We will be happy to address this. The 12-strand DNA existing in Earth humans heretofore is being reestablished to prepare you for assimilating the light being beamed to raise your spiritual and conscious connections with higher density vibratory rates. In the plunge downward from the beginning of Creation, the original 30-strand DNA of intelligent life forms was decreased until it reached the current level in third density.

DNA is the substance of light within the physical body at cellular level. When physicality first happened, so far back in antiquity that at this level we cannot comprehend when, total conformity with Creator's original materials for building reigned without question or deviation. All materials were of light.

As the materials became denser for manifesting in form rather than in only light and awareness, changes were required in the structure of the DNA elements. They became tighter in composition as the more dense bodies and substances for building were visualized and manifested.

Eventually the density became such that the original 30-strand DNA was reduced to only one strand in the most primitive life form possible to produce, which you might call sub-life. You do not know of these, as at Earth level, at least two strands are required.

Descent in density was the focus of Earth human life for a long period, thus your planet became populated with people whose decreasing number of DNA strands was a natural result of their creating intent. Just as the intent to produce life with minimal

DNA strands accomplished that, the same is true in corresponding increases of the strands as souls are seeking higher forms of manifestation. This is now happening on Earth as the intent of some souls is to ascend rather than remain static.

Do you understand this, dear one?

S: I believe so, thank you. Do you have any knowledge of a laboratory creation of light from sound? Is this being fed from your realm to scientists here?

MATTHEW/GROUP:Yes, it is happening precisely that way. Those scientists are more pure of heart than many others operating in this moment on Earth, so they are being privileged to receive this experimentation instruction from this realm. Our scientists are feeding much more than this information to Earth scientists, but in only a few instances is this being acted upon. It is a lack of the scientists' willingness to change their perspectives on what they know and wherein they are comfortable, and much that is being made available to them is resisted.

However, always with third density beings there is reluctance to receive new information, so this is not trying the patience of our scientists. However, we do wish you all would be more open, as the advantages would be so great for Earth if only our knowledge were received and used. Other, higher sources also are beaming light filled with insight, and this, too, is being met with only mild curious interest as flashes of "science fiction" without any applicability to Earth. As more seeking souls there receive the light, this attitude of science will change, too.

You have another question.

S: Yes, I do. It's about the emissions of light and very low frequency perturbations from electromagnetic pulse sources that started appearing in 1994 and have been described as "red and ring-like" or "blue jets of light" or just "lightning discharges." Can you explain these phenomena?

MATTHEW/GROUP: These happenings are not phenomena, in our view. They are totally natural events, or occasions in the course of events, occurring in atmospheres in the process of considerable change. In this case, it is simply the extra light movement being beamed from light sources and the bursts of opposition from the entrenched dark energies.

There is great movement, much more so than heretofore, because now advances are being made in unleashing the strongholds of the dark energies. That is, the light is getting them out of their entrenched status. These are not inaccurately described as "lightning discharges," but of course your scientists who describe them thusly are attributing them to only weather or celestial occurrences and not at all to the spiritual combat evidence that they are.

They are blue and red in coloration because spiritual intelligence is evident as blue and the anger of the dark energies is evident as red. But there are light colors not being seen simply because the third density human eye is not acclimated to observing or identifying the myriad other colorations evident to higher density vision. Nevertheless, these are good signs as they signify progress in the light and dark combat that is leading toward light victory. You say, "Sparks are really flying" when you refer to an argument between people. Well, apply this same concept to the heavens and you get what is being observed.

S: That makes sense.

MATTHEW/GROUP: Mother Suzanne, it *all* makes sense and it *always* makes sense. By this we mean, in all ways the perfection of God's love and light reigns eternally on behalf of His children.

EXTRATERRESTRIAL LANDINGS

March 19, 1997

S. Will there really be ET mass landings in just a few weeks? Someone wants to know if the landing dates in a report she read are accurate – I can't find my notes with the date, so can you answer without them?

MATTHEW: I can tell you what I do know – or don't, and I don't know anything about any plans for ET mass landings. No definite dates, numbers of craft or occupants or landing sites are firm plans as far as is known here, and our Council is in constant touch with all of the civilizations within your "light years" of Earth. Our information is that no landings are intended any time soon because there is no assurance of safety for the landing parties, and the fate of those who did land in years past is well known in the universe. So it's safe to say that the imminent dates that person is asking about definitely are not accurate.

S: Have any ETs recently, or ever, destroyed an asteroid that would have severely impacted Earth?

MATTHEW: On occasion they have, but not recently. Your motion pictures are having a field day with these heavenly bodies, but none is near or approaching Earth that needs to be destroyed or deflected. That can change, as can anything or everything, but if something were imperiling you, it would be deflected or dispersed by the extraterrestrials who are tending almost every other measure of Earth's great needs in this moment, too.

FEDERAL RESERVE SYSTEM

March 19, 1997

S: The next question is, will the Federal Reserve System be exposed and toppled any time soon?

MATTHEW: Well, Mother, "soon" is not to us what it is to you, but yes, eventually it will it be toppled so another more fair, honest and just system for all can replace it. The Federal Reserve System will have to fall to pave the way for a new foundation out of which a phoenix economy will rise that in time will work well for you. The reason the Federal Reserve System, which has virtually paralyzed the monetary resources in your country – indeed, globally under other names – never has been challenged persistently is that its top power is within the darkness.

Like all other institutions completely within dark origination and operation, this system will be lessened in influence and powerful grasp as more and more light is beamed into the people at the top. As layer upon layer of the stranglehold is peeled away, revealing it for what it actually is and allowing light beings to take the reins, functional national and international monetary systems will emerge to institute methods of trading and sharing all resources fairly and equitably.

There must be a system of exchange based on goods and services for some sort of receipt in return, and money – which is not inherently bad at all – was in the beginning a reasonable form of exchange. That, like all other things deliberately designed to get out of hand, did so. Now international economies are at the stage where the dark grip is becoming evident due to the light shining on it.

S: Forget "soon" – can you give a time estimate for this to be accomplished?

MATTHEW: Mother, I'm not comfortable prognosticating in timeframes. At this level all I can see are developments in the field of potential and I know the word we receive from light sources beyond our own observations. I don't ever wish to speculate on timing or give information I'm not certain about, and so far, a specific time for completion of this money-changing basis is not coming from those higher sources. They're content to let it unfold without giving a timetable for completion and therefore, so am I.

S: OK, dear. That's the end of the list, and I thank you for all the answers.

MATTHEW: You're welcome, as always. So then, we've had this entire long sitting to ourselves except for the beginning. I've loved having you all to myself today except for that brief interlude, and you have held on admirably strongly.

S: Matthew, your energy is so much nicer to feel than the heavy, stodgy group energy, but I'm grateful for their background support and I hope they know I appreciate it.

MATTHEW: They aren't offended by your enjoyment of only my energy, Mother – they've always known that. And they do feel your appreciation, so not to worry.

THE YEAR 2012

September 19, 2002

S: Next question: Will the year 2012 really be the time of the major density shift?

MATTHEW: That year has been widely talked and written about by researchers of records of civilizations that were greatly attuned to universal happenings, and in some cases the information has been misinterpreted as a major shift to occur that year. No singular major shift can be assigned any specific time because the shift is a process and it has been going on for several decades. I am not saying that the Omnipotent Power cannot manage a complete changeover from one status to another in a twinkling, only that this is not what is happening.

More correctly interpreted is that 2012 is a *target* date for completion of the ongoing process, not an abrupt end to the scourge of the darkness. But even so, it is not a firmly fixed date in your linear time but rather a ballpark figure that can be either sooner or later, depending upon the acceleration of soul progression that you record as "time."

Previously it was correct to speak of solely third density planetary existence, when the vast majority of Earth inhabitants were stuck at that mentality and spiritual level. I surely don't mean that none escaped that limitation, because certainly God's message-bearers did and some visionaries – philosophers, inventors and artists in any form whose intelligence and spiritual clarity were further advanced. But by and large, the populace *could* not yet think in those loftier densities and thus their collective thinking kept Earth's overall third density limitations prevailing.

This started changing significantly about half a century ago and has continued to advance many hearts and minds into the light of Truth. At this time more than half of the energy of the planet has reached sustained light, and this means there is no turning back into the control formerly held by the darkness. However, the free will of that force must be honored, so whether the darkness will be completely vanquished by or even before your year 2012 is not yet known, but if not, then most surely not long afterwards.

NIBIRU (*PLANET X?*)

November 17, 2001

S: Hi, dear! Kiara Windrider [author of Doorway to Eternity*] would like you to talk about Nibiru – or Planet X since that's what some are calling it – and how it may affect Earth.*

MATTHEW: Mother and Kiara, I am happy to do this. In certain esoteric circles on the planet there is much talk of "Planet X." Some call it Nibiru, some refer to it as the photon belt, and some think of it as an unknown celestial body to be identified when it has approached more closely. The thing is, no one there can speak about this with certainty and so there is the tendency to look into the cosmology of ancient records.

The theory that this is the photon belt is way off. The belt, which is more influential than some regard it, as just a meandering massive collection of photon energy, is not the same as the "mystery" Planet X. Or more correctly, mystery *asteroid* of such size that it is not identified as such. This asteroid, which has been turned into a disaster, has a tortured soul and is seeking refuge in a higher spiritual frequency. Its Venus-sized body has a hot core and an exterior appearance of such desolation that it conveys no possibility of any kind of life.

Ah, the deception this has caused unwary civilizations! That appearance of being a dead world, a totally lifeless wandering form, is actually camouflage. Totally contrary to the asteroid's desire, it is populated with beings in a last ditch effort of the darkness to capture all of Earth. You could think of these beings as mercenary-type soldiers because they are a rag-tag population gathered by the dark forces to do their bidding, with the current promise that they will live richly in a sublime atmosphere if only they will go after this prize planet Earth.

It is the topmost level of dark energies at work on this plan, and the crucial point here is, it is *only* a PLAN – it is a reality *only* in the minds of the planners! It is the desperation idea of the darkness to destroy Earth if they cannot take over cleanly – if that word can even be used to indicate taking over by capturing souls rather than by invasion and occupation of the planet by the bunch aboard the asteroid.

At this juncture it isn't known whether the planners intend to use the asteroid as transportation of their puppet army for an Earth landing or whether it will be maneuvered into a collision course. In that case, the dark forces know that the hapless army aboard would be sacrificed, but lives to them are expendable.

They don't need a transportation system like this, of course, but it is serving their twofold purpose. One, it is simpler to convince warrior beings to feast and be jolly while planning the destruction of a once-pristine and godly planet, and Two, it fits into the Nibiru philosophy being promulgated.

This asteroid is *not* Nibiru, but that philosophy is serving the purpose of the darkness. Nibiru is sometimes spoken of as a "battleship" planet, and that tallies with the present day purpose the dark forces have in mind – which is precisely *why* they have it in mind. Those who believe Nibiru is returning will find this story believable and not think to look further into a possible grand ruse. The more energy in thought forms directed into this stream, the more reality given the asteroid and its ominous approach that the dark forces wish to achieve.

This asteroid presents *NO* danger to you! It will neither destroy Earth by collision force nor will it bring forth strangers to take over your planet and enslave all life there. Yes, it is a large body that could have explosive impact upon the entire solar system if all continued as the dark forces intend, but that will *not* happen. We have been told that the asteroid will be turned off course within your time period of the next six months.

More universal light than you can imagine is accomplishing this. Much is being generated by the extraterrestrials working throughout your nights and days to keep Earth stable and prevent the polar shifts even in a moderate measure. Significant shifts have happened before to cleanse the planet of negativity, but this time that is not intended as other plans are afoot.

Mother, give your fingers a break while you read and correct typos and see if you have questions.

S: OK, thank you. .... Matthew, this sounds like really bad science fiction! Was there ever a Nibiru?

MATTHEW: This gets into, What is "reality," Mother. Yes, there was a Nibiru in the minds of people who many millennia past needed to interpret their history, to put some order into the fragments of stories they had heard and account for the world in which they were living. These thought forms added to similar thought forms manifested Nibiru and its advanced civilization. In some parts of the universe there is no doubt of the actuality of Nibiru, so in that sense, it is certainly real.

The universe in its entirety recognizes much activity and results of ongoing manifesting, but not all. All is within the God mind, or universal mind, and of course within Creator mind, but not all is known by all civilizations throughout the universe. Many manifestations are not recognized as a reality in energy registrations far removed from them, and Nibiru is one. This puts it in the myth category of those civilizations who may have heard of it, but due to the lack of verifiable knowledge, they do not recognize its existence beyond the story.

But that revolves to this: There is some truth behind all myths, so something prompted the civilizations "in antiquity" to devise that kind of history that altogether created the Nibiru known today. In the continuum, what happened millennia past is the very same as if happening now and not two different "times" in the universal history of development. Thus it is very difficult to state categorically whether something is either real or it is mythical – almost always it is both, not simply Either or Or.

May 21, 2002

The six months was up, so where was the asteroid? Also I asked Matthew: What's this about Earth's revolutions stopping?

MATTHEW: First the asteroid answer, Mother. It is in an ongoing directional energy flow, not moved out of the way by a single major jolt, and by now there is no possibility of any collision course with Earth. The warrior force that had intended to plummet toward the planet for a battle worthy of their fighting prowess has been told by the galactic hierarchy that they may choose to accept the light or they will be taken to a lower density placement for remedial learning in alignment with their energy registration.

Now then, what you've heard about your planet stopping spinning on its axis is a fantasy that those who will stop at nothing to either scare you or entertain you must be chuckling about. However, very few are buying into something as ludicrous as a single celestial body suddenly standing still while the rest of the multi-billions continue in motion.

But then, universal science is greatly misinterpreted on Earth, either deliberately skewed into 100% fallacy or in innocent error. So *no* idea should – forgive the use of that word "should," Mother, that I've often told you YOU shouldn't use in your thinking and creating, but how else can I say this? No theory proffered in good intent should be ignored or ridiculed, but rather investigated by requesting input from the channels of light sources known to be dependable.

PHOTON BELT, LIFE UNDERGROUND?

May 8, 2002

S: Matthew? Hello?

MATTHEW: Mother, I'm here. I know you have serious thoughts about the difference in two main points in what you have just read and what I have told you about the photon belt and underground living on the planet. What I have told you regarding both is correct.

There still are as many ideas about the photon belt as there are souls contemplating it, with the basic theories ranging from "It will collide with Earth" to "It will not be anywhere near Earth" to "We already are in it." And most people there don't even know the belt exists.

We have no way of knowing at this point when or *if* the belt ever will profoundly interact with the planet again. Speculations about the timing and the proximity of the belt's journey in relation to Earth are reasonable because of any potential interaction, but definitely you are *NOT* within the belt!

Mother, please listen to the sense of this: How could the photon belt have embraced Earth without your awareness of entry into that powerful momentum, not to mention the major changes in power source? You have had the same sources of power for well over a century, with increasing technological innovations. Well, yes, counting fire, much longer than centuries, but the mainstay of your power sources for heat, light, transportation, appliances, tools and surgical instruments is electricity, oil and gas.

Other sources and types of energy are known, to be sure, but in most cases, their development has been suppressed by the corporate influences that want to keep the economy under their control and not let it rush out to greet sun and water and wind and new technology as energy sources.

Thus, oil sucked from the interior of Earth provides fuel for many of those power providers and so does gas, also from the interior of the planet. Both of these are part of Earth's very life force, and their removal at such a rate that she could not begin to replace them to sustain herself, must stop, and it *will* stop as soon as souls there treat Earth's life as real and sacred as their own.

But my point here is, neither oil nor gas can be used for ignition purposes in a photon-charged atmosphere because they are not compatible in nature. In fact, they are combustible, so you can see that the photon belt, which is called that appropriately for its composition, would not enable two of Earth's most prevalent power sources to coexist with its own energy makeup. Talk about an *explosive* situation!

In an atmosphere where photon charges are more prevalent than electron charges, the predominance of the photons dictates the type of power produced: photon. At this point Earth still has a predominately electron-charged atmosphere, therefore electricity is your primary power source. Mother, even if photon power *were* available to you, how would you run your *electrical* appliances without adapters?

It is not that photons are not all around you, but that the miniscule knowledge of how to apply their power extensively has not been allowed much exploration let alone development. This will be changing. Information about how photon energy can be directed into higher technological applications is being sent telepathically from scientists here to receptive scientists there, and with the additional light now on the planet, they can act on their "inspirations."

S: Well, it's obvious from what you said that we aren't within the photon belt, but can you tell me exactly where it is?

MATTHEW: If there were defined locations in the universe, yes, I could pinpoint the belt's location as well as any other observer beyond Earth could. But as you know, the time and space calculations devised on Earth do not exist beyond there. Even the determination of your telescopes' farthest range is an interpretation based upon the definitions and limitations that are *exclusively* yours, and those are only beginning to resemble the factual nature of universal laws regarding motion in the continuum.

Furthermore, the photon belt is not a placement such as Nirvana and your solar system are, but somewhat like the force fields without dense mass, its vastness meanders. There are innumerable conscious alignments with the belt's movement, and like all other like-attracts-like thought form manifestation and attraction in the universe, the belt is composed of thought forms and is subject to any alterations put into action by this basic natural law.

Despite, or perhaps because of this, the belt does travel in a fairly well fixed orbit in relation to large celestial bodies but not in a fixed pathway with an absolute headway or direction. So it can maneuver itself within an immense area and not threaten a sizable mass but can pull into itself the heavenly debris of smaller size. That is how the belt became what it is, as if it is a sky sweeper assigned to keep Space tidy.

The impulses emanating from the belt's motion are thrown out so far as to be unimaginable. It is these photon emanations that Earth science has detected and soon will be able to harness into what has been referred to as "free energy," alternative sources from those that are stripping Mother Earth of her life force substances. Those substances will be replaced by the advanced technology of other civilizations, otherwise planetary healing could not happen, and it is from those higher plane residents that the technological information comes to us that we filter to receptive Earth scientists. When you are using photon energy for everything that now is requiring other types of energy, you will see the difference, literally, between light and dark in action.

Mother, very few people on Earth really understand this universal principle of manifestation, and it should not surprise you that those who do also are aware of their other-worldly origins and universal connections. You do not have the education to provide me with the vocabulary needed for a scientific treatise, and this isn't necessary. Many souls like you can relate to this explanation, and the science of the spheres will be given to those who can assimilate and apply it.

Now then, the other point in that article that has let you feel once again that I do not always give you adequate or correct information is the underground living on Earth. Yes, there is now, long has been, and likely will continue to be underground living, but that is not meant to be the destiny of all Earth's residents. It just is not so that someday, maybe even in your lifetime, everyone on the planet will have to live underground!

What *is* true is that in the not-too-distant future beloved Terra's healing will return her to the magnificence that you don't remember consciously, but your soul does. It is unlikely that then people would not choose to live in the midst of what once again will be a true Eden.

I do not mean that no one is living underground now! Life there is much as it has been described in that article. Although details of cities, their sizes and distances apart, and scenery differ somewhat from the actual, all of that information is valid. The filtering aspects of telepathic communication added to the density of

Earth and the human brain that dulls memories of even personal experiences, account for the little discrepancies.

What is *not* correct is that the residents of Earth's interior are the people who escaped the catastrophic devastation and found refuge within the planet when all other life there was annihilated. All life *was* destroyed at that time – there were *no* survivors in physical bodies.

The loss of all humankind on the planet was not caused by an accident, but by the necessity to relieve the negativity created by the people who had forsaken spirituality and focused on intellectual domination, conquest, greed and fear. A time of freedom from those energy attachments was a prerequisite to Earth's rejuvenation.

Although it was not the entire population who had so far dropped from their spiritual beginnings that this drastic cleansing action was required, the pure in spirit were only too willing to leave physical life. The world they knew was being turned upside down, and survival anywhere on the planet would not have been pleasant. More accurately, it would not have been possible.

At a point when it was considered prudent to initiate human life on Earth again, the soul population embodied in her hospitable interior instead of on her surface, which was still in a recovery mode for comfortably sustaining life. The souls *now* living underground came at that time, in the repopulating by the same ancestors who had come to Earth or had cooperated in the original seeding programs.

When human, animal and plant life could flourish once again on the surface, some of the interior population moved out and up and, along with other ancestral repopulating – other major planetary upheavals notwithstanding – increased in numbers until reaching today's six billion or so. Herein may lie the discrepancy between that article and what I have told you: Many souls now living in Earth's interior also had embodied during the days of Lemuria and Atlantis and have clear recall of the happenings.

Mother, it never is my intention to dismiss, much less discredit, another source's version of what *IS*, but you are reluctant to accept my information that you see as being at odds with that. I'm glad you don't read any more channeled information than you do! As I have been traveling to other galaxies during the past three of your calendar years, it is from far beyond the vantage point of Nirvana that I can give you this information with assurance of its authenticity. However, prior to this, some of the information I have given you has come to Nirvana from those higher realms, from their master teachers or others who were visiting as well as the continual communication between those realms and our Council.

But what I especially wish to emphasize here is that the little variations in truthful information make no difference! I know you regard that article's two points of deviation from my own as very significant, but actually, Mother, they are inconsequential. It is possible that some words came out of order or were heard indistinctly so similar words were recorded – this is not unusual at all in telepathic communication. Telepathy has its own filtering system and each receiver has his or hers, so the originating thought may not be received exactly as the source transmitted it. That is why some messages received through our various channels are in agreement, sometimes even with similar terminology or phrasing, and other messages are at variation in some respects.

These slightly differing views of overall Truth are not going to put one segment of a soul-searching population in one growth place based on their perspective and another segment in a different level because they believe something a wee bit different. Both views – and their myriad kindred spirit variations – are milestones on the lighted pathway, where identical footsteps are not necessary. Souls who are seeking the Christed light don't have to step in time like synchronized marchers. Their route is the same, their destination is the same, their desire to be traveling there is the same. But the souls are *unique!*

One may pass a rose bush and smile in memory of the gift of roses for special occasions. Another may see a lilac bush and linger to absorb its fragrance, thinking of that enjoyment in childhood. Another may miss both of those but spot a bluebird and recall the thrill of seeing a nest of bluebird fledglings long ago. What attracts these souls differs, their moments and memories differ, but their journey is not altered and their destination is unchanged.

CROP CIRCLES

July 10, 2002

MATTHEW: The last part of that article is "where it's at," to borrow your phrase, Mother, and I cannot give you THE correct message of crop circles, either. There is not just one approach to considering the nature of these enigmatic creations that appear overnight in grain fields.

If their only purpose is to widely inform about the very existence of their off-Earth originators, then those beings surely would choose a means whereby all people could notice them. Something in the sky could be seen worldwide, but instead, these unique signs are on the ground where very few people can see them and, globally speaking, relatively few even see them in photographs.

However, the sudden appearance of an anomaly in the sky that would equal the puzzle of the crop circles could incite mass fear. Clearly that is *not* the intent of the circle originators or they would create something that absolutely *would* achieve that, because they certainly have the powerful technology to do so.

The precision geometric designs of the crop circles are awe-inspiring to behold, and beauty can be its own sufficient reason for being. Still, their existence must have importance beyond the intricate maneuvers that create the designs. Some believe they are messages between the extraterrestrials off and on Earth, but if so, it would seem to be more in the nature of charades because the telepathic communication of those civilizations does not require "sign language."

Obviously the circles are not meant to be translated into your languages because there is no common frame of reference for one to interpret the symbols into an accurate message. And if there were – actually, living among you *are* extraterrestrial souls in human bodies who can do this – how many would believe that someone really had decoded the message authentically?

While the designs may indeed be a series of communiqués, and probably a very enjoyable pastime for those who made them, the main point of the circles is, *they are right there in your fields!* Their designers want you to know they are so close to Earth that they are practically *on* earth, and they create tangible evidence of their presence to prove this.

So, I would say the makers' intent is your pondering and discernment of their purpose beyond any word message: Your awareness that indeed a higher intelligence is that close to you and it is *enhancing* the planet instead of marring or polluting, much less invading! If this presence desired to harm or conquer you, how easily it could have done so long ago, and instead, there is no harm done even to the stalks of grain. Surely this is the best possible evidence of the peaceful intentions of the circles' originators!

Can this not be a signal that "box" thinking about the world around you must be put behind you? Definitely no explanation for crop circles can be found in "box" thinking of either science or art, so don't these "enigmas" make it clear that an open, receptive mind is essential for these times when "new" truths are being revealed?

Why am I not certain if the designs also may have a worded message everyone could understand? Well, Mother, because there are a number of extraterrestrial civilizations and many millions of souls, individual or collective, around you, and there is not simply one artist who swoops down and makes all of those crop circles. I am not telling you that no one in Nirvana or elsewhere may be tracking these and one day will announce in Earth languages the exact translations of these designs, but simply, *I* do not know of any specific messages.

I think the conclusion of that article, that there is not only one valid interpretation of the symbols, is the wisest idea to hold for the time being as long as you realize that they definitely deserve interpretation as your inner self, your godself, suggests.

INDIGO AND CRYSTAL CHILDREN

February 2, 2003

S: Do you know anything about Indigo children and Crystal children, even if not by those names?

MATTHEW: Oh, absolutely, Mother, and they are called by those names here. Well, that is *why* they have those names – they took them with them! What you have read about their extraordinary psychic powers and their natures and wisdom is true. Moreover, it is strategic, so it won't surprise you to know that these are very advanced souls coming in to be their generation's vanguard for the era of love and light into which Earth is moving.

Actually, they are part of that movement's foundation as the light coming in with them is steady, never fractured, and their service is multifold. They not only are adding to that energy on the planet but also anchoring it, similar to the service the cetaceans are performing. At soul level they know exactly, and at conscious level they are mulling over their remarkable abilities, ideas and plans that will be the basis of the transition from dark laws and unjust governing into a world of kind, equitable and peaceful relationships among all nations.

These souls are known for manifesting abilities considered "miraculous," but actually are within the innate capacity of all humans healthy in mind, body and spirit. Enlightenment of that birthright is one of the gifts they bring, and that will be realized as they become the inspiring new leaders on Earth.

ASTRAL TRAVEL, EARTHBOUND SOULS

December 18, 2002

S: Hi, dear! Can you please tell me about astral traveling and also "Earthbound souls," if there really are those?

MATTHEW: Hello yourself, dear soul! "Yes" to both. Astral travel is like anything else that requires a great deal of knowledge and practice before it is mastered. The novice traveler often is unaware of the risks and due to ignorance doesn't stay within the safe "space highways," which are marked by energy registrations that a newcomer to this traveling would not always be able to discern.

While the soul itself has the knowledge for this in safety, the part of you that decides whether the trip will be undertaken is the *psyche,* and that is where the trouble begins because the psyche is third density in composition and deductive ability. Those who have progressed to fourth density spirituality, cellular structure and mental capacity can travel far more safely, but they, too, need to observe extreme caution in this era of such shake-ups in the universe.

Although some people there are managing this travel successfully, others are not doing so well. Not all who start out end up back in their bodies. During the souls' sojourns, other entities may have entered those "vacated" bodies and have enough energy to refuse to leave when the "owner" returns.

In some cases, physical death was the outcome, as the original soul garnered its strength to oust the intruder and the ensuing struggle damaged the body's life force beyond repair. In these cases, death is attributed to a medical reason for one "dying in his sleep." Certainly those physical ends not always are due to this battle of the souls, but some have been.

When the body survives the struggle for single soul occupancy and the winner is the intruder, a striking change of personality is evident to family and friends. Since the real reason for this obviously is not even considered, some logical cause is given, such as a mild stroke with prompt recovery but with puzzling aftereffects. If the body is more severely impaired by the struggle of the souls, it's considered the result of a more serious neurological happening that affected mental and mobility functioning.

Other times there is an agreement that the traveler-owner and the new occupant will cohabit the body, and then there is a less striking change in personality, again attributed to an acceptable medical reason. In all these cases of any personality change or physical death, it is respectively the psyche's alteration or the cessation of the body's former energy rhythm that produces the results.

With those possibilities upon a return home in addition to the risks of the traveling itself, you can see that it is not really safe at this juncture to undertake this adventure. This will change as Earth and her light-receptive beings move further into fourth and on into fifth density frequencies.

A light grid is being constructed by civilizations with the spiritual and intellectual advancement to use the love of God manifested as light, and when completed, it will assure safe space travel. Grid completion will be when the balance of light and dark has replaced its prevailing polarity in this "two-sided coin" of energy usage. In higher light realms, souls' travel safety already is assured because of their spiritual energy registration.

S: Why would those intruding souls want to enter a body here instead of living in a discarnate realm?

MATTHEW: I suppose there could be as many reasons as there are souls who want to do that, but basically, it's for experiencing that is not possible without a body. Until you have conscious awareness of life without a body, you don't truly appreciate the glories that can be experienced with one. Yes, there are many trials as well, but unless you are deprived of any aspect of your mobility and sensory span, you take for granted everything from breathing to performing feats in gymnastics and other expressions of agility.

You enjoy a symphony concert, but do you consider the gratification of the performers who are making that music? How about the pleasure of working with the soil and plants and reaping the harvest? Or smelling and eating delicious foods? The marvel of childbirth!

S: I hadn't thought of that. But still, you have described Nirvana as being so beautiful and offering so much that I can't imagine a soul not preferring it to getting into some strange body here!

MATTHEW: Most do eventually accept this realm as the after-Earth-life, but the souls who do *not* are the ones we're talking about. Actually, Mother, the situation of Earthbound souls is inextricably related to what I've just explained and also to what I've told you about the souls who refuse to accept Nirvana as their next world after leaving physical life and instead choose to "sleep" intermittently perhaps for centuries. *(NOTE: "Adjustment to the Realm" in* Matthew, Tell Me About Heaven, *covers this.)*

That is who some of these Earthbound souls are, and their wishing to be back in a body is not necessarily with negative intent. Often the indoctrination in religious or scientific beliefs was so intense that their resistance to a spirit realm foreign to those is understandable, as is their motivation to re-embody as proof that their beliefs are correct. Some souls desire vengeance for the brutal killing of their Earth lifetime bodies, and others have a strong desire to prove their innocence of the crimes for which they unfairly paid with their lives.

Regardless of what these souls may deem a justifiable purpose, taking over another soul's body incurs serious negative karma for the invaders. Yes, that would seem unfair if they did it unknowingly, but these body-searching souls are given explicit guidance as well as abundant light, and they refuse both in their determination to achieve their objectives. The good news is that most of these souls eventually do accept the light and agree to residency in Nirvana.

But there are many other soul entities whose immediate past life was not on Earth, or perhaps not even in a human civilization, seeking bodies anywhere to inhabit. These always are souls with low level spiritual awareness, or dark proclivity, otherwise they would be striving to move forward, not backward, in soul evolution, and they know that taking over another soul's body with dark intent is a regression of utmost severity.

It is not only astral travelers whose bodies may be occupied by strangers. In dream state there can be a similar, but very temporary situation. Unlike the soul struggles when a body has been vacated and then invaded, in these cases the "owner" soul always is on guard, so to speak, with protective measures against a permanent intruder. But with people in a very stressed state that puts the mind, body and spirit severely off balance, this protective element is diffused in strength and low-level energy registration souls take advantage of this.

The entry may be brief, leaving perhaps an uneasy sensation but no conscious memory upon waking. Other times this may cause traumatic dreams, or nightmares, that may be a preoccupation for a few days until life activity overcomes it in the person's focus. The difference in duration is due to the strength of the intruding soul and the determination of the original soul to oust the unwelcome visitor.

Definitely not all "bad dreams" are due to this kind of visit, but in this time the prevalence of drugs in so many bodies does make them more susceptible to the temporary take-over experiences. The chemicals in drugs, including those by prescription, attack both the soul and the psyche of a person, seriously compromising the ability to ward off an intruder soul.

A common effect of these temporary experiences is depression and confusion. If this happens frequently, professional counseling may be sought, or at least a friend to listen and advise how to deal with the distressing feelings. Unfortunately, often more drugs are prescribed or recommended, and those exacerbate rather than ameliorate the situation.

The third density elements of Earth combined with the individual's energy stream also play a part in allowing these entry occurrences.

But despite all the turmoil there, an enlightened person can achieve the emotional balance that automatically puts him in a higher vibration, or energy frequency, where an entry attempt is not possible. Any soul who would try such an action would be consigned by its lower energy registration to third and lower density realms, thus prohibiting access to any body whose energy stream is in a higher frequency.

Civilizations who have achieved the spiritual clarity that places them in fourth density and beyond do not experience intrusions because those energy registrations are not encumbered by Earth's lower density limitations.

S: I see. If channels reach entities in those lower levels, even though they think they're connected with light sources, are they reaching Earthbound souls?

MATTHEW: They may be, but not necessarily. Souls with far more in mind than sharing or taking over a body to avenge a wrongful death, much less to play a violin or eat a fine dinner, are lurking for other purposes. These are the ones with the dark proclivity that I mentioned. They are only too eager to captivate the souls and consciousness of power-hungry people and through them achieve their own dark goals of domination.

S: The work of the dark forces again. When people die in the struggle of their own souls trying to evict intruder souls, is this part of their pre-birth agreements?

MATTHEW: Pre-birth agreements have latitude in some of the experiencing chosen as karmic lessons for balancing, and soul-level "in-fighting" is one of the elastic areas. Astral travel and channeling have many offshoots that in themselves are specialty experiencing, and all categories of mingling with and rising above lower-level spirits can provide the selected lesson.

Let me say this more simply: *It's resisting temptation.* This can be at soul level, which you don't realize, or at conscious level, where the conscience part of the soul gives the answer in accordance with the pre-birth agreement. But you have the free will to ignore that inner voice, and if you do that time and time again, eventually the conscience totally loses its ability to function, and that provides a constant open invitation to whatever outside influences you think of as evil.

UNIVERSAL LIGHT FORTRESS

September 19, 2002

MATTHEW: The universal light fortress is what it sounds like – protection within the light – and in the case of Earth, it is a grid of electromagnetic waves that bend with energy motion to allow safe passage of craft and small orbiting objects. This grid is the younger cousin of the much vaster protective system being erected in your galaxy that permits without interference the orbiting of craft, planets, whole solar systems. That grid is connected to grid segments covering all galaxies surrounding the Milky Way, and so forth

The purpose of this universal web is to create safer traveling for individual souls, for collective souls and for solids such as planetary bodies and mammoth spacecraft when materialized. The bumps in the astral highways are being fixed, so to speak. A breach anywhere in this grid web precludes the strength of the entire web, and the weak link around Earth cannot be permitted much longer.

This weak link is caused by the manmade grid undertaking claimed to be for providing national defense, determining and warning of weather severity, and for enhanced communication hook-ups. Not reported is that it also is a global populace surveillance system, but even that is not the whole truth of this Earth grid. It is being designed to prevent extraterrestrial spacecraft coming within the parameters of its lower level formation.

It baffles us why your world leaders are fooling themselves that off-planet civilizations' technology would not be as far superior to Earth's inferior knowledge as many other scientific projects already have proven. They do know that their efforts to keep "aliens" from landing on Earth are doomed, yet they are rushing along this grid and "Star Wars" defense equipment as if it will be a safe haven for their continuance of dark deeds. Their technological obstacles will affect only the timing of the universal grid's completion, with "later" rather than "sooner" at stake, but not going ahead with the segment nearest Earth is not an option.

The higher density into which Earth is rising is required before the part of the universal grid around your planet can be firmly established. When the light is reigning on Earth totally, no darkness could even begin to approach that brilliance.

However, nothing in the universe is isolated from anything else, and even though this entire light web-work is a major development to benefit countless souls, the emergence of one soul out of darkness into the light holds the same triumph for the universe as the grid. Every milestone for the light is heralded with universal joy and every backslid soul is a sad note for all, with renewed efforts to send more light to that soul. And so it has been for eons.

PART III

TALKING WITH GOD

MARNIE

When Matthew and the Group no longer could answer my questions about Marnie, whose family and cult made her the victim of their Satanic ritual abuse, God entered the discussion. Since this was the first time God ever had spoken to me, His reference to "the second time" shocked me – His very presence shocked me! Later it occurred to me that He must have been referring to the short message that appeared on my computer screen at a time when I was too distraught to type. (NOTE: That was in Summer 1994, when finally Matthew told me why he had died at such a young age, and the message is in "Communion with Matthew," in *Matthew, Tell Me About Heaven.)*

December 22, 1996

MATTHEW/GROUP: No, we are *not* just saying that, Mother Suzanne! We are telling you what we *know*, yet you want more assurance that our words are valid.

GOD: Suzanne, this is God speaking. I know this is the second time only that I have come in your long time of speaking with Matthew and the others through this computer. I have come to speak personally to Marnie.

"Marnie, my dearest child, please do not despair. Know that always and forevermore you are within my light and love. Dearest child, look inward at the light that has preserved your mind in health throughout the angel child's rescue and beyond. You need not suffer more. Please know that and hold it to your heart.

"In your heart you ask me for a sign of my presence. I can give you a dove that you will see in the air, in a picture, a tree, a greeting card, in a song. Wherever you see the dove, hear the dove, know that in those moments you can smile and say, 'God, you old fool you, you really are doing it.' That would not be disrespectful, daughter of my light and love."

That is all, Suzanne, my servant in this moment and beloved in all moments. No one is more beloved than another, but some are higher in my sight only because they are closer to the light. Marnie is one of the closest you will ever know in many lifetimes of doing and learning. You yourself shine brightly, but your life force did not derive from the Christed realm, that highest angelic realm closest to Creator, and hers did.

I am with you through all your tribulations with the book, dear soul, and I know of its success as ordained. Amen.

S: Matthew? Was that really God? Are aware of what He said, if it really was God? Did you ask Him to come?

MATTHEW/GROUP: Yes, Mother, that was God, and no, it was not necessary to summon Him. God is in constant awareness of Marnie's struggle. He is sending her light and love through various means, most of which she never recognizes. We believe she is recognizing you as a messenger in full caring, but do not be surprised if she has doubts of your sources' authenticity. After all, you experience the various energy sensations of our communion, and do you not still have doubts at times of its reality?

January 15, 1997

S: Is God upset because Marnie feels He abandoned her and has never given her relief from pain?

MATTHEW/GROUP: Would you like God to respond in His own words?

*S: Does God want to? And, does God ever speak to me
directly and I don't know it because He doesn't identify himself –
I mean other than the two recent sittings?*

GOD: Dear soul, you question too much in some ways and
insufficiently in others. Let us relax in our conversing. I'd like that
but *I* can't if *you* can't! Maybe first you should breathe deeply.

Ah, that is better, so let us speak of Marnie. I shall address
her directly.

"This is your buddy, Marnie, not your adversary! You blame
me for abandonment, but I did not abandon you. Your pain was
too great for you to see that it was the rescue that made you feel
abandoned. At the depth of darkness into which you had to
descend to rescue the angel child, there is no light. So of course
you felt abandoned, dear heart, because in the darkness there is
separation from me, separation from the light. Your soul understood but your psyche could not.

"It was by your choice that the mission with its inherent sense
of abandonment was undertaken. The angel child was *your own!*
No wonder she finally cried out for salvation – you had been
pushing her so long to accept the light. Had she not agreed to the
rescue, millions of souls in her lineage would have perished when
cut from their life force.

"Only in physical body could the mission be performed and
only in physical form have your despair and discouragement
come. Your soul, knowing all that the rescue mission required,
undertook and completed the job through the highest degrees of
light and love. Only from that height of connection with Creator
could the strength and power of a redeeming soul come. That is
who you are, Marnie, beloved child. Read the section I dictated
to be published and you will understand far more. (*NOTE: This*

refers to the "Lost Souls" chapter of Revelations For A New Era.)

"Let us speak of this moment, when you still feel I'm not here or there or anywhere else that you are. No doves around? What about the dove in the treetop that you thought you saw and then figured, 'Na-a-a-w'? Well, I am within that dove and I am within every aspect of your life that you will allow.

"Every moment my energy is filling you with something of your choosing. You are choosing *fear.* You are preoccupied with events whose outcome you fear and with memories of the past that was filled with fear, and by so doing, you are placing binding straps on your consciousness that won't allow fear to leave and be replaced by what you *do* want to feel.

"Marnie, dearest child of my total essence, please think only of this moment. Think of the encouraging 'visions,' as you call them, but they are memories of actual happenings on that highest angelic plane wherein you don't think you're operating, but you *are!* As you leave fear and allow the light of your angelic composition to be felt, you will leave in a twinkling those areas of fear that are *over.* The agony can be over as well.

"Marnie, dearly beloved, live with the knowledge that always and forever your godself is at oneness with my godself and know your divinity within Creator."

FEBRUARY 28, 1997

S: Good morning, everyone! You know from my prayer that I am asking for answers to Marnie's questions.

MATTHEW: Mother, this is just me, and only to say good morning, dearest soul. We are going to turn over this sitting to

God, as only He can answer the many questions on that paper. It would be presumptuous of me or even the group to even try to reply. I'll speak with you later because now God is ready.

S: Good morning, God. Thank you for coming to answer Marnie's questions. I'll type them for the record even though I'm sure you can read them just as Matthew does. That's not being presumptuous, is it?

GOD: Not at all presumptuous! Dear soul Suzanne, I commend you for your devotion to Marnie, who is the highest spirit – or soul, if you prefer – that you will know in this lifetime and many others combined. So, please type each question "for the record."

Q: Will any of those who have made my life a living hell feel remorse and make amends to me? They deny it happened

GOD: "Marnie, dearest child, you came from a realm so near Creator Source that it is beyond even the wildest imagination of most souls on Earth. But in your humanness, you are asking for those people to be at the same height of knowingness that you yourself are.

"In *their* humanness they have no mental, emotional or spiritual depth to see what they have done. They know their deeds, of course, but they are not aware of the length to which vindication of their deeds is required by their higher selves. They simply are too far out of touch with their souls to know this connection.

"In your heart you want to know if these people will be consigned to 'hell' to repent. It is a complex situation that is not within any frame of reference for your understanding even with your high consciousness, which still is within Earth's density. But in simplest explanation, there will be a combination of the 'hell' as well as the soul growth accorded each of them.

"What you do not know consciously is that all had to agree in the soul-level contracts to do or allow to be done to you what was necessary for you to experience so the angel child's rescue could be undertaken and accomplished. First came your decision to undertake the rescue mission and then came their agreement to fulfill their roles that would enable you to fulfill yours. But of course in their consciousness there is not an iota of awareness of this.

"There is no separation from the moments of their 'repentance' station within the entirety of experiencing and from the higher station they have attained by agreeing to experience such a difficult lifetime with all the ramifications of horror and being the cause of your own horror and agony. But I do assure you, beloved Marnie, that the process will embody both the 'child within' being graced beyond your ability to conceive while the personage of each soul - the person of the lifetime - will indeed have to endure the awakening of what it did, the traumatic aspects of the karmic lesson incurred.

"Dearest Marnie, I cannot explain more clearly or with more elaboration because you simply haven't the human capacity to relate to what happens within the light and the darkness and the reconciliation of all simultaneously. That 'judgment day,' if you will, is when each of those abusers will see the enormity of what he or she has done, and in the self-judgment process of each, the pain can be relieved only by requesting absolution and forgiveness *directly to your soul.*

"Time is not the vital aspect of what you are asking for, but rather, the emotional capitulation, the full recognition and admission of what all of them have done to you. That will be known to them in fullness only after their embodiment ends, and if you are still right there on Earth, this process will happen during your life-

time, but not theirs, do you see? Your *soul* will know, beloved
child, as will theirs.

"For now, let the vindication of all you have endured be the glory
given you by the highest angelic realm from which you came."

That, I believe, is sufficient for Marnie even if you are still
wishing for words I didn't use, Suzy. Suzy is lighter than
Suzanne, just as your spirit is lighter now than when we started.
I'm glad! You are so afraid – yes, *afraid!* – that I won't say the
right thing. My goodness, child, of course I know what you're
thinking: *"God's lousy at answering questions."* Well, aren't you?

*S: Matthew said that when he isn't invited into my thoughts
or feelings, they're private and he's not aware of them. But obviously you don't work that way.*

GOD: Suzanne – that more formal name for the seriousness
needed here – Matthew is Matthew. For him to know your deepest longings and most private thoughts, yes, you must invite him.
However, *I AM* you, and I am not in any way at all removed from
you in any moment. I AM your *soul,* so how could I be excluded
in some moments and not others? There can be no arbitrary separation of me from any of my children, not even those who don't
acknowledge my existence, by whatever name they wish to
denounce my very being.

There, now let's get back to Marnie's questions.

*Q. If God is absent in darkness, then only those not suffering
"hell" can experience him – correct? What about the poem,
"Footprints in the Sand"?*

GOD: "That is a simply and beautifully expressed sentiment,
but you are missing the point here, my beloved child. I KNOW

there were times when you felt totally abandoned – I felt those as powerfully as you did yourself! You are part of me, I'm *all* of you – so of course I knew you felt I had abandoned you!

"But *why* did you feel I had – because I never took away the horror and torture? How could I take away something that *you yourself* chose? Marnie, by *YOUR* choosing, I had to go through *exactly* every moment that you did, and yet, I didn't say, 'Wait a minute – *you* may be up for this but *I'm NOT,* so forget about this rescue!' I *couldn't* abandon you because *you* didn't abandon your angel child!

"Maybe therein is the pit of darkness you've been living in and it can be transmuted into the light by those words alone. I hope so, I devoutly hope so, my beloved Marnie!"

Suzy, let's move on.

Q. *Just exactly what is God good for?*

GOD: Oh, my! I saw that coming, and I'm still searching for the best words. It's not your fault here, Suzy, so just calm down. I know the question took you by surprise because you had to turn the page to see it, and once again you felt afraid that I wouldn't give Marnie a satisfactory answer.

"What am I good for, Marnie? How about for starters, allow-ing you to proceed with your intense desire to save the part of you that finally had called out to be saved? How about my sharing that *complete* experience, however agonizing and fearful and painful in every way? How about my enduring with you every memory of those many years, and how about my willingness to be whatever you thought of me, whether demon, fool, good-for-nothing-son-of-a-bitch? How about my willingness to stay within you and within all others and allow this play of *all* humanity to run its course as EACH soul on Earth has *chosen* to do?

"*Surely* you can't believe that I enjoy being brutalized, terrorized, starved, grieved or whatever my children are enduring and be left alone without a spark of spirit as in the case of the most desperate ones! Surely you can't believe that I enjoy being the CAUSE of that kind of suffering! Yet I have to experience all of this because this is what my children *have CHOSEN* to balance their experiencing so they can return to the former 'heaven' of total light that *they* had chosen to leave!

"Just think of this, Marnie, and if that's not enough, come back at me for more."

Go ahead, Suzy. I feel your sadness in realizing that everything you and Marnie have experienced has been felt equally by me. And *none* of it because *I* chose, but rather only followed *your* choices.

When you grieved so long for Matthew, I was grieving with the same intensity *even though* I knew where his soul was, I knew how OUR grieving was harming his adjustment and growth, and how I wished it could be otherwise for *all of us*. But I did not have the power to change what you had the power to choose. You may not think you chose to grieve as you did, but you would not let in the light that Matthew and so many other souls were sending to uplift your spirit.

So, let us return to Marnie's questions.

Q: I need relief from financial insecurity. Why aren't you helping me?

GOD: "I know you do, dear Marnie, and even though part of me wishes this were not so, the part of me that is YOU is *decreeing* this condition! There is a conflict between what *I* know can be your lot in life and what *you yourself* are putting in the way of that unfolding by the constraints you have imposed. Look back at what I said about placing binding straps upon your relief from fear – lack of finances falls into this as surely as everything else.

"The universe – an expression that means to many the same as God –provides *exactly* what you ask for, *exactly* what *any* soul asks for! How could it be otherwise, when I am that soul who's asking and also the provider and source of what's being asked for? You *fear* never becoming financially independent. So, you aren't asking for the prosperity you *want,* you are stuck in the fear of it never happening!

"The powers of manifestation bring the conditions of whatever you're putting your energy into, and instead of putting that into prosperity, you're putting it into fear about the *lack* of prosperity! No, you *don't* want fear and you *don't* want poverty, but when those are what you're focused on, how can your powers of manifestation bring anything else? And so, Marnie, you create for yourself – and for *me* – the experience of fear and reasons for financial anxiety.

"*Change your focus!* Dwell instead on money coming in! Be realistic. See it starting to come in a trickle of glittering gold, like sequins or golden sand, and then see it coming in bigger and more forms. See it brightening your home, your heart, your soul. Simply set the course for that which you *want,* NOT that which you *fear,* and stick with it and it *WILL* happen! The universal laws can't be denied!

"Dearest soul Marnie, my caring for you is even vaster than your own heart cares for your happiness. So, carry forward your plans and dreams with the LIGHT assurance that you will bring about the answers to your dreams, whatever they are within the reality of your being. If they exceed that reality, they cannot be unfolded as they will be in a foundation of almost senselessness, self-defeating entrenchment in what you *think* is impossible.

"But it's precisely that condition of *disbelief* that does indeed make the dream impossible! Reverse that, and be realistic in your reaching for the stars and you will become as one with them. At that point, *nothing* is unrealistic. You have returned to your one-ness with all your 'selves' and with all that I AM."

April 7, 2000

S: Do you know why Marnie still is suffering so much from memories?

GOD: Yes, my child, of course I know. This is one of those situations that is quite beyond your accepting. Not because you haven't been given answers time and again by both Matthew and me, but you do not hear what you want to hear and you are not accepting what you *do* hear.

All right, once again, it is the law of the universe that is binding Marnie to the horrors that are *over* and to the memories that have fulfilled their rescue purpose. Her experiences are still in energy form throughout the universe, and with like attracting like, she is calling these to her again and again and again by the *fear* that is holding her captive of her past. I have explained how she can release this by receiving the light constantly being beamed to her.

S: Surely you have the power to beam enough light to stop this cycle.

GOD: Suzy, if Marnie chooses to remain in that dark place of

532sdfsf22

---

fear – and she *is* choosing this! – NO, I do *not* have the power to defy Creator's laws of free will or like attracts like! I inherited those laws and am stuck with abiding by them. And remember, her rescue arrangement is with *Creator*, not with me.

    S: Then why doesn't Creator help her? The rescue is over and her monumental task is done. Her suffering isn't helping anyone now.

    GOD: Not only isn't her suffering helping her or anyone else, it is creating bushels of negativity within her and all around her. All of the thought forms being created by the combination of her fear, rage, and need for revenge is adding to like thought forms in the universal soup and making a powerful block of darkness to penetrate in your dimension.

    S: God, excuse me, please, but I don't understand how Marnie's arrangement can be with Creator when you keep saying that she is "your child."

    GOD: Suzy, even though the entire rescue mission was indeed beyond my domain, Marnie is living in *my* universe. Her life – her psyche and physical being and free will – are here. So she is "my child" in every aspect of her *embodiment* in her Marnie personage, and her choices affect this universe where I'm bound by Creator's laws to function as I do and without power or authority to do more than that.

    It is at *soul* level that Marnie is above my station, and as for Creator helping her, I simply don't know. I'm not sure if Creator isn't allowing her the same free will choices as all other souls since back in the Beginning. That's when her soul was created in the Christed realm just beneath Creator and above me, as you have been told over and over by Matthew and me.

My child, you must accept my limitations, however the reality of me differs from what you were taught.

ELLA

June 5, 1998

MATTHEW: Ella, the love of God is within and surrounding you and those whom you love. Do not ever doubt this! *Never* are you being punished by being given premonitions, as if you had done something "wrong" or "bad" and therefore God was letting you know something awful was going to befall you. That NEVER is what happens!

GOD: No longer is Matthew speaking, but God wanting to speak directly to my child Ella. Suzy, please excuse this intrusion just as I have asked Matthew to do. But this is my opportunity to reach my beloved child and tell her what has been going on and what she can expect if she will feel confidence and follow what in truth is being given forth.

As before, please put my emphasis in all places with capitals and so forth as I show you. Thank you.

"Ella, you are highly chosen and gifted in a way that few are, but you see this gift in darkness. NEVER, my child, is it *within* darkness that you are living! Not only are you protected within my loving grace, but you have these premonitions or visions *to protect you!* You have been in places at times when your physical life was endangered, so you were warned and you were moved to follow the warnings. By doing so, your life has been saved. But you do not connect the premonitions with the life-saving grace they were.

"Instead of attaching a sensation of love and warning to the spirits' alerts to you, you have attached a sensation of fear to your escapes. That is where it started and from that moment forward, that fear has been drawing in – creating! – the vision of darkness. Not evil, not wrong or bad, preying on you, beloved soul, only the darkness at work on your *mind*.

"I need you and *you* need to be just where you are – *alive!* You have involvement in major ways in the lives of your children and others as well, and all of their agreements for this lifetime would be sacrificed if your life were to end on Earth. *So you have been protected by the light all along!* Your visions can be within the light, too, if only you will allow that darkness where YOU have put them to ease away into the rosy goodness of the love and energy that is swirling softly around you."

No, Suzy not like a vacuum cleaner from heaven, but I am hoping that when Ella reads this she will smile just as you are at that bit of imagery I sent to you because I want you to feel lighter. As you were typing my words, your heart was with your own child who is in pain. Your mind stayed with my words, but I need you to be free from that heaviness in your heart.

"Ella, you have arrived at a juncture in your life when not only do *you* need to be free from the darkness you have associated with your premonitions, but *your daughter* also needs release from this influence.

"To prevent darkness from further blinding you to the real nature of your visions, your gift and how you can use it, I wish first to release you from feeling that evil is behind it. NEVER in the case of you or your daughter is evil behind it as you both think! *NEVER!*

"You had this gift of 'seeing' in less negative regard prior to that first escape from danger. There is no longer the acceptance and honoring of this gift in these ages that once there was, and I'm having such a trial in awakening my myriad Earth selves so that a return to this total communication and understanding becomes possible. So, even though I speak of this as *your* gift, as if none other shall ever have the same, it is a gift that is the birthright of *EVERY* soul throughout this universe.

"The intensity of darkness, however, is *not* a necessary design of this gift! So, please do this simple exercise. See a photograph of yourself and surround it with light."

Sounds ridiculous, Suzy? Well, I have to make these exercises simple so people will do them and not say, *Oh, I'd never be able to do that!* like astral travel, for instance.

"Ella, my child, choose a photograph where you are being reflected in such happiness that you actually *feel* LIGHT - uplifted, being lifted up by the light, *light in heart!* Then close your eyes and feel yourself in that happiness of the picture. If not a photo, then remember a special joyous time and feel yourself smiling, laughing, as you were in that moment and now feel how uplifted you are in *this* moment.

"That's because in this moment you *are* being uplifted! It is an actual transformation as the light is entering you. You need only do that exercise over and over until you no longer are tied emotionally to the fearful sensations that were in murky blackness. Your daughter should do the same with her picture or recalling a joyous time.

"Forgive my use of the word 'should,' which *should* be banned from your vocabulary. So not 'should,' just *do!* 'Should' is a different vehicle of speech, of course, but it does not take into account free will, which is the basis for all of your experiencing in this lifetime. All lifetimes, actually."

Suzy, please breathe deeply. You need another release from heaviness. Just let me flow as you have done before. .... Thank you. Now let us proceed.

"Dear soul Ella, you have grown spiritually because of your mother's influence that you have been drawn to. Now, you or anyone else could say, *I just as easily could have rebelled against that and been drawn to the opposite.* Yes, you could have been drawn instead to the *opposite* of light and love, which is the *absence of light and love* that you have termed 'evil.'

"But you were drawn to this godly influence by your soul nudging constantly at you to stay on the track that at soul level you chose to follow when you and the others in your family made the agreement. Or more simply, you *listened* to the conscience part of your soul. These are pretty complex agreements, and more widespread than you can imagine, but they work *because I AM the minds and souls of All!*

"Ella, you are NOT in darkness, beloved child, but you SEE yourself there, foundering and confused, lost and sometimes so fearful of being evil that you can barely breathe. It is time – it is *past* time, truly — for you to be free from that and to lead your daughter out of that same type of murkiness so she does not experience it for many years, as you have. *It is not necessary!*

"It is not a waste that you experienced that darkness, my blessed soul! Experiences are *never* a waste if light emerges out of them, especially if light instruction and assistance are given to others. You can tell, teach, *show* others the light that fills and fulfills your life!"

NORMAN

July 1, 1998

GOD: "And so, Norman, LIGHT is what is coming to Earth in this unique time and creating what you think is the 'coming of the end.' The end of *what*, pray tell? Many will follow the light being beamed to all and many will not. That is the free will choice of *every* life. It is not changeable. Those who rise into the light will be uplifted and be with me in body and spirit. Those who choose not to accept the light will not live in body or spirit with me, but will end physical existence and start over as almost infant stage of awareness in that first moment of gasping for air.

"*That* is what is ahead. *That* is what has been 'forecast.' Excuse me, but I cannot help but feel amused by that word 'forecast,' as if something immutable and immovable has been waiting throughout 'eternity' – and exactly what is *THAT? Hardly!* Not the tiniest speck of matter is unchanged from moment to moment!

"So, this 'forecasting' you're asking about, as if Dooms Day or Armageddon is on the near horizon – *forget that!* It is NOT the case! It is the *concept* of some, so they can create that for themselves as long as they are alive on Earth to do so, because it is solely the province of their *ideas*. Their CONVICTIONS do that creating! So, those souls who are intent upon having an Armageddon, so they *shall!* But for you who aren't intent upon having that sort of 'future,' you WON'T!

"You, my beloved child Norman, can stay within the light and rise into higher and higher dimensions of closeness, understanding, awareness. There are no strict rules that are so complex or rigorous that you and anyone else aren't capable of adhering to them. *All that is required is to live within the light!* Or in simplest terms: **BE KIND.**"

Suzy, how hopping around on the keys your fingers are! You are feeling the love flowing in this light, and your fingers are hopping like tiny bunnies on the keyboard.

"Norman, what you need to FEEL, not just know in your head, is that we are ONE! Every soul together still is *ONE!* What happens to one is never separate from all, and that is why we must make the pathway in unison within the light. Those who choose not to join us will not know of their Oneness or of their light that has become so buried in their proclivity to live in either fear or ignorance. Well, ignorance is the breeding ground of fear and greed and the results of that fallout, and *none* of this needs to be at the core of any life!

"I know you think I am naïve, Norman. Yes, of course I know your thoughts, my dear child – but how *could* I be naïve? I know *everything* that *every* being knows, I *feel* what *every* being feels! So by the very definition of naive, I am NOT it! Therefore, what I tell you is sensible, is THE WAY, THE TRUTH and THE LIGHT. I have sent all of you this message in many tongues, by many messengers, and *still* you aren't getting it! So we're having one more try at this."

Erase "try," Suzy. In your language it works, but in deeper reflection, "trying" indicates less than DOING. It indicates a rather half-hearted effort, a fore-acceptance that "this" or "that" may not work. And unless you approach something with the attitude and conviction that it IS successful, how can you then manifest it so? So we must forget "try" – like "should" – and LIVE!

"Norman, living is from the soul upward, outward, and inward. There need not be any compartment locked away for you to discover and scare you or capture you or sadden you. *All* can be lightened!

"So, beloved child of mine, I think I have talked too much, but it's a THRILL for me to be heard by ones who actually *believe* it's God speaking! It's also *of* you and *through* you that I'm speaking, yet doing so with the knowledge of *all* souls in the universe, only keeping private all of their thoughts and feelings."

Suzy, I can go on because I AM eternity and your body isn't. Your soul, yes – your body, no! Take a break!

ERIC

October 22, 1999

S: Good afternoon, God.

GOD: Yes, indeed, it *is* a good afternoon, isn't it, Suzy? All of the days on Earth have goodness within them. I have enjoyed your and Matthew's discussion today. Now I believe you have a question for me regarding something your son Eric told you. For a record of the question and my reply, would you like to type that now?

S: Yes, thank you. Eric said he has developed the theory that you constantly are putting people to the test that takes them to the limit, but not over the limit they're capable of handling. He wants to know if he's right about that. And please say anything else that will be enlightening to him about that SCUBA diving incident last week.

GOD: Suzy, I think you will be more at ease if you feed your dogs before we go further. Then they will be satisfied and happy and quiet.

S: .... God, thank you for that break. It was a lot longer than I had expected. Are you ready to comment on Eric's theory?

GOD: It is good that you're more at ease now, with all dinner times over, and yes, I am quite ready to comment on my child Eric's theory of what I do. First I shall say that you, Suzy, have the idea that since I am not separate from any of my children, that I already knew his theory. *NO?* Well, then I am not as much a

thinking part of you as I thought! But you *did* think of many conversations we have had that would dispute my testing *anyone*, and
I *know* I am quite correct on that! But I shall tell this myself to
your beloved son.

"My dear child Eric, first you must understand that there is no
separation whatsoever between me and any living form – and that
is all the animals and the plant life, not only people in their myriad forms and cultures throughout this universe. If I would be putting tests forth for any, that would be testing *myself,* you see, and
there is no need for that. Rather, I allow Creator's gift of free will
to serve each individual as he or she seeks fulfillment. For me to
step in and take over that free will would be to deny the exalted
nature of Creator.

"I am but a second level force with CO-creating abilities, *not*
creating abilities, and in just this universe. Others like me do the
same in their universal spheres of jurisdiction. That is, they and I
co-create with Creator, just as each of my progeny does, because
that source energy is of Creator, and the laws that govern this universe and the others are of Creator's design.

"It is exactly in that co-creating through *individuals'* free will
choices that my part in all of this experiencing through every life
form anywhere universally happens. Most of the life forms you
are not familiar with, but I assure you, there are many of them with
intelligence far exceeding that of humans on Earth, and furthermore, there are no things between you and them that are hidden
from me OR from your own souls!

"It is at *soul* level that we all are inseparable. I rejoice when on
a *conscious* level some of you realize this, but most of you do not,
not while you are residing in a dense atmosphere that doesn't permit the all-knowingness that those in higher dimensions are thoroughly aware of. It isn't just at the *conscious* experiencing level

that I AM you, you ARE me, of course, as our *souls* are ONE. Therefore in any and all life forms throughout this universe, I AM that I AM Totality, and each of you is an inseparable aspect of that.

"You needed to know that more clearly than you do before I could speak directly to your theory. No, my beloved child, I do NOT give tests! I experience the same degree of risk or ease that each of my children does in his or her *choosing* of each! I am not in the habit of disagreeing with any of you insofar as how you exercise your free will, whether it be 'stupidly' or 'brilliantly,' which is all in the eye of the beholder of the activity and its result, is it not?"

Suzy, I feel there is some disagreement between you and me as to what I'm saying here. Do you wish to comment, as I am as confused as you. How could it be different, my child, since I am not exercising my eyes as "omnipotent"?

S: I'm not disagreeing with what you're saying, but Eric does understand who you are, so I'm confused about why you're telling him all that.

GOD: Child, do you really believe you know better than I what he understands of me?

S: Well, maybe he hasn't read everything I've been sending him. Anyway, God, you haven't mentioned that dangerous diving situation last week for Eric and YOU as an inseparable part of him, or vice versa. Who alerted the dive master to look for Eric and then share his air so Eric didn't die from lack of oxygen? Since you are both of these men, or they both are parts of you, did you in your "umbrella" self handle this lifesaving situation or did Eric's guardian angel do it?

GOD: My child! You are assuming too much here! I had not completed my message to Eric, I only interrupted it because of your feelings that were confusing me. So let us address your questions.

Yes, there is a guardian angel with every life everywhere, so that angel's constant and diligent presence always is prepared to be in a lifesaving mode. However, this was a risk of death, not a death risk, if you see my difference. *No?*

There was not the onset of the pressure that could, and no doubt *would* have been life threatening, or, a death risk. But the angel doesn't wait until danger is so nigh that physical death can happen without instantaneous intercession, and that intercession can be done in any number of ways, with the quickest and easiest method – *avoidance* – the angel's usual choice.

Now then, you don't know if Eric called upon me not to let him die, do you? He told you that he thanked me afterwards, but all you can be sure of is what he has *told* you. Did he think that he was in such danger at that moment prior to the intercession? *No.* Did he willingly put himself in that position to deliberately incur such a risk? *No.*

Granted, he did foolish things in his sense of adventuring and discovery, but there was not in his mind an intent to put himself at life-threatening risk, nor was there any wish on his part to end his physical life by that specific means. Those are all ingredients in the equation of how or by whom intercession was given so that Eric's life never was in danger.

Let me be clearer. His life COULD have been in extreme danger had not the dive master, as you call him, interceded. I believe your question is: *Who* alerted that man to intercede? Yes, it likely was the guardian angel, because I as Eric was completely involved in Eric's episode throughout the entire experience, oblivious to the danger before it was announced.

You have heard from Matthew that I have many emissaries to carry forth my wishes. Guardian angels are some of those. They are the primary gatekeepers of both physical and spiritual lives of their assigned person, but they cannot – CANNOT! – interfere with that person's free will! *Nor may I do so!*

Eric had no wish to die. Since he was not exercising any free will choice for dying, his angel could act on his behalf to insure that such did NOT happen. I don't have to give each guardian angel individual instructions, you see – they already have their instructions that hold true for the Earth lifetime of their assigned person.

S: So it's as simple as Eric's time on Earth wasn't up and that's why there was intercession so he wouldn't die?

GOD: You would like things to be easily explained, my child, yet you are not satisfied with the simplest explanation. No, it is *not* as simple as what you proposed. It *is* as simple as what I explained, Eric not choosing to die.

It is in the nature of the happenings that I mentioned, with many unseen and lightning quick thoughts and actions at work so that Eric was not harmed by spending such time deep in the sea that his own oxygen supply would not cover life to reach the surface and he needed the sharing of the dive master's supply.

There are many facets of everything that happens to anyone in every moment — facets unseen, unrecognized, unfelt and unappreciated. But that is the level of awareness prevailing on your planet, where the atmosphere is far denser than it was when spirituality was a part of every life, including the plants and animals, not only human life.

What would you like to draw upon next to clarify this for your son?

S: First, may I please read everything you've said?

GOD: You *know* you may! Have I ever denied you that, dear one?

*S: No, but it's more polite for me to ask than to assume. ....
OK, thank you. I asked if you could enlighten Eric about the diving experience, and I shouldn't have restricted "enlightening" to
just that. So, is there something else you can tell him?*

GOD: There is no end to what I could tell Eric, but I would
prefer that he talk with me personally. Actually, my child, your
beloved son *does* talk with me a great deal, and sometimes he's
aware that I have talked with him.

For instance, he does attribute his business success to his attitudes and character, and he is feeling the inner harmony that is the
natural product of the energy he is putting forth in honesty and
conscientiousness. He may think such as, *"Thank you, God, for
my prospering,"* and I let him know that I am *with* him but not
responsible for his conscious choices to deal honorably, thus he
can cherish the inner peace knowing that he himself engendered it.
That is balance!

*S: Thank you, God, for our talk tonight and your patience with
the long interruption – and with me. We make a pretty good team,
don't we?*

GOD: You delight me no end, my child! YES, we *ARE* a good
team. So are Eric and I. And now I sense that you've had your fill
of this discussion. Not that I am rushing you out, but I'm responding to your awareness of the midnight hour as well as a sense of
contentment that I have answered your questions.

S: Yes, I do feel satisfied with what I can send to Eric. We'll talk again soon I think, because I suspect that some of my list of questions for Matthew will get turned over to you. Thank you again and – what can be said instead of "God bless you"? Creator bless you?

GOD: Suzy, I am smiling with delight! You could simply say, *I love you.* That is the zenith, the alpha and omega of all feelings.

S: Then, thank you and I love you. Good night, God.

GOD: Thank *YOU,* and I love *YOU!* Eric, I love YOU! Without reservation and without judgment, I love ALL of my children. Good night, beloved little Suzy.

GOD: *MORE OF WHO I AM*

January 13, 1997

S: Is God encouraged by progress here that we can't see but that can be seen from your vantage point?

MATTHEW: I believe so, but I'd think that you would prefer His direct reply.

S: Do I just ask Him, like saying "God, can we talk"?

MATTHEW: I'd say so!

S: Well, then, God, do you know my question and feelings about what Matthew and I have been discussing? How will I know if you are the one responding, if you do?

GOD: My child, I'm glad you felt assurance enough to type in there "GOD:" and not "?:". You *always* can have assurance if you will just allow its sensation to pervade your uncertainty.

As for "progress" on Earth, I weep with each soul who is suffering in any way and I rejoice with each soul who is feeling joy. I am the soul of all of the worst and all of the best, so I cannot be inseparable from the best and not inseparable from the worst. Am I happy about what I see happening on Earth? For those who are happy, yes, I am, too. For those who are worrying that their tyrannical power is diminishing, I feel that, too. Do you see?

S: I think so, but I meant as the total God, the entirety of souls in this universe, how do you feel?

GOD: There is no "entirety" of separate pieces, there is *amalgamation.* The souls are inviolate during their physical lifetimes and remain inviolate in spirit, so they influence within the body of God just as they influence the play unfolding on Earth. It is simple, not complex, but I see that you are not grasping my words.

As a child of mine, you have equal importance with the life of Jesus that Christian religions exalt as perfect in my eyes, and you have equal importance with the soul who is causing misery and death. There are equal amounts of my powers and love within every soul who is born into a body you recognize or a body you do not recognize or a body you cannot even conceive of in appearance. Yet, you wish me to see something that doesn't exist beyond the view of me on Earth, that I am only a loving and merciful God.

With equal aspects of what you think of as good and what you decry as evil, how can I be except what I am? In one stage of my Totality, I *was* purely light and love. Then parts of my creations descended into the darkness Matthew refers to, but they were nonetheless inseparable parts of my whole. And thus they remain.

That is why I cannot give you the answer that you wish in your heart, dear child, that I am saddened and appalled by the injustice and brutality. Nor can I say that I am gladdened only by what I see of the light being spread on Earth. I can reply only as the amalgamation of the *two* sides of each soul. Each soul has its potential for goodness and darkness, or godliness as it was in the Beginning and the evil, as you see it, in motion. My child, can you relate to what I am in all truth telling you?

S: I'm sorry, but I just don't know. Please let me read what you said. ..... Thank you. I'm not sure I understand everything, but what you said doesn't seem consistent with what Matthew has said about a "totally loving God."

GOD: Then let me correct Matthew. There is resistance to who I am in "entirety" anywhere religions prevail. First, I AM that I AM. And what I AM is what you and countless – well, I could have an actual count if I wished to investigate and pass on to you, but I don't want to do that right now – so I shall say that I am the countless beings who have lived in any form in any place within this universe in any speck of time since its Beginning.

I am not a separate oversoul – or parent, if you will – who can see my likeness in a child of myself but am disappointed when the child doesn't grow into my measurements of good or bad. I have *no* such measurements for my children! There is that energy balancing of the polar opposites that Matthew calls light and darkness, and that's as good as any differentiation for the two opposing forces.

Those opposing forces keep the universe spinning, so they are not soon to be changed from their oppositeness or everything would go haywire. As for souls, like everything else in the universe, they are energy, my original light energy as I was co-created by Creator and the highest angelic realm. However, when free will became "abused unmercifully" – I am acceding to using your words because it's your sentiment, but it is not correct in my eyes, dear one....

Let me start again. I am each person who is judged in such poor light by others who cannot know the heart and soul of that single one. None of you on Earth is connected in awareness at soul level, so your judgments can be quite off kilter insofar as a particular soul's *purpose* in this lifetime. Each agreed to play his or her part in the balancing act, and I know how often Matthew has told you about the need for balance in each soul so that can extend to all of Earth. To all of the universe, for that matter.

Suzanne, I see that I am straying from what you originally asked: *How do I feel about what you and Matthew were discussing?* But I did reply to that, just not what you wanted to hear. Shall we go on?

S: Then "personal God" means that you respect each person's life as much as any other?

GOD: Yes, but I know your question about *motive* and *intent* counting for more than the evidence. There is the difference, perhaps, that you want so much for me to bring into this commentary. Do I *WISH* that *all* of my parts were within the light in which I was created? **Yes!** Who would *not* wish that perfection of Creator to be returned!

But I do not hold forth condemnation or punishment to any faltering part of me. I am here to respond to what you call prayers of the "godly" just as I am bound by the laws of Creator that are set up within the parameters of my operating powers if the choice made is *not* within the light. Do you see?

S: I'm not sure I heard your last statement correctly. If I did, your meaning still isn't clear to me.

GOD: I know that, of course, but I intend to give you frequent opportunities to question rather than my rambling without your understanding any of it. So then, to clarify: I am whoever is living at any time, all the time, anywhere in this universe. I cannot be a separate entity or a power beyond that given to me.

Nor can I make new laws of science or nature that you also call *my* laws. They are *NOT* my laws, they are *Creator's* laws! Within those I was created and am bound to honor. I don't object to those laws, but I do object to having them ascribed to me only because it is part of the non-understanding about me that prevails in your minds.

S: If you are the total of darkness and light and you really want the light to prevail, isn't that denying the darkness what it wants?

GOD: It is gratifying to see you thinking, my dear child. Hatonn would be pleased. *Why?* Because he is one of my major aspects when it comes to communications and records, and he adores deeper thinking beyond the superficiality of most thoughts emanating from Earth. He's been given a bum rap there because for ages one of my children has been claiming that what she's putting out is from him, and that's not so, but that's another story.

You are worried that I'm taking sides, or better said, *can't* take sides. Then who better to set you straight, my child? I am as much the gentleness and searching and on the lighted pathway as you wish to be, yet there is the part of me that equally is, and cannot deny, that soul whose interests and actions and motives are what you call evil. I am not separate from that soul, and whatever that soul does and all of its effects, however "ungodly," as you think, become within my composite and are an inseparable part of me. So, to say that I could "take sides" of myself is just plain unscientific, isn't it?

S: Then it seems that we're really just on our own, stumbling along thinking that prayers for anyone's safety or health are reaching you, but actually, all you're doing is being aware. Is it, then, that any actual beneficial intervention is coming from other sources, like the angels, spirit guides, souls in Nirvana or highly evolved extraterrestrial civilizations?

GOD: Is that arrangement so bad, my child? …. You're waiting for me to continue, as if I didn't say it all right there.

S: Those other sources are you, too, aren't they?

GOD: *You see!* I didn't intend for this to become like your analysts of the mind who desire you to see for yourselves rather than be told. But it was immensely heartening to me that you came to that realization, just as it was for you, dear Suzanne.

My beloved child, you can see that I am not the God that for all those years you believed me to be. You still cling to the idea that what you were taught is correct – OK, that at least most of it is. But most of it is *not!* Religion and spirit, or spirituality, are *not* the same. Well, maybe for a moment now and then in Earth time they were, when some of the people received the truth I sent by various messengers as I intended, and those who did thought of it as "religion." But actually it was *spirit* – seeing, feeling, LIVING the light and love in the ministry of my children who carried my Word.

Especially in the case of my child Emmanuel, whom you call Jesus, were the messages quickly subverted into what the self-serving leaders of that day needed to keep their positions of authority and control. Greed and power got in the way of the truth every time. So your religions of today teach the lies inherited from those early leaders who turned them into *religious* teachings, and woe to those who disagreed!

Matthew has explained this and still you haven't released all of the hold that your Christian indoctrination gained over your own reasoning powers. Oh, yes, you are opening to the truth because you don't want your son to be giving forth incorrect information. Of course you don't! But it's difficult for you to accept the damage that has been done by the suppression of the truth that time and again I have sent to Earth.

And where has this gotten me? More and more fighting – even killing each other in *my name!* – between the various religions that have been formed by deliberate distortions of my messengers' words, that's where. Each religion thinks it's absolutely right and is the *only* right one. Oh, my! And because every one of those souls who believes whatever he or she has been taught is a part of me, and I am *all* of them, I love all without reservation, you see.

S: God, thank you for talking with me. I guess you know that I'm not really comfortable with what you've said, but maybe with more time to think about it, I will be.

GOD: Child, with humility and respect and divine love I hold you, enfold you, and allow you to experience in accordance with your own needs and wishes. In no moment shall I be separate from you, in no moment shall I be disappointed in you, in no moment will I fault you or judge you, and never shall we be more or less than who we are. And it is the same with *all* of my children. Amen.

S: Matthew? Do you know what God and I talked about?

MATTHEW: Yes, Mother, and I know your dismay that God seems so different from the Almighty and All Merciful God of your religious orientation that still is holding your beliefs very strongly. God would not speak ill of Himself, and He would not be dishonest with you, even if parts of Him are those souls in whom dishonesty reigns. You demand only light, and therefore you receive what you demand.

S: Well, I need to read this again to really digest it all, but Matthew, I do have the gist of it and what you've told me and what God has just said aren't the same. So what do you say about that?

MATTHEW: Mother, no, I haven't explained God as completely as He did Himself, and sometimes in my fervor to make a point about love and light being so desperately needed on Earth, I have ascribed only that to Him. But please remember that I have told you that each soul is an inseparable part of God, and think of the many instances when I have mentioned the necessity of balance. Think how often I have explained the playing out of karmic lessons and why judgment of others' actions is not the way to go because you cannot know what roles to achieve balance are at work. But I acknowledge my omission in not pulling all of that together in one fell swoop so you understood that God is *all* of the light and dark playing out the karmic balancing.

May 26, 1997

S: So I'm speaking with God now?

GOD: Yes, dear one, you are. You and I have discussed already that you are in communion with me more so than if you were in some building erected by a religion ascribing "God's word" to its formation.

Now then, you just asked Matthew how I can be "perfect" if I'm every soul on Earth and he was thinking about asking me how to respond. I told him I'll do this myself. So, my child, shall we now talk about whether I am "perfect"?

S: I don't mean any offense, you know that, don't you? But since you are a synthesis of all souls everywhere and none of us is perfect, how could you be perfect with all of our flawed parts?

GOD: Suzy, my dear child, as to my "perfection," you said it as well as anything I could come up with – the "flawed parts." No, *of course* I am not perfect! I'm not at the level of perfection.

In Creator ALL IS PERFECT. Then there is that level nearest to Creator, the Christed realm, where co-creating began and where all co-creating *still* is of that original material, only love and light. This is the level of soul energy from whence Jesus and my other messengers embodied in this universe. To clarify, their souls embody or are only in energy essence wherever that intensity of love and light is needed in the cosmos, not only in this universe. That realm also is where Creator bestowed to all souls Its gift of free will with its inherent ability of manifestation, or co-creating with Itself.

It was in the co-creating of Creator and those Christed realm souls where I – and the gods of the other universes – came into being. So you can see that within my range of knowing and powers and the other gods, too, there is less ability to co-create. With Creator, each of us gods co-created the universe over which we reign.

While perfection does still reign in that Christed realm above me, once *away* from it, the souls had free will to co-create as they could envision or imagine. That's when the imperfections began. At first this was in all innocence, because the process was new. And once established as to what joinings and what powers were allocated to each co-creation, perfection could have been restored and maintained, but the free will element descended in desire and intent. From that point on, imperfection was co-created because the elements, while the same, were not joined in the perfection of their origination.

Now then, if you would like to question me further, I'm at your service. However, if you'd rather talk with Matthew, then he and I both are at your service.

S: God, are you saying that there is no perfection in you or any souls in your universe?

GOD: Yes. My child, please read what I have just told you and you'll see why there is not.

S: OK, I will, and thank you, God, for talking with me. Now may I talk with Matthew again, please, with total protection of the light?

GOD: As you've often been told, but I'm happy to repeat it, you are within the light and thus protected in every moment because you have asked for this. ALL who ask for light in their lives receive it *just for the asking!* And now, my child, greet your Earth son Matthew.

October 30, 1997

S: Do you have constant communication with Creator?

GOD: No, but only because it isn't necessary. The means is open always. We are aware of everything, you could say, without chattering about it. There is nothing of me that Creator is oblivious to, just as there is nothing *you* are doing or feeling that *I* am oblivious to. And there is total noninterference both ways–that is, between Creator and me and me and you. The same functioning and reason directs both of these noninterference bases.

Let's go back to our conversation that was interrupted the other day, about free will. You understand free will, Suzy, you just don't like it, so let's talk about this. Free will seems to you a curse, and *believe* me, as the frequent recipient of it—you must understand the understated humor here—I *do* agree! However, there are lessons that can be learned, chosen lifetimes that can be experienced, *only* because there is the pain that to you seems intolerable. There must be balance in every soul's overall experiencing, and I'll tell you why it isn't automatically there and how it has to be regained.

When the original "fall from grace"—let's call it that—happened with the original darkness entering the light, then the balance that is *only* within the light was knocked askew. It's not an arbitrary decision of Creator that every one of Its parts cosmos-wide has to come back into It for the reintegration to occur and all lightness to prevail. That is, it's not just an idea of what would be nice. It's *essential* within the laws of physics, in your word, that govern not only Earth energy usage and cause and effect, but cosmos-wide this principle is so. And until all of the original light energy is "back home," there will be this askew condition prevailing.

Therefore, each soul is endowed with knowledge of the pathway back to Creator, and each physical lifetime of any soul is given the direction to fill some gap in the learning. The problem was created when too much enjoyment became focused on what you call "evil," and the free will principle of physics became blocked at the top where the "evil" resided in a sense of peak control and authority. So, the decree had to be made—and Creator did this—to dislodge that control so the power of decision-making, free will choosing, once again became the independent province of every experiencing aspect of every soul. *(NOTE: "Creator's Decree" in* Revelations For A New Era *comprehensively covers this.)*

S: How does Creator's decree affect you?

GOD: Well, I am overjoyed in my synergistic self, of course, but in the individual selves that are my essence, I'm basically unaware. You are one of the very, very few souls who know this, you see, and the billions of souls who do *not* know this are quite a majority. So, even though an energetic level of truth and the universal application of this decree are in effect, the results will be slow to be registered in the actions and motives of humankind on your planet. Or anywhere else. It's not an instantaneous *en masse* result.

S: Why can't the intensity and enormity of the suffering of people on Earth, or anywhere, be ended by Creator's "divine grace"?

GOD: Now then, how would *you* feel if you needed to fill in a gap in *your* experiencing so you could move forward and suddenly, that course wasn't available any longer. *Ohhhhh, wellllll?* No, dear one, there have to be *all* the choices so that *all* the souls have the opportunity to experience and grow.

Why is the child so battered and tortured and eventually is allowed the peace of dying? Such innocence, you say, and such pain and helplessness—who ever would *choose* that? And how could adults, or anyone larger than the infant or toddler or young child, how could anyone be so filled with evil as to *want* to live that kind of abusive life? Yes, it does take an understanding that goes outside the sentimental curve of your experiencing to accept that their respective souls *chose* these roles for progress in the pathway toward the light.

You can't imagine either causing or feeling such excruciating pain, and I can't explain something to you that you have no emotional basis for comprehending. Well, dear little soul, that is because your nature is beyond those levels of experiencing. You could say, "been there, done that." You have been a sufferer in many lifetimes and you also have caused suffering to others, and in this lifetime there was no need for your being at one end or the other of this spectrum. Your life has not been free of grief and other sorts of mental and emotional anguish, but overall, this is not within the seesaw effect of the karmic lessons, in your terms, that are still required for evolution of the majority of Earth's souls.

I see that you are holding your belief in abeyance, as if the words make sense but you are resisting feeling the truth of them.

S: I don't know how to feel about that—it's not all that simple. God, would you like to talk about El Nino, volcanic and earthquake activity and other effects of the global cleansing? Do you consider them that, part of the cleansing?

GOD: Yes, let's talk about something more acceptable to you, my child. Well, any one of you on Earth who considers these "natural phenomena" to be part of the cleansing of the planet obviously are of me just as much as you are of me, so I do in those cases consider these increasingly serious "acts of God!" to be cleansing in nature. They're all in the overall effort to release negativity from Earth and allow the damage of eons of neglect or outright abuse to be relieved so that a desperately required healing of the soul of Earth can happen. What would you like to know specifically, as I can't deem anything beyond your wish for that confirmation.

S: Give me a minute, please. .... Thank you. Is all animal and plant life being affected by whatever is causing deformities in frogs? What will be the logical progression of this strange situation?

GOD: First, Suzy, it isn't strange—it's the natural progression of the effects of powerful chemicals on delicate reproductive systems. It's that same basis in all maladies being ascribed to one cause or another, but essentially, it's a superabundance of the chemicals toxic to all animal and plant life that are proliferating Earth. That is *why* Earth is reacting so increasingly violently, to lift the negativity that is jeopardizing her very life and breath.

You don't see the damage that is being done to the lungs, the heart and the other internal organs of Earth. But she—your Earth, your Gaia—is different from you only in shape—*literally in shape only!*—and NOT in different condition from you. Earth is in the form of a sphere. None of her life forms is. But whatever is affecting Earth is affecting each of you, the creatures who live upon her. There is no more separation of you from Earth than there is of you from me.

Let us give this a simplified explanation with a beginning. In the beginning, there was perfection. Only light and light-filled intent reigned in a place that was truly called by the name Eden. Then negativity filtered its way through other parts of the universe and arrived on Eden in the form of what you would call "dreadful" personal treatment of beings by other, stronger beings. That was the beginning of negativity *vs.* positivity on your planet, now no longer the Eden in the perfection of balance. The original balance left, you see, with the first pinpoint of negativity.

Once that polarity was present on the planet, her life forms had the ability to reject the negativity by replacing it with light or to allow its proliferation to eat away at the *very life* of Earth. The latter is what happened.

The beginning of the loss of balance was Creator's endowment of life as thinking, feeling forms with free will. But by the time Earth was ready for inhabiting—whether she thought herself ready or not—there was such proliferation among the original beings who started the planet's colonization of the less-than-fully-developed human beings, that already the division of dark and light was formed so tenaciously that only an infusion of light could bring the rapidly deteriorating planet back into balance.

There is a confusion between negativity and the "darkness," in your mind, dear one. Let us depart from the other explanation and address this so that it can be clarified for all time. Negativity is neither "good" nor "bad." Negativity is not the embodiment of "evil" or "darkness" and it is not the opposite of "goodness" or "light," it is simply the opposite of positivity.

Yet, we say that negativity is "bad" only because it is usually connected with behavior or situations that are distasteful to "good" people. Or, "evil" is the name given to negativity because evil is so closely allied to "darkness" in your terminology, yet what is labeled "evil" is only negativity in action. It is an aspect of energy being directed, but the energy itself is impartial, neutral, without a label.

There is the sense of division, but there is NO division. It is the "two sides of the coin." It's that simple. There always have been the two sides, but the choice of which side to exercise—"to smile upon you," shall we say—is what determines which side is prevailing in any area at any time.

Now then, back to what has brought Earth to her precarious health today. Negativity, when exercised, brings a most terrible lopsidedness to anything requiring balance, and hardly any life form is not seeking balance. For planets to survive, just as any other life form, achieving balance is *absolutely necessary!* Souls have a way of circumventing the absolute need for balance in every moment only because *my* life force is sustaining every one of you on Earth and many "you's" you can't even imagine in your graphic imagination.

But a planet, a sphere, requires balance constantly so that its orbiting path may be steady. When the orbiting path becomes erratic, that signals the first of the potential "death throes" of the planet. All the forces of universal nature then are not allied, but are allowing the negativity to be "attacking" due to the positivity being out of alignment. None of this is meant to be good or bad, but just the natural forces in operation. You see?

Earth could have chosen to be so out of orbit that the natural result would occur—she would shatter and be absorbed by gravitational pull of the nearest orbiting bodies or forces, and that would be the end of Earth as a planet. However, with reinforcement of light forces, or positivity conductors, Earth could right her motion and stabilize movement of orbiting. This is what she chose, and to do this requires a return to "health." That is what the alleviation of the negativity is all about.

To be sure, there will be what you call "disasters" in numbers of injuries and deaths, too, as you consider them, and geographic changes are coming. This is not news to you, Suzy, as you first heard of this long ago in your timing, and you wonder if anyplace on your globe is going to be safe for human life, and you are concerned about the animals as well.

Dear little soul, safety is something peculiarly obscured from truth within Earth humans. Security is *the soul knowing itself*, its direction, its course of learning. *This* is security! You're thinking in terms of a few years of living in a specific form, that body, and the safety of that body, of many, *many* bodies, the safety of your children and their families, and the areas of seacoast or islands being safe. There is nothing I can guarantee you about this, nor is that meant to be. All is in accordance with what Earth programmed for its continuation of life as a sphere, as a habitable planet.

All life forms now existing on Earth at soul level are aware of the changes forthcoming, and each human soul and animal as well, chose to experience at this vital time in the history of your planet. You helped create the conditions in "previous" lifetimes. You are enduring and helping in the course chosen by Earth in *this* lifetime. That is what *all of you* need to know! OK?

S: I guess so. It's out of my hands anyway. So, what are we supposed to learn from the deformed frogs appearing in several places? Is the cause of their situation the same cause of AIDS, cancer—all diseases— and birth defects in humans?

GOD: First, Suzy, *YOUR* life is in your hands and you *know* this! Think about everything we've talked about, everything you've heard from Matthew, from *all* of us who talk with you!

As for the frogs, they're symptoms of what is happening to every form of life on Earth. They're such vulnerable little creatures to lower degrees of toxicity, more so than many other forms of life, that the abundance with which they have been assailed with malformations is particularly noticeable. They volunteered to be used for the purpose of alerting your scientists to the plight of ALL life on Earth. More studies and research will happen before the connection with all life forms will be accepted by science.

It's ironic, isn't it, that when the truth of these scientific "discoveries" is manifested on Earth, those privileged to absorb this information choose later on to curtail the fullness of it? There is a sense of fear of ridicule or rejection among the less powerful or less notable scientists. But most assuredly, when the filtration process is in effect, the fullness of the truth *is* infused into the minds of those being dealt with most admirably by our panel of universal scientists. It's just that once the information is on Earth, it's treated the way so much of the information from realms beyond your own is treated, as *"That's bunk."*

Your governments should be ashamed of themselves, truly, because they are lagging well behind the timed phasing in of universal truths and are holding back the other life forms there from opening into the fullness of spiritual blossoming during this embodiment. In short, you are being short-changed in your learning choices because your governments are withholding many truths. So are your church leaders. Earth as her whole self is saddened by the individual slowness of her peoples. Particularly in regards to treatment of each other and the animals, there is a severe lagging over the timeframe of spiritual enlightenment chosen by the souls now embodied there.

S: So even YOU are saying that literally billions of souls are being victimized by the free will decisions of a few powerful people!

GOD: Oh, no, that's *not* what I'm saying! And it's not what I *meant,* but I was stopped short of the full story when you started typing your impression. *Souls,* not bodies, is the issue here, Suzy. Yes, a lot of what's transpiring isn't what was originally agreed upon, but adjustments are being made at *soul level.* Those who truly are "victimizing" others, as you say—but "not living according to their original agreements" is what *I'd* say—actually are victimizing *ONLY* their own soul evolution! The ones you see as their "victims," those who aren't proceeding with their original chosen lessons due to the free will of the few "victimizers," *are leaping ahead in soul growth,* whether it's on the planet or beyond, after leaving their embodiment life there. But of course they don't *consciously* realize this!

Dear one, you are in no frame of mind to accept this because you can't get beyond the consciousness of it all, so I as you—how could it be *different!*—want no more talk of this now. With total love and adoration of self, for you and me and all life within the universe and the interconnectedness of ALL, this is God, your servant and your *self.*

April 2, 2000

S: You have said that you experience exactly the same joy or pain as every one of your children anywhere because of your inseparability with all of us.

GOD: Many times I have told you that, Suzy.

S: Yes, but when all of those countless lives in the universe merge at the top, your combined awareness is a product of synergy more than the sum of the whole, right?

GOD: Yes.

S: Then with all the knowledge and energy generated by those billions of souls, you know everything—the omniscient God—and have all of their combined energy to use—the omnipotent God. What do you do in THAT status?

GOD: *Ah!* Well, first, those attributes are given to me in *name* but to Creator in *meaning.* You *know* I'm NOT the "be all and end all" that Creator is! It's more realistic to know me or try to picture me—*feel* me!—as a sibling in good grace with you. That's more what I am in truth and essence anyway.

But I can tell you what I do in my highest powers. I move mountains, I part seas, I rotate the planets, I open doors to knowledge that as yet is unknown within this universe. I talk with

Creator, I talk with my counterparts in other universes. I weep for the lost child, the frightened puppy, the wounded deer, the smallest plant that has been trampled needlessly. *That* is the essence of my Totality, as there is no separating the energies of each component from any other. Do you understand?

S: Well, yes, but if the part of you that is me hurts someone, who also is a part of you, is your entirety allowing that to happen?

GOD: Oh my! Above all else, there is Creator's free will law, and if someone uses that to harm another, I *can't* interfere. Therefore, I not only experience *exactly* the hurtful action of the first, but also *exactly* the hurting sensation of the second. I can't escape *any* of the suffering of humans or any other life form anywhere in the universe, just as I can't *not* experience the exact rejoicing of any. So it's not a matter of my "allowing" this free will exercise, you see.

S: Well, do YOU like what some people are doing with their free will?

GOD: You're asking me to pass judgment on those whose free will choices *you* don't like, aren't you? Please excuse me, my child, as my question had a twinge of judgment sound itself, didn't it? At least now you have good reason to stop honoring me at a height I don't deserve!

S: I don't know about that. Since you feel the combined physical, mental and emotional pain of everyone simultaneously, has that weakened your powers so that the dark forces gained such a foothold on Earth and anywhere else in the universe?

GOD: This is not so easy to answer. I am *not* weak, that's for sure. It isn't that the intensity of pain is not overwhelming for each individual bearing it, but even in combination of *all* that – which is unfathomable to you, of course – weakness is not a part of my Totality. There is pain, yes, but not weakness. And an alternative to this arrangement is not even offered. That is, there's no option for me but to endure as each of my beloved children endures, each of my beloved creatures in the fields and in the seas endures.

There is no separation of energy. It can be harnessed or directed by specific means, by thoughts and feelings and intentions and actions that can be called its "attachments," but energy never is compromised in its neutrality. Therefore the energy which is my composite essence and shared by every life form in this universe is never weakened because it is not diminished, not lost, not transmuted into other universes. I believe we're getting into physics, and who knows better than I how little you know of this field?

S: That's true enough! How do you heal yourself from all that pain?

GOD: I can't be released from any pain that is still being felt by any souls. As they are healed, so am I in that aspect of my "entirety," as you still think of it.

S: But you also experience the evil of those who cause such suffering to others. How do you feel about that?

GOD: My child, think how a baby bird feels when it is pushed from its nest by a different bird. Think of its shock and fear at falling, its pain from physical injury, and a fright it cannot even understand as to what happened and what is coming next. I feel the same frightened, helpless way about those parts of me who have so fallen from light that they delight in what you call evil. What will become of them?

Do I abhor the suffering they cause others? *YES*, and I send light to reach the souls of those beings who cause the suffering. But it is up to each individual, as inviolate parts of me functioning independently, to respond to the light or not. I am saddened beyond your imagining when darkness flares, especially when such innocence is suffering, often killed, because as you know, not all chose what they're physically enduring.

With the increase of light being willingly received by my Earth children, the major source of what you call evil that has constricted the energy of Earth for eons is changing. But notice that it is *Creator's* decree, *not* mine, that was required to untangle the stranglehold of free will from the peak of darkness!

October 26, 2000

S: Matthew, is God satisfied about the response here to the incoming light?

MATTHEW: Mother, you know I don't speak for God unless He requests it and He hasn't here, so would you like to speak with him about this?

S: Yes. God, would you like to speak with me about this?

GOD: Suzy, my child, indeed I *would!* I always welcome the opportunity to communicate with you at the keyboard, where you have much more repose in our chats than without your attachment to that electronic marvel.

So, you want to know if I'm satisfied with the response of all my children to the increasing light that is being sent continuously. How can I say "satisfied" when parts of me are in such pain and terror and other parts of me are *causing* that pain and terror? You mean *overall* satisfaction when you ask me to offer up a "yes" or "no," don't you?

There are many "yes-es" and many "no-s," but do those cancel out each other? No, but there is less of the light being registered within hearts and minds than I would wish, so I can speak to you with that much of a reply that isn't the "hedging" in your mind.

You're wondering how I would change things if I had free rein without that free will law. I *could* not change anything, dear child! I cannot bring the connectedness down upon what are the parts, you see. It is not that free will is preventing my sense of wholeness, but rather that the independent, inviolate parts of me that always have been operating in their own directions are exactly what myself and my selflessness are about!

That is puzzling you, so perhaps I can state it more clearly by telling you to look at yourself and *your* children. *Aha!*

S: I see – thank you, God. Is your proper name Yahweh?

GOD: No, nor is my name recognizable in the sounds within your auditory range. I'm afraid I can't give you an approximation that would be pleasing to my ears!

S: OK! Do the synthesized feelings of every one of the life forms in this universe fall into the emotional spectrum of Earth humans?

GOD: It's difficult to describe sensations for which you have no common reference. Earth humans' feelings are in quite a dense, harsh range in comparison with those beings in lighter evolutionary stages. But yours are higher in frequency than other life forms that are just emerging from human rootstock in many places in this universe.

I believe it will be easier for you to know that yes, I do feel exactly the same feelings you do in our bonded connection and the same with all other life forms on your planet, and best you not try to understand the synthesized sensations of the universe.

S: Very well! You said beautiful things about Matthew and gave good reports on my other children. Thank you for those.

GOD: I don't believe that I deserve thanks for what those souls are doing themselves, but I understand that you mean the thanks to be for the words I spoke about them.

S: Yes. Just one more thing, please. What did you mean the other day about my being of "Matthew's lineage"?

GOD: Matthew's soul is ancient, of the light from the beginning. Not as your son, but as the composite of all the soul experiencing that includes his soul, which did experience prior to your soul becoming an explicit sensory aspect of his. But once a part of the soul that was the originator of all the experiencing, you and he have never been separate in the knowingness and have chosen to be together in human and other lifetimes for a period of long, *very, very long,* longstanding.

S: That's a lot of time together! Thank you, God, for talking with me today.

GOD: You are welcome, and *I* thank *you* for letting me talk with you. We talk *with each other,* my child. Never must I be "impressed" with your sense of wonderment that I would speak with you, but let me exalt in your wonderment of knowing that *never* are we separate.

We must *not* stop meeting like this! I wanted to feel one more smile with you before we say goodbye for this moment. And now I say, Ciao, knowing full well that you don't consider that a "God-like" word of leave-taking. Actually, I wanted to say "Toodle-oo," but you'd just ascribe that to your imagination, wouldn't you?

S: Probably! You usually speak to me more simply than Matthew or any of the others. Why?

GOD: Because my relationship with you is so simple! You don't make long charades or diplomatic or esoteric conversations with yourself, do you? Then why would you and I converse in those unusual ways, ways that would be too absurd to ever happen with just yourself. So, there you have it—we ARE simple, dear soul!

May 2, 2001

S: So, why did Sylvia lose her lawsuit against that huge corporation?

GOD: Well, I sure don't want to be held personally responsible for that, but please do not think that I accept this as a final judgment. Light is *not* going to forsake this situation! What Matthew has been telling Sylvia, to persist in this until there is a just resolution, is right. She needs to continue with her convictions that the light will prevail and it *will!* This case is *not* over! I am interested, of course, in the just outcome that will benefit many. The corporate corruption that she is battling is another area of heavily entrenched darkness on your planet that's "coming to light." *(NOTE: Sylvia did persist, and over a year later the corporation offered her a major settlement.)*

S: But do you personally – or some force you designate – intervene in unfair situations?

GOD: My goodness, child, *all the time!* Well, not in the exceptional case of Marnie, which you know is out of my jurisdiction, but in situations on Earth, where I have special interest in its pristine beauty and glory returning, indeed I *do* intervene. Sometimes these occasions are due to angels coming to Earth, divine intervention, spirits helping – there are many designations for the help you receive from any of my helpers.

S: But are you in your entirety doing anything?

GOD: Quite a bit, Suzy! I'm *glad* you smiled at that! But in the cases of "divine rescues," it isn't necessary that my full powers prevail. It would be like sending a hurricane to provide one drop of water to a tiny thirsty seed.

S: I see. So then what are you doing?

GOD: Actually, I have addressed this before, when you asked what my "omnipotent" self does. It isn't necessary that my entirety take charge of anything individually happening on Earth. That is for my helpers to handle, but I am aware of EVERY happening to EVERY soul. How could I not be, as each is a part of me and I experience exactly the sensations as each is experiencing them? I've spoken to you about this on *many* occasions. Anyway, my entirety – and I shall use your word for I AM – sees to the higher motions, like the universal bodies staying in order and orbit.

S: I do recall that now, God, so please excuse me. Is it really so that everything that ever has been, is now or ever will be, already is known? If that's true, why would you ever have to wonder what will become of any of your children? I remember your comparing the "dark" souls to baby birds pushed from the nest and being frightened because they didn't know what would happen next.

GOD: You are the pesky one, dear child! In my entirety, yes, all is known, but with free will choices abounding until the final physical breath, what is known is the *potential* for something to happen or develop from a process.

S: So then it isn't really correct that everything actually is known–only the possibilities are known. Is that right?

GOD: The possibilities and the probabilities, beforehand, and certainly, the happenings afterwards. Think of this, Suzy – if all were *absolutely* known, if nothing required any independent thinking or decisions or activity, then why would there be any need for multiple experiencing? What would there be to learn? Why would *life itself* be necessary? We could just fast forward to The End, which is the Beginning, and let all lives of all times reside at that initial point of Being.

S: That makes sense, but it certainly is different from the omniscience ascribed to you. Does Creator know? Or is omniscience incorrectly attributed to you and maybe to Creator, too?

GOD: I guess you could say that by comparison with what individuals know, Creator and I know so much more that omniscience isn't far off. But *we* did NOT give that word to us! Do you think it is another strategy of our opponents to so far distance us from you and everyone else?

S: It could be. But I suppose some people hold you in higher respect or reverence because of that.

GOD: My dear child, what I *do* know at all times are the attitudes and sensations of all of my children! And believe me, those who truly respect and revere me do not need me to know everything that according to the definition of omniscience I "should"!

S: OK, then! Did reptilian civilizations start as descendants of the Christed realm or did they start in this universe?

GOD: So you're back to those. The *energy* of those souls who embody as reptilians—I mean those you call "bad," for simplicity's sake, because others are "good," you know—didn't originate in this universe. That energy came in through the portals created when universes melded. That was a provision of our gaining some advantages in the melding, but frankly, I didn't foresee just how much damage and for such duration this would cause. There, *that's* quite an admission, isn't it?

S: And how! There goes omniscience right out the window!

GOD: Which is *exactly* where it belongs, Suzy! Now then, it is so that some among the reptilians have long been oppressing human populations not only on Earth, but in many other places in the universe, too.   They are the mutated descendants of the primeval force you call Lucifer, and have proliferated with what I can say is alarming powers and numbers.

In this time of universal cleansing, not only your planet's, the direct and primary effort of this essential change is to permeate those reptilian souls with light. They are without conscience due to the light eons past having been eroded from them. It also is so that some of the reptilian descendants, far more in number than the pure bloods, are a combination of human and reptilian genetic orders and are not to be penalized by their heritage, which in most cases is not within their awareness.

I should—no, *you* never should say should!–clarify what I mean by those souls are not to be "penalized." Penalty is not a harshness except in your language and effects. It is more so a neutralizing of the darkness by the light so that a state of equilibrium can be obtained. This balance is required before the light can start to become predominant within the soul. Therefore, I hasten to say that it's in this context that I use "penalty."

S: I see. Since the inclination for evil started with Lucifer's free will choices and he was in Creator's First Expression and you were created later, do you still feel responsible for that energy in this universe?

GOD: "Evil"–that's what you mean here, isn't it?–was initiated by the misuse of Creator's free will gift to all Its creations before I came into being, that's so. But when I came along in the line and was given this universe to manage, all that transpired after that is indeed my responsibility. So it isn't an assignment of responsibility for that energy pattern, as that was not of my making, but it is up to me for *correcting*, shall we say, and I do wish to banish it so that love and light from the Beginning can return.

Suzy, we have had a most enlightening and enjoyable long talk today! I feel that finally you are knowing me on a more "personable" level than you did for so long, which your *entirety* concept of me welcomes! And now, my beloved child, I bid you good day with celestial blessings as you chart your other activities.

June 4, 2001

S: God, do you play with animals wherever they are?

GOD: What an endearing question, my child! Yes, I do. I delight in the animals that are loved and tended well, like the shepherds of biblical times enjoying the feel of the fur of their sheep or goats. It is no different in this date on Earth. I delight in *all* my creatures, even those who are in your eyes fierce. I weep for and suffer just as do those who are neglected or brutalized or wantonly killed.

S: Will you please tell me what you're going to do to save the whales and dolphins?

GOD: That is a request for me *to save them,* is it not, and not a question? But of course I'll speak with you about this. My emissaries are diligently working to defeat this intention to destroy these beautiful souls that are the anchors of light on planet Earth. It is my intention that those who would willfully do the bidding of the darkness shall not be permitted by law and by activity to continue.

The US Navy is not "in the loop" insofar as understanding the dark intent behind the destructiveness, as they are thinking only in terms of what they are told–necessary "defense" against the "enemy." They are not thinking about the harm that would befall massive numbers of whales and dolphins and other sea life or the domino effect of such damage, and they have utterly no idea about the sacredness of these highly evolved souls, the cetaceans.

The "dark" intention for mass destruction of these sacred souls will *not* be permitted to happen! I can't deal out of any equation free will, because that's not my invention, as you so well know. In fact, it is my responsibility to *preserve* that capacity or capability in each soul's embodiment. But when it comes to allowing free will to destroy those lives in the oceans, which are the most highly evolved souls in embodiment on the planet, that *cannot* be permitted, and whatever has to be done in the way of light prevailing overall, *will be done!*

S: I'm so glad to know this! But what about the whales that are being killed legally by Japan and Norway?

GOD: I'm afraid those come under legality in the countries of the killing origin, so in those cases, the souls of the people who permit and actively kill will have to be softened, lightened, one by one. The "big lawmakers" may not cotton to this change, so the efforts to voluntarily curtail this practice have to be made on an individual basis. That's also true where ceremonial killings take place.

S: How soon will we see merciful changes?

GOD: Immediately, my child! The Navy will not be given the

authority to continue the destructive testing because the outcry against that will be amazing. It may not be widely publicized, however. More than likely the testing will be quietly shelved after another effort or so to justify it for "national defense."

The part of the reptilian civilization that throughout all Earth time has been manipulating the weakest and most power-hungry souls who have embodied there will be in a rage and will plunge ever deeper to wage battle with the light forces. So do not be surprised to see other areas of what you will consider, and rightly so, to be inhumane, but know that the torture, maiming, killing – *yes, outright wanton slaughter!* – of human and other life, the animal and plant kingdoms who are the very life of Earth herself, cannot last much longer.

S: Is this battle taking longer to win than the light forces thought it would?

GOD: I don't know. I think that collectively the light forces did plan to vanquish all darkness by the year that keeps being mentioned, 2012. That is indeed a critical time in *your* planning and calculations, but it is meaningless beyond Earth's timing machinations.

It is not that there will be no victories on huge fronts prior to that date. I think that if 11 more years had to pass in the same measure of killing, sorrow, rage, fear, grief and terror, that indeed desperation would befall every soul of mild and gentle nature and turn the hearts of peaceful light warriors into retaliation for the dark forces' massive and widespread activities. Oh, indeed one of gentle nature has the capacity to rise up against a foe, and with swords blazing! My child, destruction is in *every* heart on Earth. Those who feel the most self-righteous would like to annihilate the most "ungodly," you see. These hearts and minds are at the fringes of the opposing powerful groups, and the sheep are all the masses within those slender parameters.

S: I see. Well, I certainly don't see everything. Is there no limit to the brutality that you will tolerate in one of your souls?

GOD: Surely you're not asking if I will intervene with powers I *do NOT have*?

S: You told me that you intervene in unfair situations all the time, remember? Isn't it unfair that ruthless killers are annihilating innocents? Where do mercy and divine grace – whatever allowances you have to protect the helpless and Earth herself – come into this light vs. dark battle?

GOD: *Ah!* I should protect the "innocents"? What about when those "innocents" were the ruthless killers and the roles have been reversed? You would ask me to step into the karma that these souls are choosing to work out for their spiritual advancement?

S: No, but Matthew and you yourself have said many millions of souls are suffering far more than the karmic lessons in their pre-birth agreements.

GOD: We're both right about that, Suzy, but I still can't step in and stop this merry-go-round! Those souls who indeed are suffering beyond the limits of the lessons they had chosen now are choosing to leave embodiment in great numbers via disease, starvation, massacres, and natural disasters before the end of their original contracts, which at soul level have been amended as being completed. This could be considered the "mercy and divine grace" you are wanting.

I realize that from your standpoint, this is no relief from the darkness of oppression and tyranny over souls still on Earth, but once out of that realm, the departing souls escape from those controls over their lives. They join the light forces against those prevailing dark forces on Earth – that is part of their reason for leaving, to fight the light battle from this higher plane of light. Remember that I told you this is a matter of *souls*, not physical lives?

S: All right, I see. What about the energy of the whales that were anchoring light energy here until they were killed? What about those whose sonar has been distorted or damaged by the sonar testing?

GOD: My goodness, child, you *are* protective of each and every lamb of God, aren't you? That is fine – I'm not finding fault! I realize that you cannot see the overview of the energy or the soul breeding places and healing phases.

As for the whales that are killed, it's true that their energy no longer is within those bulky carcasses designed to anchor the light within the oceans. However, their energy may remain there to join the light workers on that liberated basis of "free spirit" or it can work in the universe with the light forces in body who are stabilizing Earth in these times of greatest changes ever on my Eden planet.

S: I see. Overall then, you are satisfied with the progress of the light forces even though the dark forces still are causing terror, hunger, endemic disease, torture of the body and mind?

GOD: You are pointing fingers in either despair because that is what you see, my child, or in criticism because any of those situations still exists. This is a play set in motion and it cannot be stopped, frozen in midsection, and the players nevermore growing from that point upward or forward.

It seems that you have no intent to judge others, but nevertheless, my child, you are placing *your* values, *your* ideas and what you need for *your* heart to be lighter, on all other souls. They do not have the same lessons or the same qualities of character to even identify rationally with what you need for *your* soul to be at peace!

It is not a simple situation at your level of understanding life and learning, of remembering. It *is* simple from here – getting things back into balance. I *do* wish it could proceed as you would like, as all others also pure in heart would like! Impatience with the slow dirge-like procession of killing and grief and control seems to be the emotional blanket forever covering the planet.

Earth herself is weary of this. She, *most of all*, has suffered almost unendurably, and her consciousness, too, is asking for stepped-up light for her healing. The light is coming in such grand measure, my child, that you need to take this into your brain and process it that way, because emotionally you are set back each time you read of a brutality to any life.

So, I'd say that you may wish to read this and tidy up the areas where my words are not spelled correctly or you would prefer to soften the language, choose a better word, insert an omitted word – all that sort of work you have been trained to do. Please add our talk today to the others I want in the third book.

S: OK, but God, I don't think you answered my question about whether you are satisfied with the light's progress here.

GOD: I think I did, but it may not be to your satisfaction. Would you like to tidy up our conversation as you read again my words and evaluate my response?

S: Thank you. .... I still don't think you told me whether you are really satisfied with the progress of the light against the dark forces on Earth.

GOD: I see, my child. Very well, in a word, **NO!** How *could* I be satisfied when so many of my soul aspects are crying in torment and deprivation and others are the cause of this? When many of my children are enchanted by Satanic worship that abounds in such widespread rituals of torture and killing that your mind could not handle it? When some of my children have fallen so far from the light that they rule with tyranny and destroy all who oppose them? When so many of my children are living in fear and horror or are dying because of the deeds of these others who also are my children? When deception and corruption abound to the point of no truth being illuminated except when the light is so strongly exposing it that those who believed the lies are devastated upon learning the truth?

But my dear Suzy, I am able to see the broader horizon, the full measure of this conflict, and when I see the light that is emanating today from a soul that yesterday was hazy, more inclined toward control by the darkness, I rejoice in that lost one – the "prodigal son" – returning. When I see big areas, like a town in your thinking, where light is emanating from hearts that formerly were cold and dark, I rejoice!

Would I like to see the *TOTAL* of Earth life in peacefulness, love, sharing, caring and service one to another? **OF COURSE I WOULD!** But do I have the power to snap a finger and have this be so? You *know* I do NOT! So I send my love and light *every-where, to every soul,* and I may as well rejoice in the pockets of light rather than dwell in the pockets of darkness and weep, you see.

S: Yes, God, I do see as well as I can, because trying to imag-ine all that you must be feeling is overwhelming. Do you ever feel that way yourself?

GOD: If you will just think of me as all of my children, then you must know that I do indeed feel correspondingly overwhelmed.

S: Yes, of course. I'm sorry–I get stuck in my single-self feel-ings and lose sight of what you've told me. Will you please explain exactly the limits of your powers on Earth? I know I've asked sim-ilar questions, so maybe you're expecting me to know this, but I really don't except that you have to obey Creator's laws.

GOD: Well, first, my beloved child, your "single self" is exactly why you are having this Suzanne lifetime, and your entire range of feelings and what you do with them is your purpose for being there! *Never* is sense of self to be equated with selfishness or egotism. I don't mean that a self *cannot* be selfish or egotisti-cal, but there is a huge difference between feeling self-ness and those characteristics.

As for the limits of my powers there, I feel the same confusion as you, and *as* you, how could I not? So I shall give this a good effort. I do not mean to sound weak and totally unlike the All That Is omnipotent being you still think me to be, because I *do* have powers, of course, but also I have limits. They're not like a barbed wire fence, let us say, with well-defined boundaries and exact limi-tations for maneuvering and pretty harsh effects for trespassers.

What I MUST observe without exception is Creator's law of free will being supreme over all other laws. I don't mean that the other laws are weaker, such as like attracts like in the energy streams and the principles of manifestation, but nothing within my power is capable of subverting any of my *own* soul aspects' free will choices. So in that sense, you could say that my "father/mother ruler" has given me far stricter moral and spiritual guidelines than any rules given on Earth, and you can see that the "supreme" energy potency associated with me is not without limitations.

Let me give you an example. Let us say that you see a star and think it would be nice if you could put that star in a different galaxy. No reason is needed, only the capability of performing something that appeals to you. You don't have that capability for good reason. Do you know what would befall any civilizations living on or near that star, depending upon that star for heat, light, orderly stability? No, you don't, and therefore you don't have the power to play with the celestial bodies.

I *do* have the power and energy to do that because I know exactly what would happen if one star were taken out of its orbit and stuck in another place. I *don't* know how taking the free will gift out of universal experiencing would upset life on a cosmic basis. Creator *does*, and only It has the capability of amending the power of free will. And that Creator *did*, as you know, in Its decree that the topmost darkness had to free all the captive free wills of the souls that force had penned into its cumulative energy mass.

I believe you are beginning to see my position of the god of this universe with more of my perspective, dear child, although I must admit that it is not an easy one for any human being to fully comprehend.

S: I do understand more clearly now, though. Thank you, God, for your patience with me and for all of your answers, too.

GOD: Child, it is my delight, my *joy,* to communicate with you in a sense that you know absolutely that I am saying these things to you, that it is indeed God answering your questions, *respecting* your questions!

———————————————

My many futile attempts to interest a publisher in the books and later, after I formed Matthew Books publishing company, futility in getting my print order filled, prompted a ton of talks with God. He wants these few passages included.

January 13, 1997

GOD: Suzanne, you and I have chatted so often that I could, but I don't want to bother counting all the times. You think you're playing mind games, but each time you chatter away with yourself, I am aware. It is not always I who answers, but sometimes I do. I don't tell you what to do, but often I tell you what I think, and you say, "Gregory *[my guardian angel]*, is that you?" or "Matthew, I know it's not you because you wouldn't talk like that." *No?* God is not what so many think, the vapor essence without face or voice or contact or would use only "proper" words. *No way!*

So, I am aware and correspondingly concerned about your attitude of momentary hopelessness about the book. As Matthew has told you, I mandated this book and the ones to follow, and the Council of Nirvana is my supervising arm. When I give orders – which is often, by the way, it's just that there is no punishment from me when they aren't followed – but when I give an order for something of the measure of importance I place on this book, it DOES happen. I know exactly when, but you wouldn't understand my "time" even if I did my best to explain it in words you do understand.

Very well, I shall do my best. When the energy of the book – in which there is an amalgamation of many energies – when that energy flows in alignment with the correspondingly strong and like energy sources within the universal code for publishing time, *voila*, there it will be by name and worthiness.

You see, I said you wouldn't understand. But that is a facet of the translation of energy into Earth terms and it affects everyone there.

That's all for this minute. In abundance of light and loving energy to you and all whom you love, dearest soul, this is God, leaving in full appreciation of your communication, including what you did *not* say.

March 10, 1997

S: Matthew, if you're sure God wants to talk with me, of course I'll talk with Him. Good morning, God.

GOD: Suzanne, please listen to your son. He can speak for me on these subjects you have been addressing this morning. He and I would say the very same thing, and you wouldn't like it from me any more than from him, isn't that so? It's not that I'm unwilling to tell you myself, but Matthew knows far more than you are willing to attribute to your "little boy." Here he is not anyone's "little boy." You would be the proudest mother in the world if you could know him as he is in his full soul.

Well, let me see what I can say to encourage you. You are challenging me a lot lately. I love it! You had removed me from your awareness far too long, and I'm joyfully welcoming this close communion. Know that you just have to say, "God, get over here and tell me what's up," and then stand back in your thoughts and let me give you the answer you're seeking. You tend to bluster your way through my reply, and then assume I never did get back to you.

Ah yes, the books. Back we go again to needing reassurance, eh, Suzy? Well, dearly beloved little soul, I am human enough so that I understand. You aren't whining – you just want something intensely. Naturally I know the full scope of your feelings, and believe me, they are well founded because this has dragged on far longer than you were originally led to think. However, the course of the first book is straight, it is sure and certain. Put your energy into the second book.

You're not even mentally arguing with me, my child, and I thank you for that. Actually, you're doing admirably on patience and faith, and I thank you for *that,* too.

April 28, 1997

S: Good morning, Matthew and all Friends who may be with you.

MATTHEW/GROUP: Mother, we have to laugh at your prayer for light protection with elaborate confirmations that God also is welcome in these sittings. Of course, He is laughing, too – as we laugh, so does He. Now you're wondering if we talk with Him and get clear messages. Yes, all the time. Frequently we discuss the various aspects of our greater service, and He speaks not necessarily in words, but certainly in clear reply infused with light and love.

MATTHEW: You have the usual list of questions, I see. Yes, Mother, now it's just me, your "little boy" speaking, as you were thinking since you're feeling my more lively energy. I can handle this easily alone as the energy connection is so strong today. Would you like God to say something about the books?

S: Hi, "just you" sweetheart! What made you think of God saying something about the books?

GOD: *I* did, dear one. I was nudging Matthew to let me in a moment. I'm here to say I'm pleased that you are working diligently on the second book. These books and the others to come will comfort and enlighten many souls, millions of my children, as you shall see.

When? How about *soon*? Will you accept that "soon" is about as close as I wish to tell you and you will still feel heartened? *No?* Then how about the end of the calendar year?

July 19, 1998

GOD: Suzy, this is God, nudging Matthew to let me in here. You have been disenchanted with me on so many occasions that I'm surprised you're giving me the time of day now. *Why are you?* Because you still believe in me in the same vigorous way that you believed Santa Claus was real, benevolent, kind-hearted, generous - all those good attributes you gave that jolly old fellow for years beyond the other boys and girls. Well, with me, a far deeper and more spiritual relationship, yes, but you're thinking right now: *Why the hell did you tell me over a year ago that the books would be published by the end of LAST year?*

Surely we don't have to go over that again, Suzy, that not for one second are your thoughts and feelings unknown to me! You are having natural heartfelt concerns that Matthew's work ever will be published. I let you down there, didn't I? I did say the end of the last calendar year, yes, I did, and here it is in the next calendar year with July staring at us. So what can I say about THAT?

Well, I can say that the human element that is God, in your frank terminology, screwed up. Oh, God can't make mistakes? Oh, ho ho ho, *not!* Just as you can laugh at that, I can be rejoicing that we are feeling the light flowing in laughter at the same moment I also realize you are serious and require a reasonable answer.

First, I ask that you forgive me. And now you can say to anyone you think will accept that you chatter away with God that he said he screwed up and asked you to forgive him! Go ahead, we both can laugh when you tell people this.

It isn't easy for you to understand, dear child, and maybe I understand only because I'm living each and all lives thoroughly, totally, in every moment. Suzy, only if you were actually this "umbrella God" that you think of me could you see everything, of course. But maybe like my other children who share your dilemma of why I have let them down, you can accept that if I am you and you err, I also err because I cannot avoid it. Now put that into the perspective of *every* soul on Earth!

That time in your dimension was not a mistake, not even a miscalculation. What I did *not* do was take into account that free will can change midstream even when the current is running so swiftly and surely as to be almost at the end of its journey to the sea - in this case, the sea of publication. And my omission is why I'm asking for your forgiveness.

What happened is that powerful forces of darkness came in a swoop and derailed a great many projects of light, including those manuscripts. Yes, in a time that is even more right, this darkness will be dispersed and the books will see the light of publication. So, shall we make our pact to cooperate once again in friendship as our joint selves? There is abiding love!

December 2, 1998

S: Well, Matthew, that's not good enough after all this time, so I'll do what you suggested and see if God has a better suggestion. God, hello?

GOD: Hello, my child.

S: God, will you please tell me what I should do now about these books that you "ordered" to be published?

GOD: All right, Suzy, let's talk about this. Here's my answer to what you "should do now." You shouldn't think in terms of *"should."* This word has its place to be sure, but not as it's too often used, as a directive, a *demand,* that one turn away from a direction intuitively chosen and switch into a direction of another's choosing.

But you are serious about your work, dear daughter, and I never mean to make light of it, but to put light *into* it and surrounding it. Light *of* it is essential, so I guess I was right the first time, but now with a positive slant.

Think of a stream of light in which you see the books named *Matthew, Tell Me About Heaven* and *Revelations For A New Era.* See that light stream glowing and moving steadily toward a brightness that exceeds the brightness of the energy stream itself. That is all you need to do as your part in getting these into print.

The universe is handling this now. Just give it a helping hand and forego the negative outlook. You know the power of thought in bringing to you what you want, so leave behind your frustrations and helpless feelings or you'll just get more situations to give you those feelings.

Of course you can do this! You believe in me so how can you not believe in *yourself?* You know they are one and the same!

August 4, 2002

GOD: Those feelings of frustration are back, but this time I tell you, they are totally understandable. You have been told time and again that you are in control of everything affecting your life. Well, just as I have my limits, so does your control over the printing have its limits. What you have control over are your *reactions,* and in this case, your reactions are justifiable.

Moreover, they are not impeding the progress of getting the revised editions printed. Suzy, beloved child, I have only respect and yes, awe, that you have shown such exceeding patience, diligence and perseverance for more than eight years, and your energy poured into these feelings and service are in the light momentum of the books.

All I can tell you beyond this is what I've mentioned in context of everything transpiring on Earth during this time of monumental changes there, this time of unprecedented changes throughout the *universe.* The darkness is battling mightier than ever against all sources of light, and these books with their crucial information for my children are some of the foremost targets of attacks on Earth. This energy is so entrenched around the books that all light being beamed to the soul derailing your efforts is not phasing her.

Keep the faith, dear Suzy! When my wishes are not met, I continue "the good fight," and this is what you need to do, too. I'm doing this now on so many fronts that you cannot imagine it, but not for a moment do I forget these books! How can I – *you* do not! Furthermore, they are *my truth* that I have mandated will be available to my children on Earth!

You have much material for the third book that needs to be organized and polished and more will come. Work on this and keep focused on what you want – this information *"out there"!* – knowing that your faith will be justified that these vital books will "come to light" because I have ordained this!

January 6, 2003

GOD: It is time for others to get into this situation. I am not saying that the light is failing the books, not at all, but a new kind of light service is required. Yes, Suzy, I mean that legal assistance is necessary to dislodge the free will of the one who is exercising it to prevent the books' availability. You will be led to the attorney who will manifest this in conjunction with the light. Remember, my child, I work in wondrous ways, and you may consider this one of them!

JESUS

April 7, 2000

S: Good morning, God. You've said you would tell me about Jesus' life – can you do that now?

GOD: Good morning, Suzy, and of course I can. There was indeed a man named Emmanuel, whom you call Jesus and therefore I shall here, who was born to be one of my major messengers to Earth. However, the story about him as related in the Bible is not the same as his life.

His life was by pre-birth agreement just as was yours, Matthew's, *all* souls who incarnate for the same purpose – to remember who I am and who each of you is. Therefore, his life has the same significance as all others, but with this great difference: Jesus had the *conscious* awareness of his mission and he lived more closely to his agreement than almost all other souls ever born on Earth. Therein is the big difference between that son of mine and all my other children except those few souls whose agreements also included the same Christed realm origin and mission as did Jesus' life, to carry my message to Earth.

Jesus was born by the same means as all other human babies, the union of his mother and father. That is a good method, so *why not?* His divinity as my child did not require a star in the East to proclaim his birth, nor did his life require the "supernatural" attachments that are heralded in the book so revered by many, the Bible. Most of the fanciful happenings that book attributes to Jesus, to include that most unusual means of his conception and even his mother's and that manger birthplace, not to mention his "resurrection," are not so.

That story was made up to suit the aim of the church leaders to distance Jesus far above all other souls on Earth, and by intent, that distanced me from my children as well. The deception and corruption then was not much different from now–greed and desire to control others seems to have no end!

Never would I set apart one of my children above another! Nor did Jesus do that, because he knew the Oneness of all! As Matthew has told you and others have also, it is in this context of that *distant* soul wherein most of the fallacies lie. (*NOTE: The "Cultural Resources" chapter of* Matthew, Tell Me About Heaven *mentions this in more detail.*)

Several years ago you heard from one of your high sources that Jesus wasn't meant to die on a cross and in fact, did *not.* That was quite a jolt to you. You didn't want to include that in the book and did so with great reluctance because those were the instructions you received persistently from a source you identified as "the Council," but it was *I* who pushed you on that.

Actually, Jesus never was put on a cross at all. By order of the San Hedrin he was flogged and banished from the country. In the eyes of those who ordered that, to make him a martyr would give greater impact to his message whereas getting rid of his presence would eliminate his influence on the populace. Or so they thought. But the influence lingered, so they proceeded to distort his message and make up others that would achieve their own objectives, and in time, those falsehoods became Christianity's recorded story of Jesus.

What actually happened is that with Mary Magdalene, his wife, Jesus left that area and returned to the East, where he felt safety for his family. He lived a much more earthy life than your Bible version portrays. Why should he not have married the woman he loved? Why should he not have enjoyed sexual relations with her and had children to love and nurture? Why should he not have moved where he wished, studied what he wished during his long lifetime? *None of those natural human desires diminishes the importance of his message one iota!*

His teachings were heeded by some, ignored by many, and despised by those whose control he shattered with his revelations. Those true revelations were "shrouded in mystery," to say this more mildly than the deliberate falsehoods they were. His true message was clear, simple and forthrightly expressed. Furthermore, it was clearly *understood.*

His message was given to him by me, but it did not reach you as I intended. The Bible eliminates many of his teachings and distorts others by efforts of the kingpin of changers, the Vatican itself, as the primary mover and shaker of the deceit that long ago replaced the original records.

You are only beginning to see the lies that have been established to serve the purposes of the forces that wish to rule the universe. Yes, the "dark forces," as Matthew calls them, are very, *very* real. I don't call them that myself, but rather the DIS-serving ones of my flock. However, by any designation, their intentions have been the same, power and control, and their goals have been thwarted in the same way, by love and light.

Child, would you question beyond this?

S: God, considering the importance of your message to Earth, why have you let the distortions go on this long?

GOD: Two words: free will. All right, *more* words: Not *my* free will, but my having to observe Creator's law of free will in all of my children's use of it. I'm speaking of those who caused the distortions and those who freely believe without reservation what is in the Bible.

With so much of what you call "evil" in your world that the Bible claims started in the very beginning, in the Garden of Eden, is it not logical to question if the **True Word** might have been strategically changed during the millennia that have passed since Jesus' teachings? Is it not logical to question if those who wrote about Jesus but did not know him got the stories about his teachings exactly right? Is it not logical to question, as the records that became the Bible were interpreted and the versions translated, if those who worked with the material may have expanded or deleted portions to reflect their own beliefs? Is it not logical to question why the "word of God" would be the basis for killing each other to uphold the *very same* word?

Suzy, I could go on and on with this, but to what avail? The situation is what it is, millions of my children believing the lies, and as long as they do, they do not know me or my son Jesus.

S: What about the miracles Jesus performed – or are they just more stories to create the distancing?

GOD: Calling them "miracles" is what created the distancing, and it was *not* Jesus who did that. He knew *exactly* how he was enabled to do what he did, and furthermore, he told the multitudes that they could learn it, too.

His awareness of his pre-birth agreement led him in his early years out of public view to areas in the East where there were teachers of the ancient arts of levitation, directing kinetic energy, vision beyond your vision and hearing beyond your hearing, healing without tools or medicines. Those master teachers had not perverted the truth of this innate capacity that's in *all* of my children as their birthright.

Through them Jesus learned how to use his mind far more greatly than most others, and with his fascination for developing the capabilities he saw in them, he practiced and practiced. He had no more innate capacity to learn than other souls, but most had put constraints upon their minds and didn't even think how much more they could produce and achieve than what they saw around them.

Those who banished Jesus did so because they *knew* this truth, that *every* soul has the same innate capacity as he did. They couldn't deny what so many had seen, so they made the feats unique to Jesus and kept the truth suppressed to retain their power over the people. Thus the reports of the "miracles" are sketchy in today's Bible, again by design. Enough to create the distance of the mystery, not enough to show that constantly there were incidents in which Jesus amazed people. However, those incidents were recorded by people who profited directly, people who witnessed them, and people who were told firsthand about them, but *those* records are *not* in your Bible!

With very few exceptions, people today are continuing in that same limiting belief that Jesus *came to dispel.*

S: Did he and his family go to France and did French royalty come from that beginning?

GOD: Yes, and there are records that prove this, too, but as you can surmise, producing them would cause quite a stir in many circles! However, the French royalty of recent centuries is not the same lineage as the beginning royalty stemming from Jesus' descendants. What changed is by intent of the darkness, to state it most simply, and surely by now, no surprise to you.

So, my child, I see you have another question.

S: Will people here ever know the truth about Jesus?

GOD: I cannot say whether the truth will be revealed "soon," but most assuredly it WILL come forth! That truth, like other truths, must again be revealed so that purity upon my very own Eden will be restored.

But to answer your exact question, Will people ever know the truth? *Will they open their hearts to the truth?* is the question, Suzy! The truth of *everything* is being given left and right, and it is being obscured or attacked by those whose power will be gone forever if they cannot stop the steady progression of questioning, of self- and truth-discovery among people on Earth.

This is the time of *TRUE* revelations, dear child! That is the purpose of your work with Matthew and the others who have given messages for the books!

February 25, 2003

S: God, hello! I need to ask you a few things.

GOD: Hello, my dear child! Shoot!

S: Are you really satisfied with your part of the book? Have I included everything you want? And are you still absolutely sure you want all of that information about Jesus in it?

GOD: Suzy, in a word answer to all your questions, YES!

S: Well, OK then. So I didn't miss anything in searching through all of those files?

GOD: I don't think so. That was quite a task! However, I would like to add a message and before this "goes to press," I may come to you with another. For this moment, though, my note is short and sweet, not the "something momentous" you are expecting. My beloved child, from *Creator* come the momentous pronouncements, not from me!

"To every one of my children reading this book, I LOVE YOU! You know now that I AM you, you are me, and what could be more sustaining for me to impart than this? All I am doing now by this messenger of the light is sharing my limitless love, understanding and respect, and I embrace every one of you in eternity. You are LIVING eternity, not moving toward it! Salu, amen, I am forever with and within you."

EXPLAINING GOD TO A CHILD

In 1994, soon after Matthew and I started talking, a mother requested that he explain to a young child who God is.

MATTHEW: Mother, let me give this a moment of thought, please. .... All right, thank you. I'll be speaking as if your friend is talking with her little daughter and having a flower at hand, but of course, my examples have to be adapted to fit the family.

God is kind and gentle, but He is very, very strong, too, because He makes everything in the whole world! He made you and me and He made everybody else, too.

Everywhere you look, you can see something God has made! The biggest things and the tiniest things. He made mountains and rivers and oceans, the sky and the sun and the moon and the stars. He makes rain and rainbows and snow and grass and the wind.

He makes baby birds and puppies and kittens, all the animals everywhere. They are very important to God because He made them all.

God makes trees and flowers and plants. He starts them with special seeds. See the tiny seeds in this pretty flower? All flowers have seeds that will make more flowers just like them.

There are different kinds of seeds for everything. Mothers and daddies have very special seeds. They love each other and their babies come from God at just the right time. Mothers and daddies know how to take good care of their babies.

Dogs and rabbits and all other animals have their own special seeds, too. When their babies come from God, they know how to take care of them. When the babies grow up, they will have their own families.

God also makes things you can't see, but you can feel. Especially God makes LOVE! That's how we feel about each other!

You feel happy when Daddy and I play with you and make you laugh and when we say what a good girl you are. You know we always take good care of you, so you aren't afraid. We teach you what you need to learn. We do all of this because we love you.

And you do things to make us happy because you love us. All of this love we feel for each other is God's gift to us. He gives this gift to everyone.

Even though you can't see God the same way you see Daddy and me, it's the very same kind of love that you and God have, too.

Love is everywhere! When you touch your puppy, it cuddles up to you. It isn't afraid because it knows you are gentle and will take care of it. You love it and it loves you and both of you feel happy.

God's love is part of your happiness with the puppy and the puppy's happiness with you. God flows like a little river of love that connects you and the puppy.

It's that way with everybody! It's the same with people and all the animals and even the flowers and trees, too. That's why you want to be kind to everyone and take good care of every living thing.

You can love as much as you want! You can love Daddy and me as much as you want. You can love your friends and your puppy. You can love our neighbors and all the animals you see. You can love the flowers and trees. You never will run out of love! It is God's biggest and best gift to everybody.

Sometimes people do things that aren't nice. Then God feels sad about what they are doing, but he never stops loving them.

Maybe sometimes you do things you are sorry for, and you try hard not to do those things again. If you ask God to help you to always be kind, He will. God always will help you do good things!

God always knows what you are thinking and how you feel. So you can talk with God whenever you want to. You can feel His answers in your heart.

God always has loved you and that will never change. You will change because you are growing up and learning new things, and as you get older, you will look different. When Daddy and I are older, we will look different, too. Your puppy will look different when it grows up and is a big dog.

But our love for each other will never change! God never changes in that way, either. He always will love you because God IS love, and He is part of your life forever.

When it is the right time, God has people and animals come to live with Him in Heaven. That is a beautiful place where everyone is good to everyone else and they always are happy. You miss the people who go there, but you know they are living in that beautiful place with God. And

when it is the right time for you to live there, you will be with all the people there you love. And the animals you loved will be there, too.

You don't have to understand everything right now. You will grow and
learn and understand more.

The most important thing God wants you to know is how much He
loves you and everybody else and the animals and plants. God's love is
forever and ever.

Mother, probably that was too much. Or maybe not everything that needs to be said. Maybe a young child would interrupt
with questions that would lead into directions I didn't think of on
short notice. Maybe the explanation could happen like a story
being read and a child would listen until the end – I have to doubt
that, but I don't know. Maybe parts will be helpful piecemeal, as
the child asks about those things.

As I was talking, I was thinking of a child the age of
Esmeralda, whose Earth age would be two years but here that is
equivalent to a child of three to four years there. Although she
doesn't have complete understanding of all God's powers, she
does know that every life not only is from God, it IS God, and
God IS love.

I think it would be preferable if religious dogma could be kept
out of discussions about God because even at the simplest level,
those put a distance between Him and the child. And absolutely
it would be wrong to put God as a punisher if the child did something the parent considered bad!

Explaining God has no short and simple approach, does it?
However the explanation goes in actual use, I would stress God's
love of everyone and all in the animal and plant kingdoms so the
child can learn to treat all with respect and nurturing. In the final
analysis, though, it is the parents' living example of God's love in
action that needs to accompany their words to their child.

PART IV

MORE FROM
OTHER WORLDS

MESSAGES FROM NIRVANA

Readers who are familiar with *Matthew, Tell Me About Heaven* know about life in Nirvana, the proper name of the realm we call Heaven, as Matthew described it. Here are insights into the lives of two other souls who are there and one who moved on from Nirvana to serve in a different world. All names in the three messages have been changed.

CAL - 1998

S: Thank you for asking, Cal. Yes, I would like to ask you something –how were you when you arrived in Nirvana and how have you adjusted to being there?

CAL: I'm glad you thought of that, as it may be comforting to my family to know about that. I had no pain after the first shock to my body from the wreck, and that was a blessing, maybe divine grace, because my head got the brunt of the injuries. They know I was unconscious on Earth for a day before I left, and I want them to know that during that time I was given soul strength to ease out of my physical life. Actually, I was aware of both my body dying and my soul living endlessly.

I was totally within the light during my quick passage here and felt the consuming love that people who have near death experiences tell about. I felt that I was within music. There definitely was music, not coming at me, but enveloping me. It was so incredibly beautiful that I can't describe it because it was unlike anything you've ever heard.

When I arrived, friends and family from both this lifetime and my past lives were here to welcome me. It was a joyous time for all of us, and none of those from my past lifetimes were surprised about my recognizing them. Well, neither was I surprised, so you can see that my adjustment was instantaneous with my entry, and I didn't require the medical attention that is given to people who die in much worse conditions than I did.

I can also add that I've just signed up for a refresher class in electronics. It's an interest I never pursued there, and although I have some insight on this from what I know now are parallel lives, I didn't carry over any fresh expertise with me. But this is more like a hobby than preparation for work. I'm planning to get into more beneficial ventures soon, a real service of some kind, and maybe some more serious classes. But definitely I'm not interested in doing any more accounting. After 30 years of that, I'm willing to let others do that if they want to.

Anyway, you know I haven't been here all that long, so that's about it, Suzy. I'm grateful that you accepted my wife's request that you contact me. I am as connected as ever in love with my family and friends. Lily knows this, but I told her again in my message that I downloaded to Matthew for passing on to you. But of course you know that. Thank you for receiving that message and for seeing that it gets to her. God bless you, Suzy.

GRACE - 1999

S: A friend called to ask if you could talk with someone who arrived in Nirvana about a month ago. Her name is Grace Horton. Can you pick up her energy streamer from our friend if I give you his name?

MATTHEW: Mother, that isn't necessary, but I thank you for thinking of it. You "called me" when he was talking with you and I made the energy connection then. I have talked with Grace and have her message with me, so please record this as I download her actual words from my storage capacity.

GRACE: Hello, dear friends! I am more eager than I could imagine while I was there to tell you about life *here*! No one there can do justice to the marvels of this place. It is awesome! I did believe that something lovely would be in my next life, but I couldn't begin to imagine HOW glorious it would be!

So, I shall explain some of these glories to you. First, I arrived in a body that was beautiful. As you know, my Earth body took a beating and wasn't *par excellence* at the end. And because I left a body that was less than anyone would desire, it was such a marvel for me to travel *sans* that baggage and step into this really quite beautiful form that's alive – and I mean REALLY *ALIVE!* – with health and excitement.

My travels have been few so far as I've been settling in, you could say. It's somewhat like a move on Earth – dumping all the stuff you don't want and never needed probably, and taking the meaningful things and setting up housekeeping. So, remembering things I especially enjoyed around me there, I *MADE* them all right here! So, in a way, you sure *can* "take it with you." Well, *make* it, some of it, anyway.

I did have help, though. Friends gave me the extra energy I needed to get all the house furnishings ready. Restoring full health to this kind of light body and also the brain – or "psyche" I guess is better – is not the same for everyone. It depends upon how you were there, throughout your life, really, and not just at the end. Well, I was fairly steady, would you believe, judging from how quickly I was stabilized and ready to start living an active life here.

No, it's not necessary to have my "old" furniture here, but it delights me, and so that's why I'm doing things this way for now. Also I've been told that a transition from Earth to life here is easier if some of what's most familiar and comfortable is reconstituted here.

We can let go of it, divest ourselves of *anything* we wish at any time. The same process of creating – envisioning and giving that vision energy to form the image – is used to de-create, and poof, it's gone. It's literally, "Now you see it, now you don't!"

Abodes are something else! I was allowed to choose right off the bat, and for beginning, I'm in a small house – my preference over an apartment in a big unit, and I mean B-I-G! So, I'm settling into my little house with scads of flowers blooming all around it and in it. Can't have too many flowers, and *that* should let you all know who's really talking here!

Suzy, I'm picking up that you're wondering, *What do I do with my time?* There *is* no time! I had read this, but until you're in the midst of a "no-time zone," it doesn't make sense outside of the math. But what *is* it, then? It's a sensation of accomplishment, of doing and getting there. I've already gotten somewhere by participating in the furnishing of my charming little house, by helping the friends here construct furniture for my comfort and pleasure.

You cannot believe the happiness that abounds here! We know that the conditions where we left are not ideal for most souls living there, that's for sure, but we have a higher understanding of the *necessity* of those conditions. And it's obvious from here that there is soul growth in those situations that sometimes you choose and sometimes you don't, but that doesn't affect the learning. You can get "points" for experiencing what you didn't sign up for if they are growth experiences.

For instance, if you signed on to be healthy and somehow something slipped up and you were in an "accident" and bedridden the rest of your life, if you learned patience, tolerance, peacefulness, or whatever needed to be better filled in on your soul's overall curriculum, well, you get credit for all of it.

I won't impose upon your mother further, Matthew.

Yep, Suzy, I gave that message to Matthew to give to you and yet I've been talking to you, too. *Weird,* huh! Do you want me to show myself? Well, I'm doing it, so will you please describe how I look so I'll be recognized. Or maybe not recognized, but this is how I *want* my friends there to see me. Long dark curly, wavy hair. My skin is not as white as it was – well, I was *sick!* I wanted it more olive, like you see it. And my lips are red because I'm choosing that after such a long time of not using any cosmetics to speak of. Suzy, please do not be wondering if anyone will recognize me. I think they will. If not, well, I am within their hearts, and I think they can feel me there.

Mark called you, I know that, but I wasn't that close to him in our lives on Earth. However, I admire his interest in the discovery of alien life and I can tell him, *Keep trying, Mark!* There are troops like you wouldn't imagine and we can see the effects of their work to save Earth from collapsing due to all the roughhousing humans have been doing in their ignorance and belligerence and greed there.

Anabel, I miss you. I'm not lonely as you know it, but there is a slender thread of light that is not touching where I want it to. You aren't there, connected to me as I thought you would be. I was so sure that all it would take was my departure to connect us permanently and that we'd both be aware of it, and that hasn't happened.

I *know* you love me! I really wish that you would look within more quietly, maybe, and with less pain, and then we can be connected the way I thought we would be. Well, we ARE, but you're not realizing it. Just mentally you are, but I mean within the whole spectrum of what we *can* do in communication, you haven't reached that point of letting go of Earth entanglements that can be negative – the grief, the regrets, the missing. And that's natural. It's just that we'll be what I told you we would as soon as you are welcoming me into your soul level being and then into your consciousness without the negative part of grief.

So, then, I said I wouldn't impose and here I am prattling on and on. Well, Suzy, do you want to ask me anything?

S: Grace, now I'm imposing on you. Matthew and others have explained this message transfer business, but I don't get it. Prior to this sitting you gave a message to him for downloading to me, and then in the middle of it, you were talking to me directly. How does this happen?

GRACE: I'm not in the same timeframe you're in. I gave the message to Matthew "before" and also I'm in it "now," but they're actually the *same* "times." Here it's not restricted to "before" and "after," as you are. That's your need for scheduling and understanding the here and now, but "now" is *always*. OK, that doesn't explain it very well, but just please understand that I am within the message even as it is being transferred from Matthew to you, "downloading," he said. Well, any other question? Actually, I know there is.

S: You spoke of friends helping you furnish your home. New friends, old friends? Would any of them would be recognized by your friends here on Earth? Do you have any special messages for anyone here?

GRACE: Oh, *sure* there are friends here whom I've known for, ooh, eons, and some Anabel would recognize if she were here. I know that Daniel is a name that will ring bells there. And I have a special message for that rascal Dick! I'm not up to my old tricks at all, but there are jokesters here aplenty. *That* should be easily recognized, but basically, my message is general news for everyone.

Suzy, I know you feel like all novice channels do. Forgive me for calling you that, because you're *not*, not after five years of this, but in feeling so insecure about doing "soul contact" requests, you still feel that way. Yes, I know it's because Matthew's messages to you via mediums were your "lifeline" for many years and you feel such a heavy responsibility never to disappoint anyone who asks you to contact some soul. But that's not really your mission anyway – you *know* that, so this is like a special favor.

There really isn't anything else I want to say right now except that this is *FAR* more than I could imagine it would be when I was in that body on Earth, but it's very much as I remember it now that I'm back here. I'll say "Ciao" for now and wish you all the best of light when you look within and without. I love you all, dear family and friends.

Goodbye, Suzy – thank you!

(Three months later)

S: Matthew, I'm not sure, but I think Grace wants to speak with me – could you find out, please?

GRACE: Matthew buzzed me that he'll step aside, so good day, Suzy! I was going to say "good morning," but I see it's mid-afternoon there. So, I greet you with good cheer and thank you for talking with me again.

S: Thank you for coming, Grace. Did you speak to me about a week ago, saying you would like to talk whenever I could get to the computer?

GRACE: I said something like that, yes.

S: How often are you aware of my thoughts about you?

GRACE: Well, when you think of me very strongly, I am aware of that. I probably don't know every time you think of me, the way Matthew knows, but if you really want to reach me, that intensity always would work. That's a connection we are aware of with everyone there, and then we can choose whether to talk or not. Also, we can initiate a contact when we want to talk, but almost no one hears us.

Now, can I help you with those questions? I know they're really Mark's questions, and I'm happy to answer them. That's why I spoke to you about talking again.

S: I see – well, I'm pleased that you're here and he'll be pleased to get your answers. Last time you said something about more ETs nearby Earth than he can imagine. He'd like you to tell him more about those, if you can.

GRACE: I can do that. First of all, some of them are on the ground right there. They don't look any different from the majority of people, but they sure are different in their capabilities! In most cases, they simply agreed at soul level to substitute their higher light for the denser essence of Earth-born folks, and that's why such marvels keep appearing on the entertainment scene, for example. But there are others too, in all areas where influence is necessary for bringing about the changes for more peacefulness and kindness and truthfulness on Earth.

As for those who aren't on the ground or under it, in those vast places that are virtually unknown, there are *massive* numbers of them in the skies, most of the time out of sight of the human eye. There are probably thousands of little ships hovering around, and those quite often are seen, and even occasionally some mid-sized ships. But there also are huge home ships and operating centers, and it would be a stretch of your imagination to see these mammoth ones. They aren't all that far from Earth, but they are clouded in a sort of preservation atmosphere that's either in the form of clouds, or by using a frequency fluctuator to speed up their vibrational atmosphere, they can stay in hiding when they're practically right next to you.

Some of your pilots see these things "be there and then not be there" in such rapid succession that they KNOW something of alien technology is about. But those pilots are usually considered crazy or they're discouraged from believing very long that they really saw those "phenomena."

Is that enough on that, Suzy?

S: I think so, Grace – thank you. It's exciting to know about their numbers and proximity. Here's Mark's next question: Do you have any way of knowing if he may already know an alien in an Earth-born body or if he will meet one, or if he'll be in contact eventually with ETs who will openly identify themselves as such?

GRACE: That's not something I would automatically know just because I'm here and not there. It's something that would have to be investigated, and I'm not sure I have entry to that part of his records – to any part of his records, really. His questions until now haven't required that I get access and look at the symbolic fields and get interpretations.

Lord knows I wouldn't trust myself to interpret *anything* – that's definitely NOT something I could say is "my bag." Not that it wouldn't be fascinating, but it's not automatic endowment, you know, and I wouldn't trust my judgment with something like that.

Anyway, people tend to put too much stock in what any channel says, and that's not wise. I can see a lot more clearly now than when I was there – *of course!* – so I can see how far afield even the honest ones are just by virtue of their not staying on course in clarity. You *are* clear – you must know that, you've been told enough times!

I know you feel stuck in this niche of not having any chance to get out of it and spread the word you already have received from Matthew and the others. Suzy, don't picture yourself caught in a tight little place with no out except through the province of others who will buy into this material and get it published.

There are ways of this universe that you can't imagine, and that's fine, no one there can. Even though the words are not that unrealistic or surprising, the *activity* – the actual motion and effects of universal laws – is at work, and the belief system there just isn't divine enough to encompass all of this in operation.

So, anything else? I'm glad you smiled and are feeling uplifted on that note.

S: Grace, I'm so glad you came today! I think we would have enjoyed knowing each other if we'd had that chance.

GRACE: I think so, too! Suzy, let's let it go now, OK? I feel that you're satisfied and I've said everything I can to Mark. I even managed to make you smile a few times, so I think I've had myself quite a good day! Goodbye now, and let me know whenever you'd like to talk again – I'm here!

S: Thank you for today, Grace. Goodbye, now. Mash?

MATTHEW: I'm here, Mother. I'm VERY here! I'm taking a little vacation from my travels and I'm sitting in this chair beside your desk, observing you smile or look amazed or whatever as you were chatting with Grace. Can you detect anything different about this chair?

S: No – nothing's moving, no depressions in the blanket. But I'm glad to know you're here! What is *different, dear?*

MATTHEW: Well then, nothing, really. I had hoped I could wiggle this blanket enough for you to see it, but it didn't happen. I *could* have done it – I don't mean there isn't sufficient "fire power" for that – but I didn't wish to be that disturbing to the energy movement in the room. Just to make the blanket move a little bit would have supercharged the atmosphere in the room considerably.

(Two months later)

GRACE: Suzy, I think I'm losing the connection. OK, there we go. You started fading from me just a bit. I've been rambling, so let me pull in my natural tendency and make this point to Mark: NO brotherhood members of what are called "alien civilizations" are going to be landing soon! More than likely what will take place is that those already on Earth in either disguise or hiding will emerge first and reduce or take away the fears that might – just *might* – hit the multitudes if thousands of spaceships descended *en masse.*

Very likely there will be communication between the ones who are Earth souls, or whatever word is better there – ET folks will do – and those in "space." Obviously coordination will have to take place or it would be a fiasco, and then Earth people *would* get bent out of shape.

When I said they're not coming "soon," I didn't mean not in your lifetime, Mark, but that as clearly as I can determine between the different "time" of this place and yours – well, years are passing very quickly there now anyway – but maybe 5 years is a time-frame to be thinking of. *And maybe not!* It's definitely not scheduled, that I can tell you, so if you're hearing otherwise, like specific dates, don't believe it.

It's all in readiness as far as the *plans* of the "aliens," but there are many variables connected to Earth. All the folks of space, of origin anywhere, are in place, but not willing to supersede Galactic Federation plans, which are to hold off on a mass arrival. It's the collective mentality on Earth that's the pivotal thing here.

Mark, I know how fervently you want to be in the vanguard of those who can meet with the aliens, so here's a nice surprise for you – I've been informed that you *KNOW* one! Of course, he isn't known as that, but because of your longstanding interest in peaceful communion and collaboration with non-Earth beings, one who is there in human form but of alien origin and mentality and gifts has made your acquaintance. I've been assured that someday you'll know this.

Suzy, that's it – that's all I can tell him.

S: That's fine, Grace – I think he'll be delighted! Thank you for coming again.

(One month later)

GRACE: Mark, you are a *persistent* fella! But, you people are not far off your estimates of the ETs surrounding your planet. It's not easy for me to see all of this and not want to just shout to the whole world: *"HEY!! They're here, they're here! We told you so!"* If I could, boy, *would* I!

Well, the best I can do is tell you that you're on the right track. Stick with it. There's a communications glitch, but it's in the technology and not the spirit energy. It's not an easy one to fix, but it's sure better to have something mechanical that can be fixed instead of a totally blind mind that *can't* be fixed.

So, Suzy, want to ask any questions yourself?

S: Can you explain that communications glitch that's technical rather than "spirit"?

GRACE: Sure, at least a little. There is equipment used to measure distance and frequencies between Earth and a point to be determined by each user. The idea is that if there are spacecraft within the radius of that point in space, you can pull them in with sounds that are "off the wall" rather than within the frequencies operating in Earth's atmosphere.

The concept is good, but the equipment is faulty. You need to discover the causes of the static that's simply giving you false signals. You're not recognizing that or that the data you want is really there, just covered with the static. So, get some clarifying apparatus on that equipment and see if you can strain out the static.

I've been told that you should hear the beeping responses because the troops you're beaming at are homing in on the signals. These are English language or other language-speaking beings, you guys! They know you're trying to communicate in a common language – numbers and frequencies – but it isn't necessary. So, talk!

But get that static cleared up and then see if you can broadcast a signal – the Morse code would be a good one to send out. We'll see if we can make a contact loop involving the folks here who are set up for monitoring all ET activity relating to Earth.

Believe me, you'd *gasp* if you saw how many troops there are and how many souls here are monitoring all the movements! No commanding or coordinating is done from here, just watching, being aware. Some people on Earth are benefiting from this monitoring as some are connected here expressly for this reason.

Anything else, Suzy? Well, I see there is, so shoot.

S: Thanks, Grace. You have talked about your ET interests and their activities, but can you tell me more about your whole life? Maybe what you're doing that's like a job or going to school? What are you doing up there?

GRACE: I can't help but laugh! I know exactly what you mean because I can read your heart and your mind a lot faster than you can type words on that computer. OK, yes, I can certainly tell you more about what I'm doing.

I can see that you're referring to something that could be likened to Matthew's former medical transition assistance work and now his tutoring and consulting and advising. Well, that's advanced, I'll tell you. Remember, I'm new here, and we don't start out with those heavy loads of responsibility. Matthew is *extraordinary*, Suzy! Someday you'll see that for yourself – before you're here, I mean – that's what I'm told.

Anyway, my service at this point is studying the mechanics of taking apart weather anomalies and softening their effects in our atmosphere. And I do mean "our" – like, *yours and ours.* We aren't all that far from you, you know, and furthermore, we have such close bonds with you all that we aren't separated in very many ways. By our lighter density and the respective weather, yes we are, but still it's your AND our atmosphere I'm working on.

I know that sounds almost too weird to believe, but that's the easiest way for me to tell you. That isn't at all how I'd describe it here, but you don't have our words so how could you begin to know what I mean if I use our vocabulary? There aren't any synonyms or similar expressions there for this process. It's something that can't help immediately, but in the long run, what I'm doing will make a good difference.

It's not that I can harness the winds of Earth or act as if I'm a global umbrella in those major storms. I'm studying how to contain the energy so that it can be dispersed rather than congregate and then explode. I should have said dispersed in a routine and slow and easy way instead of just sitting for a while and then acting as if it's got the whole world by the tail and then, watch out – here's another hurricane or tornado!

It's going to take a while for this to have any effect, you know? There's a lot more still to come by whatever designation it's given – cleansing, purification, increasing the light, lightning

Earth's burdens of negativity, ascension process – but it all adds up to the very same thing: A lot of geological activity with pretty heavy damage is still in store.

There's no way out of this, you know. Energy is energy, and you can't say, "Shoo, baby, go dissipate." Actually, that's what I'm working on, how to get to that status of being able to handle things so that if rain is needed, it comes, just enough of it. When it's done, it goes away until it's needed again. The rhythm, the pattern is set, you see.

S: Whew – that's quite an undertaking, Grace! Would your friends here be surprised about that?

GRACE: I shouldn't think so. Does this seem odd to you guys? Don't you remember my fascination with weather, particularly the stuff that caused such quaking and shaking? It wasn't just curiosity, it was a soul contact – that's what I've discovered. So it's a natural that I'm working in that same area where I've been before, because this isn't all new to me – I'm remembering from delving into this before. But now I'm advancing and will have more to offer in the way of real energetic application next time I'm around on Earth. Or somewhere else, if that's what I decide. That's a ways off, so let's not carry this out too far.

Suzy, let's pack it in, OK? Your mind is still with me but you're trying to think of another question and can't, and that's a sure sign that we've said all we need to. You're great to listen and pass on my messages – I'm grateful and will come just any time to answer questions, yours or Mark's or anyone else's. And if you just want to say "Hi, Grace!" I'm up for that, too. So, thank you, and I'll be around.

JEREMY – 2001

After a time of "remembering" and more advanced training in Nirvana, Jeremy went to another planet in the galaxy where his specialized knowledge and skills were needed.

JEREMY: Suzy, I'm glad you asked about my current endeavors. It is my honor to be given the opportunity to work at this height of light energy that is being strengthened in its velocity toward Earth directly into the oceans. At this time it is required that more light be poured into those waters because there is a need to thwart the most damaging effects of the sound testing that otherwise would have killed thousands of whales and dolphins as well as other marine life. That testing would have increased ocean waters in temperatures that to human comparison would be past boiling, so you can see that the work we perform in this height and breadth of energy band is critical to preserve that facet of Earth.

I know that you have been told the importance of whale spiritual energy as anchors on the planet of the light forces' energy streamers beamed there. That is true, and that of course is the purpose of my work in tandem with these other souls whose service is the same as mine. We chose to rise into an orbiting within the galaxy that would permit the garnering of light rays from other celestial bodies and direct these beams to Earth.

This in no way deflects the light from serving its full purpose for all other places and life forms, but it permits us to focus the powers of the light instead of having it diffused in space. It is the concentration of energy band that is preserving, to the extent we are able, the health and lives of marine life.

Suzy, you have been typing for quite a while. I understand that a rest now and then is welcomed by you. Also, if you would like to question me, I would entertain that request.

S: Thank you, Jeremy. I'd like to read what you have said. ..... Thank you. First, can you explain to Cyndi how you could give your personal message to Matthew to pass on to me and in between talk with me as if we are face to face? I don't understand this communication well enough to explain it if Cyndi asks about it.

JEREMY: Suzy, it isn't easy to comprehend something you can't relate to. Cyndi, consciously you don't understand this, either, but I can assure you, beneath that veneer of Earthling awareness, you not only understand this, you are in spirit working with me! But for the explanation of how this happens on a conscious level you can comprehend, please compare this to an orange on a tree. It is stationary, but its properties are the same as the orange that has fallen and still is rolling. Those identical properties emit energy bands that keep the stationary and the rolling oranges – and *souls* – connected.

Let us say that Suzy is the stationary soul here, and I am the roving one. There is the soul connection that is the same as the energy connection of the oranges. My message through Matthew was the connection needed for the original contact between Suzy and me, and now that we have this glue, you might say, she and I can converse at any time regardless of our respective energy placements or embodiments.

What do you think of that explanation, Suzy?

S: Well, Jeremy, I thank you, but I think it's simpler just to take this on faith. Cyndi has far more understanding of physics than I, so perhaps your analogy will be helpful to her. Are you in a body or in free spirit status?

JEREMY: I'm in a body. It's lighter than yours but not as

light as Matthew's. I could have made that more inclusive by stating that bodies here are not as dense as on Earth and not as light as in Nirvana. My appearance is a male humanoid, I think you'd say most accurately. This body is taller, sturdier and frankly, in the universal view, more handsome than most Earth bodies.

However, at this level, the technology inherent in the energy of this lighter density permits materializing any form at will, so I could change this body into whatever shape and size would enable me to perform this service most effectively. I, like those souls working with me, do this quite frequently in aid of collecting the energy streamers and harnessing their power into a direct beam for the most potent absorption by Earth's light workers and from them into the areas of their manifesting focus.

S: Are you part of a different civilization or are you part of a group of Earth human souls working toward the same objective?

JEREMY: My little group is Earth souls on loan to another civilization. We could be considered the visiting advisers, trainers or specialists, and the civilization in which we are living right now could be considered an apprentice army of light workers. Spiritually they are evolved, but technologically they are not, and our purpose here is to teach them what they need to learn about harnessing, directing and intensifying the energy streamers so that they are optimally effective. The vantage point of this planet in relationship to Earth provides an ideal channel for intensifying the light as it travels from here to Earth. That's why we're here rather than there.

S: Are you within our solar system?

JEREMY: No, but we're in the same general area of the galaxy as you are. The light coming into this area from far distant sources could be wasted almost totally if we were not here working along with this benevolent civilization to harness it, bring it into a purposeful use and direction, and see that it is beamed as most needed to Earth. The light we've been sending is not directed only to the oceans, although you could say this is our "passion," but rather dispersed to help achieve balanced energy on the planet.

There is another aspect of our service here, and again, an advantage offered by this placement in relation to the position of Earth. Without us in this position, the abundance of incoming light could be so diffused by the time it reached the other light workers on and around Earth that they would have a much more difficult job performing their specific services.

They are helping the planet maintain regular orbit and helping the natural forces allow milder dispersal of kinetic energy so that it does not require the cataclysmic action that otherwise would be needed. We could be likened to the light gatherers and senders, and the alien civilizations surrounding Earth could be considered the engineers, technicians and hands-on healers. You could call us the Wayshowers who are beaming light to the Dispersers of healing energy on Earth.

S: Jeremy, what is your special assignment?

JEREMY: Well, you're dealing with linear time and awareness, and of course you would because you have no other frame of reference. But it's not that after I died and went to Nirvana that I first became knowledgeable about this civilization or with this service group working with the "locals." It's something that even

as I was living on Earth I knew at soul level and actually was participating at that level. Part of my agreement – soul contract, if
you will – was to get a good grasp on the feelings, emotions, pas-
sions of and for sea life there as the over-layer of impetus I needed to qualify me for this higher level energy work.

That's why I didn't stick around very long, dear Cyndi. I wish
I could express the closeness we share still. I know you feel it, but
you ascribe it primarily to our shared interests in whales and dolphins, achieving the communion between them and us, sharing
the joy they feel and so abundantly give. All of that is part and
parcel of the bond between us. There is no difference except in
our individual pathways, our separate focuses through the conscious work, from the unity of our souls that is our everlasting
bond.

Suzy, I know you'll be sending her this full transmission, so I
took the opportunity to get in another short personal note there.
Do you have another question?

*S: Yes, and I appreciate your willingness to answer all my
questions. Jeremy, I'm trying to think of things that Cyndi would
ask if she had this opportunity.*

JEREMY: I know this, Suzy, and that's one reason I invite
your questions. I am offering as much of myself as occurs to me
will be enlightening and encouraging to her.

*S: Do you know Steve Baxter? And how well do you
know Matthew?*

JEREMY: You bet I know Steve! He's still in Nirvana, but
our mutual interests and experiences on Earth have cemented us

big time. Some of the projects I'm involved with in this location are forwarded to him for refinement of ideas, maybe suggestions as to course change or a different intensity of energy voltage at the target. I'll tell him we talked, but you do know that if you wanted to speak with him yourself, you can do that. Oh, I see – you don't approach souls except by request, but you welcome them if they come to you. Well, I think that is the epitome of consideration and graciousness.

As for Matthew, I know about him rather than having a buddy kinship with him. You know that Matthew is working at a high level and the service he is performing is an exalted spiritual function, but you don't understand the individual spiritual evolvement that has occurred since your son and his cumulative soul have continued growing and serving since he left the Earth plane.

I think that if you could know this, you would be in utter amazement. It would be like your being the mother of a king with a domain covering half the Earth and reigning in such benevolence that all of his subjects honor his name. Yes, I know that for your comfort, that makes him sound too much like God or Jesus or another of the great messengers, but that is exactly what I meant to convey to you, Suzy. That is the same league in which your son is serving.

S: Jeremy, that's a lot to contemplate. He hasn't talked about his service more than "just the facts, ma'am." Are you aware of my conversation with God about the Navy's sonar testing?

JEREMY: No.

S: OK, then please tell me what is being done to stop that and any other plans to kill whales or dolphins.

JEREMY: The work of this group I'm with is aimed at interrupting the dark proclivity that is ordering those tests to proceed and is legalizing the slaughter of whales for commercial purposes. So we're working on two fronts. We're sending the focused intensity to the oceans to ameliorate the effects of the sonar and other forms of destruction like sewage, chemical and oil pollution and over-fishing, as well as directing light energy to the souls responsible for those acts being carried out.

There are just a few souls who favor this destruction, but the darkness is firmly entrenched within them and so we have to work around them. We have to get the masses of souls within the light so that the quantity of protests cannot be overcome by those few powerful souls whose efforts are absolutely engulfed in darkness.

S: Do protests from the public like the letters I've written really help or are all protests just ignored? Maybe change can come only from sources like you and other high-level energy healers.

JEREMY: Suzy, don't ever underestimate the amount of light that even one person's caring can generate and how far-reaching its effects. It's like one vote in a close election that makes the difference in the outcome, or like one lighted match in the darkness that lets the scattered in hiding know someone is signaling that he is alive. The amount of light within your heart can be without limitation, and if you are so moved to write a letter, there is an incredible amount of light generated by that combination of your caring intent and your action. Now think of this in context with all the others who share your caring for preserving the life of the whales and dolphins!

S: But when one is killed or dies from manmade injuries, does

the negativity created by sadness, anger, maybe helpless feelings
of those who are working to save their lives set back light progress
anywhere on the planet? Jeremy, I'm asking you questions that I
didn't think to ask God.

JEREMY: Yes, I see what you're saying, Suzy, and yes, there
is merit in your idea that this light and dark battle is one step forward, one, maybe two, back before progressing again. But that
idea is tailor-made to fit within linear time concepts, which don't
apply beyond Earth. Furthermore, light is not understood there
except as science defines it, which is without the comprehension
that light comes from the highest power in the universe – LOVE –
and that light is the functioning aspect of love made available for
our use.

Love *IS*. There's no qualifying or measuring it. Can you
measure the love you feel for each of your children? Well, neither
does God measure how much love energy is being put forth to
save His creations, the cetacean family, or stop any other desecration of the paradise He made on Earth.

Once a heart is open to love, darkness no longer can reign
supreme, so just as there is no measurement of the light infiltrat-
ing, there is no accurate measurement of the darkness being transmuted. I can certify that more light is there on Earth than when
we started talking, and still more than in this moment will be there
when we finish.

S: Jeremy, thank you for telling me so much and for your serv-
ice to preserve Earth. If you ever want to pop in and send a mes-
sage to Cyndi, I'm here.

JEREMY: I know, and I appreciate that. I know also that you

are very hesitant to make these soul connections and in fact, have stopped taking requests, so I feel especially grateful that you were willing to receive my message for Cyndi. And just one more word for her, if you will, please.

My precious Cyndi, just know that we're only a breath apart – not even that far – and I'm showering extra light on your efforts. Don't give up! With the eternal bonding of love and purpose, in the light we serve side by side.

Suzy, that is it for this time. I'm back to work and I'll give you a respite before you carry on with your next project. I'll let Steve know you mentioned him and did so with great caring and a brilliant smile. I'll also thank Matthew, although he's completely aware of my thanks as well as this extra communion we've had. And so I shall say aloha, adieu, and adios for this time.

... AND WAY BEYOND NIRVANA

AESCHYLES
2000 and 2003

When I was organizing his material for publication, Aeschyles popped in to respond to questions in my mind and we had another enjoyable long conversation as he answered those. His new information is integrated into his original message.

After Aescyles' first visit, Matthew told me the name of his home planet is Cat-a-lon, the closest English sound to its actual name.

S: Matthew – hi, dear! You probably know that I have a long list for us to talk about today.

AESCHYLES: Hello. This is not Matthew. You felt right away it could not be, didn't you, because this is not Matthew's usual tenderness in greeting. Moreover, it is not his energy field. So then, who is here with you this day? You have trouble with names, so your son tells me, and he also said that you would never "buy into" Aeschyles. But please use it for me. I will stop and let you question.

S: Pardon me, did you say Aeschyles? If so, did I spell that right?

AESCHYLES: Aeschyles is only the phonetic spelling of the sound that most closely resembles my name as spoken in my language, so there is no correct or incorrect English spelling and that one you're familiar with is as good as any other. Why am I here?

S: Of course I'm wondering why you're here and who you are! Are you a light being?

AESCHYLES: Dear soul, yes, indeed I am of the light! Your son, who will come in later, will assure you of this. But for the moment, please remember that you have demanded that only lighted souls may contact you, so to reach you, I could *only* be of the light.

As for my purpose today with you, I have a worthy message to give to the people of Earth. Now you know that I am not of your planet, but am an extraterrestrial and therefore not of your Heaven, either. I shall identify myself further by description, yes, but first, I am to give a message about the help my nation is supplying to Earth during this time of its energetic transition, and indeed, your own.

May I call you Suzanne? I don't wish to overstep our communion relationship. Is there any order in which you wish this information presented, any schedule I can follow for your convenience?

S: No, I don't think so, and yes, of course you may call me Suzanne. But first, I have to tell you that I am totally surprised that you are here and I'm not feeling as clear as I need to be. Give me a moment, please.

AESCHYLES: Yes, indeed. Please call me by Aeschyles to feel more comfortable within our conversation.

S: .... Aeschyles, thank you for that break. Were you invited by

*the Council of Nirvana to make a presentation for a book? Was it
their decision that you enter this sitting?*

AESCHYLES: Suzanne, I am most keenly aware of your hesitation to accept my words, and that is all right. That will fade and
be of no consequence as we proceed, but your caution with me is
admirable and understandable.

Yes, the Council approached our nation, which is nearby in
terms of geological aging and experiencing, or in your term of
"light years," not all that far away. The Council requested that my
people tell you, for your putting into a sequel to the other volumes,
about our own history. You could say our "truth or consequences"
history, which brought us to the brink of global destruction before
we were saved. It is *how* we were saved that is the primary point
the Council wishes me to pass on for consideration by your own
people.

I see confusion in your mind. Do you wish to ask me
questions?

*S: I'm wondering why Matthew didn't introduce you, why you
just showed up.*

AESCHYLES: You have a pretty full day lined up with your
son, I believe. At least that is the appearance of that paper on the
desk and what I have been told, also. And might that not be more
to your caring – would that not be "liking" in better English gram-
mar? – than my presence?

So, if Matthew had introduced me, might you not have said, as
you have before, "I'd prefer just us to talk this day"? And then my
visit to this area would have been in vain, as without hesitation I
would honor your feelings. So it was decided with few dissenting

opinions that without introduction I would speak.

I must add, I was told also about what you may call self-doubt that has been "beating you up a lot," in words I quote, during the past many months. Thus I say to you, it is not meant to be such a blissful ride through Earth lifetime that you – or "one" in your terminology of wide application – not now and then reflect with distaste upon the mark to date.

With respect to you, this is what you consider failure to get published the information that is of utmost importance for your people to know. This is not your failure, Suzanne. The publication will come, and it is this additional assurance to that which you already have been given that I mean now to express.

Shall we now get to your other questions so I can clear your thoughts before I give my people's message to your own?

S: Well, thank you for saying that, Aeschyles – I can tell that Matthew has been talking with you. I am wondering if you are from a human civilization with bodies like ours.

AESCHYLES: Suzanne, it was not only Matthew who was talking with me about your need for reassurance, and you may wish to consider that God Himself has spoken with you about this.

But yes, we are human indeed, with bodies not exactly like yours, but certainly similar. If I may "crow...." Maybe I am using inappropriate slang words to make you feel more at ease with me, and I do desire your ease. But perhaps I am achieving the opposite, Suzanne, and that is not what I wish to do. I wish us to feel comfortable one with the other.

I do feel a lighter spirit in you now, so my words must have been received as I desired.

My people are of the light brotherhood and we are especially eager to assist in such an occasion as this, a request to share our knowledge and experience, as that is what we most of all have to offer of benefit to others.

Our appearance exactly? Very well, I shall do that now. In mass, or density, we are much the same as you, but we are more uniform in form and features than you. You are varied in these respects because Earth was populated by several diverse extraterrestrial civilizations. Only one such civilization started the population program on our planet.

Yes, just as you, we inhabit only one planet, so you know that definitely we are not of those majestic, almost unimaginable powers with whom you have talked before, those whose powers range across galaxies and are universal in effects. We have no power to do other than what we do, which is to travel and impart our experiencing and survival to others in similar states of war in which once we also were engaged. There is great wisdom to be gained from our history, which is so similar to your own, and that is what I am here to tell you.

All right, Suzanne, back to appearance, as I see your desire to have an image.

S: I'm truly sorry my thoughts interrupt you, Aeschyles, and I wish they didn't, but I seem to really need to see you.

.... Thank you. I'm not sure I received the right image, although it was very clear. From your strong energy naturally I was expecting a male figure, but first I saw a tall, very slender feminine figure wearing a form-fitting white gown. As she moved closer in, I could see that she has skin like porcelain; masses of long, dark curly hair; vivid blue eyes; perfect delicate features; and bright red lips. Really, a stunning woman with a seductive outfit, self-assured pose and demeanor. Then, suddenly along-

side her was another woman, identical in every respect except that she had long, flowing, glistening blonde hair. Is this really what you sent?

AESCHYLES: The women of our culture sent those themselves via my thought waves for transference to you. But you do see them as they are, and quite clearly. They may choose how they wish to appear by virtue of our having successfully developed our abilities to manifest through visioning, or visualization. Our women are not, in your fleeting thought of them, "ladies of the night" in temperament or attitude or activity, be assured. I believe they meant to convey purity and still a passionate essence to you, as that is their true nature.

S: Do men and women have monogamous relationships, such as our marriages?

AESCHYLES: I would have to say, and I do so respectfully, that monogamous relationships and marriages are not synonymous on your planet. There is a commitment in love and intent in my homeland that is stronger than your marriage vows, but no documents are registered to attest to the absolute fidelity in body, mind and spirit that is the foundation and the actuality of these unions.

Nor are there laws governing what you call divorce. You consider sexual infidelity and other issues you conclude are beyond resolution as justification to legally sever the marriage, often with acrimony, bitterness, monetary arguments and, most detrimentally, the effects on the children of the fighting over their custody and care.

None of that is within the nature of our people. If a couple decides to part, it is done with civility and harmony because the only purpose in separating would be the soul evolution for both parties, and their mutual decision is respected with the same equanimity as the union's beginning. Our children understand this as well, and in the case where a parting ends family unity, the entire family enters into the discussions. Because all is done on the basis of love and soul growth, there is no desire to influence children toward one or the other parent's "side." The ensuing home life differs, of course, but never the attentiveness of both parents to their children or the loving bond and respect between the adults as they grow in separate ways.

Yes, our babies are born in the same way as they are on Earth. There is no such thing as barrenness, no infertility of either the male or female person. Without exception, each union committed in thought and purpose is permitted to have as many children as the couple wish if the higher judgment sees that both nurturing and education are in tandem with the couple's wisdom and desire. Thus every infant is greeted with joy.

Our children grow and learn more quickly than yours, but that is more from observation and supplied information than it is a matter of our ability to know enough to compare with exactness. Matthew showed us a seven-year-old child on Earth as typical in growth of mind and body. A child in our world of age comparable to your seven years is taller and, in almost every instance that we observed, is endowed with greater knowledge and wisdom. That is not meant in any way to demean the intelligence and abilities of your children. The difference is a province of this higher frequency in which we live, where all sensitivities and mental agility are advanced beyond Earth's density limitations.

Our civilization recognizes that the zenith of balanced selves is androgyny, which requires the assimilation of both male and female energies, including sexual. Thus all attractions of mates is recognized with honor, and on Earth there is great opposition, even danger presented to couples of the same gender. Sexual activities in our civilization are "refined," I believe is the best word, and again I speak respectfully when I say that many of your people indulge in what we consider "crude" activities devoid of loving feelings or mutual desire.

Suzanne, as you realize, I have been addressing the questions that keep arising in your mind, but I don't wish to overburden you with information.

S: You're not! All of this interests me greatly, and I thank you. Aeschyles, could you please send me an image of yourself?

(As he was sending his image, our energy connection weakened, then was strengthened.)

Suzanne, thank you for calling me back and strengthening our energy bond. I felt myself slipping away like a forceful tide going back into the sea. May I take out a moment, please? .... Thank you. Now I shall answer the questions in your mind regarding the images I have sent and then give you something else of my own devising.

First, I shall tell you that our women do not usually wear the apparel you saw. That would be for formal occasions, and just as you choose less formal clothing for other kinds of activities, so do our women dress more casually and conveniently for theirs. Short, loose colorful robes is their usual preference in their homes, and they wear longer, more fitted outfits when work or interests take them into what you could consider social or business areas.

You are questioning also the attire in my image, which you perceive correctly as the short armor of ancient Roman or Greek warrior days. I chose this because it is appropriate for what I shall speak about, the warrior temperament of Earth peoples. That temperament is as outmoded in the universe as this outfit I am wearing. I could wear a business suit representative of money, job, career – business endeavors leading to financial wealth – being your idea of success and the fulcrum of your efforts and desires, and that, too, would be outmoded in this day of global and universal change.

(Aeschyles sent another image of himself.)

I appear now in raiment to represent the seekers of the light of the universe. They do so that they may be consciously elevated into that glorious state of Oneness and share that light by radiating its energy into all reaches of the universe. So you see me in flowing and shimmering raiment, with large wings of feathers, all in white with golden glow.

The wings are not representative of angelic status – angels themselves do not have wings, as you have been told. The image of wings is symbolic of soaring beyond beliefs and philosophies not based in truth, but based in perceived separation. Leaving those limitations is to soar in the radiance of love and soul connection, the essence of the spiritual Oneness our civilization has achieved.

This is what you must aspire to, to be awarded in allegorical terms the raiment of radiance merited by that level of spirituality and morality and wisdom. Within fourth density vibratory level in spiritual attunement this is possible. There is a most considerable energy bandwidth between fourth level and third, the level still prevailing on Earth, and few Earth souls have risen above that global energy.

But the elevation not only is attainable, it is *promised* to you seekers of the light in this time of transitioning energy fields throughout the universe! I am able to tell you from my people's experience that you can and *will* achieve this level of light essence if you wish it, if you work at it, if you visualize it and believe it. TRUST. FAITH. Know your soul power, take it and rise with it!

You have the opportunity to lift your eyes to meet the souls who are helping you raise your focus, your hearts and spirits so you will *choose* to live within the light. Multitudes whom you call extraterrestrials, but many actually are your ancestors, have come to offer their assistance in various forms. On behalf of my people, and as our assistance in this multilevel effort, I have come to tell you in terms of our own history about this opportunity for pure joy-producing spiritual awareness on Earth.

We were not always at this high level. Our struggle was more than similar to yours – it was almost a parallel of your own. We are not the oldest civilization in the universe by any means, as you would know because we were a population program from elsewhere, another galaxy. We do not date ourselves by the same means you do your fossils, but rather by being directly told that over seven million years ago in your timing calculations our ancestors were brought here and a colony established.

They were more primitive than our current civilization, but still higher than yours today insofar as your remembrance of your origins and your God and Creator connection. There was a small number in the beginning, perhaps a few thousand, and they were encouraged to build a society on the same spiritual basis they had been shown by their populating civilization.

During the evolution of that beginning society there came the weakening of the spirit and the resolve to adhere to the principles that had been founded by the ancestral civilization. As the part of our history that is required for the proper perspective of our rise and fall, this must be clear: It was the weakening of spirit that led to the fall.

The dark forces are ever vigilant for places where they can gain a foothold, and with the accursed abuse of free will, the beginning populace of this planet did not hold fast to tradition, belief and faith in godself, knowledge of origin, or spiritual clarity. The original knowing and living the God connection dropped from that harmony to the level of competition and conflict, then to violence, brutality and wanton killing.

It took a few million years to reach that level, which came within the last 50,000 of your calculated years. Then the inevitable negativity created by that kind of activity had its inevitable consequence: the brink of planetary destruction. Our planet had only a few souls who had not reached that self-destructive depravity and loss of spirituality, and it is thanks to those few souls who held the faith that we are the culture, the harmonious, peaceful and God-aligned civilization of today.

Those few savior souls were born *into* our populace, not born *of* it, and in this way, they could be likened to those souls upon Earth who are most revered for their godliness and savior essence. From that same level of Christed energy from which Jesus, the Buddha, Tao, Mohammed and other revered ones of your planet who came with messages from God, so came those human saviors to us. They were able to slowly bring us back from that most precarious near-self-destruction level and open our eyes to our inseparable connection with the universe.

The messages originating with Creator and God always have been the same, only the messengers change to meet the needs of the people to whom they come. Some civilizations heard but did not heed the messengers, and those civilizations did self-destruct.

Others, hopelessly captured by manifesting in negative areas of production, refused to even hear, and they, too, were ended by their free will choices. Ended by the intent of the dark forces is more accurate, as the influences and then soul captivity were of the darkness. God does not punish, you know that, but He must honor Creator's gift of free will, and thus must allow self-destruction if that is what a soul or a civilization is intent upon doing.

Suzanne, I am late in saying that I am using "God" as the name of the supreme being of this universe because that is your name for Him, and not with any intention to exclude equally worthy names used by others of your civilization. Sometimes your people call God "Creator," but they are not the same. Creator rules over the cosmos, which is all the universes, whereas God rules over only our universe, abiding by the laws of Creator.

To give an example of the difference between them, it is by Creator's decree that never again will nuclear destruction take place in our universe, and it is God's responsibility to see that this decree is followed. Therefore He is permitting extra light to enter here from other universes where the height of awareness of Creator is only increased by shining into this universe.

In addition to this and with subjective pertinence to Earth, many civilizations with advanced spirituality, intelligence and technology have been summoned by God to assist your planet in this time unequaled in changes. Sharing the story of our salvation is my people's participation in this assistance.

Our civilization heeded the messengers those many millennia past and thus did not perish. Your people are at that same point of near-annihilation. It is the hour for choosing to embrace or deny the love and light that will preserve your civilization. The countless universal kindred spirits already preserving your planet are ready and eager to help each of you who is willing!

Suzanne, I am like you in more respects than we may differ. I, too, have a family, I have children, I have disappointments, I have responsibilities, I have aspirations that I haven't fulfilled. This is true of all souls in my nation. We are evolving too, as I mentioned before.

You see, now I am lighter in your energy stream – we are closer in energy alignment. That is not because I have lowered my level, which would not be wise or necessary, but because I have elevated you through my heartfelt speaking and your own wish and energy focus to rise up to meet me. So, *inspiration* is the word that we want here, is it not? *Inspiration* is what I wish to bring to all people on Earth!

I express the desire of our entire civilization to be in your hearts and beside your spirits if you wish us to assist you in rising, rising, rising in your sights, your dreams and focus. Only by looking into the light for these dreams can you help others find them.

Your poor and sick and hungry and disenchanted – all of those souls are just as important as your finest, most noble and knowledgeable elders. Not one soul is less valuable than another. Do not ever let the body and the circumstances mislead you into not seeing the full potential, the love and power of God living in that person.

So, regard each and every person, *every* life within your animal and plant kingdoms, with the height of respect you think is worthy only of God. All are manifested of God, each is a *part* of God. Think of each life in the universe as deserving its godself recognition and you can put into perspective the laws of Creator that govern each soul's every aspect of being. The purpose of each soul is to grow enough to understand this and live within it.

I wish to say a bit more and then I shall say "Goodbye." What you call "evil" is truly a matter of perception. What you call "good" is the same. But what is *absolute* is one's choice of living within the light or living within the darkness. Darkness is not the opposite of light, but the absence of light. Darkness is the absence of God within the consciousness, the absence of conscience and rightness and justness, of harmony, of balance within the self and the society.

When darkness prevails, the angels fall. Let me explain that, please, and then I shall end this as you have been more than patient with this long time. Angels can fall, indeed. The story of Lucifer is not just a tale for personifying an event. There was a force so close to Creator that it was not separable from Creator until the introduction of free will choice and manifesting capacity.

Since only angels existed at that stage of manifestation other than Creator, there were only angels who could fall. Angels still are falling. And just as surely, those of us who did not originate in angelic realms may rise or fall. All have the choice!

Now is the moment when each soul on Earth must choose whether to live within the light or the darkness. Among you are souls whose light is so radiant that we can detect in simply our viewing that the soul is in a high station. We see twinkling lights, the announcement of souls awakening to their godselves. But we see also many souls whose light is only a dim spark because they are still slumbering in the delusion of separation.

This era at hand is being heralded by us and all other light beings as your opportunity to triumph over the darkness that so long has been clouding vision and hearts. The unveiling that even now is well underway is due to the light of God and Creator shining ever more and more powerfully upon Earth. My people stand with you in your journey to rise with your planet into the higher levels of light.

That is the message I have come to bring to your people, dear Suzanne. I do not wish to be overwhelming in duration, but I do wish to be so clear that there can be no misunderstanding of my intent. Sometimes my oratory is more than my substance, so I shall count on your help by reading this and we can work together to tidy it into a clear-cut message.

I discern questions in your mind, so may I answer those for you?

S: Thank you, Aeschyles, but before that, I'll take a reading break. .... You have given a huge amount of substance! Actually, you have said many things that Matthew has, and I am grateful for this confirmation. It's rather embarrassing to admit this and I'm doing so only because you probably picked up my reaction each time I read your information that so perfectly matches his.

AESCHYLES: Suzanne, yes, I did pick up your reactions, and what I picked up is that you want so much to prove to the world that your son's information is correct that you look for evidence to confirm this. If only you could know him as his soul, you could spare yourself any uneasiness about the authenticity of his information needing any confirmation whatsoever. It comes from a height that of itself is the verification of truth. And as you have been assured often, you receive transmissions clearly.

Now I repeat my willingness and pleasure to answer your questions.

S: Thank you for putting me back in line on Matthew's information. Aeschyles, where is your home planet?

AESCHYLES: We are very near Sirius, the Dog Star, so you now know approximately where we are in relation to you. You are wondering also about the name of our planet. ... Suzanne, I see now why they alerted me to your difficulty with names strange to you. You felt my energy pushing at your head, but without the name already within your knowing, you do not have it in your word bank for me to pulse into use. I can spell it, I was just told, or Matthew will discuss this with you later, and if you will, please, that would be my preference.

S: Mine, too, Aeschyles. From your location, what does life in the universe look like?

AESCHYLES: We are one small planet among, oh, "mega-zillions" of places wherein life abounds. Some is like ours, some is like yours, some is higher than we can even imagine, some is so primitive that it could hardly be called life, and some is at such a base level in morality and spiritual awareness that you may not wish to even know of it.

S: It's obvious that your civilization is higher than ours in spiritual and intellectual attainment – at what density level are you?

AESCHYLES: Fourth, but we are very nearly graduated into fifth, and therefore are seeking an impetus to rise into that higher elevation of awareness and clarity. We have been told by the greater council that this can be achieved by such as I am doing in this moment, on behalf of all my people, willingly offering our assistance through relating our experience that, if heeded, can be of immeasurable value to you.

I was more than willing, I was *eager* to make this consider-able space journey to be with you and spend this while in exchange of information. It is not a great undertaking – that is, the mechanics of the trip are not – and most surely I am joyful about being invited to participate in this God-mandated flow of information through these books.

We are called a civilization by God and Creator, and we ourselves regard us in such light. You also regard yourselves as a civilization, but you acknowledge that some of your numbers live by UNcivilized thoughts and activities. Their positions of authority or power force their attitudes and wishes upon the populace throughout whatever domains they control. Thus, in your population globally, there is much UNcivilization from people to people and from people to animals and to your planet homeland.

That is the easiest way I can explain the most important difference between our civilization and your "partial" civilization. I was asked to describe this to you in that way as it was thought it would be the most graphic and most understandable way for you to see yourselves alongside us and have the clearest perception of our two populations. This is necessary for my people's message to you to be understood and respected in the nature of assistance we offer.

Now, you have other questions for me.

S: Yes, Aeschyles, I do. I followed your message quite easily and I think it is very clear – and certainly timely and vital! You mentioned "space journey," so apparently you really traveled rather than make telepathic contact from your home. So why did you make a trip instead of just connecting telepathically? Did you come with companions or alone, and did your traveling require a large spacecraft or can a small one make the trip? How much time did this take?

AESCHYLES: Thank you for thinking of all of this, Suzanne.

These are interesting points that I would be sorry to have omitted and would have done so without your prodding.

Yes, I could have stayed home and our communion would have been just as clear and my awareness of the situation on Earth would be just as keen through visual observation as well as the knowledge abounding in the universe. But just as you wish at times to visit places you know about with keen interest, so did I wish to actually visit, where full sensory assimilation of minute details is such a far greater pleasure than merely looking at pictures and reading descriptions, shall we say.

I make this journey alone on a small craft that is so similar to those you see in your entertainment forms that you might not be surprised to see it in your airports. That is, you could recognize it from "Star Trek," for example.

With the assistance of higher civilizations during these past 50,000 years of our rising up from near-self-destruction, we have mastered the mechanics of astrophysics – engineering; fuel, which is almost entirely solar; and time/space energy direction. Our commonalty with you is the materials we use, which you have on Earth but have not yet combined in the correct alloy proportions to achieve what we have. We can see forms of advanced technology in existence there, but they are hidden by your governments.

In your time/space consideration, my starting point would be four light years from you. However, both your "time" and "distance" in miles and light years are your designs alone and do not apply beyond your planet. So, travel to Earth and Nirvana within the continuum, where your time and distance calculations have no basis, requires only a day and a night of your calendar for a leisurely trip.

There is the mathematical aspect and then the engineering aspect, and all is within the capacity of manifesting – the materializing and dematerializing for rapid movement and then rematerializing once in the atmosphere of destination. Our spacecraft and travel are just as common to us as your modes of transportation are to you, but ours are more efficient, more comfortable and more accessible to all of us than vehicles and travel are to your people.

First I went to Nirvana, where I dematerialized the craft, and my travel mode between there and Earth has been astral. It may interest you to know that I have seen thousands of other small and even some immense spacecraft in the area of Earth, some so close at times that they hover only feet above your surface without your awareness.

S: Aeschyles, all of that is fascinating! Do you or others of your civilization often travel to Earth? Are any of you living among us?

AESCHYLES: Hmmm. I see what you are thinking here, Suzanne, and yes, some of us are within your midst. It amazes us that you accept the unusual folks with just *"Wow, how did he do that?"* But you have no basis for understanding their frequency and energy level, so you can only regard them with awe.

I prefer to say no more. That is, I am not going to identify our people on your planet, but the very fact of their presence does add foundation to our wish to be of assistance to you in these changes of energy level occurring and additional changes forthcoming.

S: I can understand that, Aeschyles. Please tell me more about your people and your planet. How large is your planet in comparison with Earth?

AESCHYLES: I am pleased by your questions about us! Our planet is no larger than your own. It has an atmosphere that is rarer, or higher in frequency, but that is no surprise to you because it supports the needs of people living in the higher frequency of spiritual clarity and universal knowledge. Shall I describe the environment?

S: Please do!

AESCHYLES: The beauty of Earth in its unspoiled areas is supreme, you should know this. Our planet as a whole cannot match the unspoiled glories of Earth, which was God's own Eden. However, much of our environment is lovely, a lesser form of description than beauty, I believe.

Our bodies of water are less in number and smaller in size than yours, and we do not have the extremes of height, such as your mountains and ocean depths. That variation itself is beauty, to you and to us as well. We are plainer in elevations and also coloration, but all is harmonious in the visage as well as the balance of the planetary surface.

We have an even climate, not the extremes of temperature or weather violence such as your tornados or typhoons or earthquakes, for instance. As you know, that is a matter of releasing the negativity prevailing on Earth, and our planet did experience similar upheavals long ago as its own negativity was being dissipated.

Since our climate is quite evenly moderate, we do not have the truly awesome beauty of your changing seasons, as you call them. Nevertheless, there is enough of a change as we rotate so that it keeps us smiling about the times of new blooming or the slightly cooler days.

S: Is your sky blue? Are there clouds?

AESCHYLES: Yes, I would say that our sky is blue. It is not the intense crystalline blue of Nirvana nor the far gentler pastel in that realm's soul recovery stations, nor is it the azure blue of your own sky. We have a green-tinged blue, which you might call aqua in its lighter tone, and it is lovely indeed. But I must say that I am greatly enjoying seeing the skies of Earth and Nirvana.

We do have clouds, as that is the natural law of preventing a planet from losing its vapor and, in turn, its oceans and lakes. But our clouds are in keeping with the higher vibrational tone of our world and do not have the ferocity of storm clouds on Earth.

S: Your sky sounds lovely! What is your population?

AESCHYLES: We have more souls than you, about 10 billion, but considering that we are your approximate size, it is not a monumental number more. Never are there areas of such intense crowding as your cities nor areas of wasteland where no soul would or could easily and happily live.

S: Do you have varied areas like our cities and small towns and also secluded areas where only a few live?

AESCHYLES: Our living areas insofar as numbers do differ from yours. By virtue of our entire planet being habitable, no place would be excluded from the favorable living environment, but yes, there are areas where more people live than in others, just as you have cities, towns, hamlets and the lone house in the woods. I do admire your own, Suzanne, as I, too, am much attracted to the natural beauty of trees and uneven elevation. My family and I live in a rather secluded wooded area similar to this neighborhood where you are. We didn't always choose this, as formerly we felt that the flavor of metropolitan culture and sophistication was exciting and we enjoyed being in the center of that, but as our family grew, we all were drawn to the simple country life, you could say.

Our world has no cities as large as your largest because the majority of our people choose to live in smaller clusters, in the many thousands rather than the many millions of residents. No one feels crowded or too close to neighbors, noise, activity – whatever may be less attractive personally. There is no allocation of living space or areas – all is by choice. It is natural, just as with you, that people cluster as loving families or in groups who share interests or like the same type of environment in the sense of natural surroundings. We do have charming areas throughout our world, and since travel from one to another is by thought or easy access to spacecraft, distance is not a deterrent to physical closeness whenever that is desired.

S: Aeschyles, excuse me, but are you in Nirvana and with me in spirit only or are you here in a body that my third density vision can't see?

AESCHYLES: Suzanne, I have been wondering if you would question this. Yes, my friend, I am with you in this room so charmingly filled with mementos of your family and travels. I have been back and forth between Nirvana and in your presence throughout our conversations. It is lovely for me to actually be near you in my etheric body, as I am now. I believe you are not yet ready to see a tall strange male figure suddenly appear in this room and still maintain your composure.

It is one of the great delights of my journey, this acquaintance with you and your dogs and your surroundings. Prior to our "meeting like this," I spent some days in Nirvana, enjoying its remarkable beauty and vibrant activity, and when I depart from here, I'll return there for another brief visit.

I know that often I say "here" meaning my homeland and "there" meaning yours, but that is for your understanding my information, and my reversing those for accurately speaking of my whereabouts would only create confusion, would it not?

S: Aeschyles, I'm very happy that you are here even though I can't see you, and I can totally relate to your family's desire for that change of lifestyle. Please tell me about the economy in your civilization.

AESCHYLES: There is an equitable disbursement of the economic wealth of our world. It is not that anyone is pressured to give up a part of his share so that another, less enriched in the economic sense, can have a decent portion, but rather a level division of wealth is inherent in our makeup.

We do not have the great disparity of work remuneration as you. Wages for all work activity are on a par with work classification, and there is a plateau above or below which no wages rise or fall. No undue amount is awarded someone who excels in a sport or is a fine entertainer or heads a corporation, such as in your world. And there is no such thing as enforced taxation. This system is offensive to no one and is a pleasure to all, I assure you.

S: What types of work do you have?

AESCHYLES: Many of those that you yourselves do, as the needs of our people are much the same as your own. Education is a primary interest and focus, and teachers and students number in the "mega-millions." Culture is very important to us, and many are involved in the various aspects of the arts. Construction of homes and public buildings employs a great number, as does their design and landscaping. Farming and other aspects of food provision are large employment fields, and so are administration and transportation. No jobs go begging and no one goes begging for a job, and since we can manifest at will, no jobs are menial or tedious.

S: Do your women work?

AESCHYLES: Those who want to, do. All of us who wish to participate in education, business, government or any other work endeavors may do so. There is no discrimination on any basis whatsoever, and since our higher density affords rapid learning, everyone may choose his or her work and changes in those choices may be made as rapidly as individuals' interests change.

S: It sounds ideal! Are there similarities in our respective governments, at least in composition if not integrity?

AESCHYLES: A well-worded question! There is hardly any point on which our governments can be compared, only contrasted. Our highest government is a global one, with representatives chosen in honest and respected elections with none of the campaigning such as you have.

You are thinking, how do I know so much about what goes on here? Excuse me, I just slipped up with "here" because at this moment I *am* here with you. We know because we *study* you! Just as you study the languages, geography, art, history and so forth of your planet, we study your entirety now as well as what you call your "past." We also study many other planets and their civilizations with the same interest that you study Arizona even though you may be living in Texas.

To continue with our government, the global order that is feared by some on Earth is alive and well in our world, with the vast difference being the *intent* of our respective governments. In ours, there is no "hidden agenda," as many of you term it. Only open and totally admirable purposes exist for any of the laws to keep order and harmony among all our people.

I would say that our only similarity in governing is a rising from localized representation through the ranks of larger areas and on up into the global body. The highest person is called the senator, and at the next level down are our representatives. Below the representatives are the agents of the areas, which you might call regional agents, who in turn are assisted by local agents. Then we have – Suzanne, I'm getting stuck here. Please give me a moment.

.... Thank you. I think you could call the elected people closest to the citizenry, who would be like your town council, simply that – town council members. That council would not begin with a capital C, as the name of our highest governing body, which includes the senators and representatives, also is called the Council, with a capital C.

You are surprised that these designations are the same as your own. Well, I gave you designations that are synonymous in nature, we could say, so you could more easily see the similarity of our respective governing structures. No, English is not one of the languages of our world – as students we study all Earth languages just as we do the *one* language that serves our entire civilization.

S: I'd say that one language for all of you is an enormous benefit! What about law and justice systems, or aren't they necessary in your advanced society?

AESCHYLES: Not in the sense of your own, which are largely devoted to establishing guilt or innocence of a crime or in trying to get restitution of property or rights that have been stolen or denied. But we have a body within the Council that is held accountable for all laws of the land, their fairness, their enforcement and their respect by the entire civilization.

Suzanne, I know that Matthew has told you that a utopia such as you once imagined in Nirvana does not exist anywhere. So certainly in a civilization such as ours, which does bring me pride in our collective accomplishments, it does not exist. The pride I mentioned is not of ego or vanity, but of those accomplishments of our entire civilization. I have helped form and therefore am most familiar with this sort of system that still is required for keeping the planetary balance that is so necessary for individuals to keep their balance.

All governing must be done with spiritual integrity as its foundation. Occasionally one or another soul here is subverted – the dark forces are never far away from anyone, anywhere in the universe – and it does happen that a formerly wise and respected leader succumbs to the false promises of the darkness. Then an honorable and trusted system of review and removal from authority is necessary for the good of the land. Usually the person is in disgrace, and it is a sad occasion for all when this happens. But there are no prisons, there are no public humiliations or recriminations or, as you have, media frenzy and "circus time."

S: Thank you for explaining all of that, Aeschyles. I know that our time designations don't exist anywhere else, but what is "daily" life like in your world? Do people work a certain part of a time segment, and students devote the same to studies? What about vacations?

AESCHYLES: Although our time segments, if you will, are not of your devising, we do have measurements, otherwise things could be hectic and imbalanced due to disorganization and lack of order. These segments are like the time measurements Matthew has described, a series of events set forth toward a goal, the accomplishment of that goal and the setting of another. There is a structure within which we operate, though, that resembles what you call "daily" job or class attendance, and since we do have day and night just as you, our resting or change of activities comes at night time.

Yes, vacations are usual here and are very similar to what you have, but perhaps not as longed for or so sorely needed for restoration of mind and body and spirit. We visit dear ones in places that require travel, both astral travel and in our crafts to other homelands or on our own planet. We take short periods to enjoy whatever activities most appeal to us as a family or a friendly group, and there are the short enjoyments of a social festivity or a cultural event to honor an artist or a writer of renown.

Although we do have sports similar to your own, the spirit of competition is for each person to achieve his or her ability standards and not the emphasis you put upon winning. Also we have splendid cultural events similar to your concerts, dramatic and comic productions, and special exhibits of art and other manifestations of diverse talents.

The price of admission to all of these differs greatly from yours – none of our finest offerings are denied anyone, neither by the cost nor by limitation of performances. Joy is abundant in the grace here, and it shows itself in these ways of entertainment quality and provision as well as in the most spiritual ways.

For individual entertainment we have modes like your radio and television programming in form, but not content. Our programs are aligned with our interests in learning on a more casual basis than in a formal educational setting, so some are much like those you have that are documentary in nature. Others are filmed versions of our sporting and cultural events, and some are composed for purely relaxing with comic situations.

As you are surmising, none are based in violence that is anathema to our nature. It is unfortunate for your people that violence is so prevalent in your most frequently viewed TV and theater films. That is resulting in a generation attuned toward violence as a natural outlet of their insecurities about world events or questions of life's purpose.

S: Many objections are raised here to that kind of programming but so far, it's still with us. Aeschyles, do you have animals similar to ours?

AESCHYLES: Indeed we do have animals, with both similarities and considerable differences from yours. None of our animals are fierce. Just as we have evolved out of warring temperament, so have our animals evolved out of their former "food chain" temperament, where the larger and more powerful devoured the weaker and smaller.

There is complete peace among our animals and between the entire range of species and our humans. We feel the same affection – yes, *love* – for those who bond with us, just as you do your dogs, Suzanne, and many souls on Earth feel with their pets. The bonding of human and animal life is to the benefit of all.

I see you wondering if my family has dogs and hoping we do, but the truth is, no, we don't. Definitely dogs are on our planet, but I'm speaking only of my family's animals. Ours are more like your domestic cats, and we have them in abundance as they do create more of themselves just as all animals do on Earth without intervention. But here, never is there carelessness or neglect about the care of any animal. All are of such importance to us that we would neglect their needs no more than our own.

Always the relationship between animals and humans, or other classifications of cognitive beings, is of essential value in spiritually evolving souls in all civilizations at levels up to seventh. At that level and above, the souls have no form. That is, there are no dense bodies, but even so, the animal and human or suprahuman energy is closely aligned. Plant life also, as that cannot be ignored in the overall essence of either God or Creator.

Each living soul – each *life* is more accurate – is composed of energy, and since energy is of Creator, every creation is also of Creator, and in this universe, of God. Thus, a tiny ball of fluff is just as much a creature or creation of Creator, or God, as any other. Its charm and open, loving nature and loyalty – the same characteristics you admire in a person – are recognized and respected in our animals, and our interaction with all of them is on a plane much higher than your own.

Yes, there are animals for food for the humans of our world. But the treatment of those animals throughout their lives and most surely, the means by which their lives are ended to become human nourishment, are with caring, mercy and painlessness, and with our thankfulness for the nourishment that they willingly provide. Sadly, this cannot be said for the treatment of most of your animals.

Earth animals, too, are sentient beings far beyond the awareness of most on your planet. The non-recognition of this truth allows many there to see animals as "dumb beasts," neither needing nor worthy of love, kindness, loyalty or mercy. This lamentable situation that has caused much of the trauma of Earth herself will change as your civilization rises into the awareness of the interconnectedness of *all* life.

Do not forget the order of plants in Creation, because that interrelationship gives and receives in equal measure. Your Devic kingdom, unseen and unknown to most of you at this point, is closely allied with the care-taking of your plant kingdom. Few there have recognized the sacredness of your trees and the other plants, which have their own consciousness and thus know of their value within the entire planetary life system.

S: That sets your civilization way ahead of ours, but many of us do recognize the value of all life and are striving to promote that awareness. What is normal life expectancy on your planet? And please describe your equivalent of Nirvana.

AESCHYLES: Oh yes, such a vital aspect of our civilization! First, we are not programmed for physical or mental deterioration as are you, and life here can be extended in robust health as long as each individual wishes. However, there comes a point of fulfillment, I believe is the best word, when perhaps hundreds of years of active living is considered "enough," and that person elects to leave for the next stage of experiencing.

At that time, the person is given a joyful departure ceremony in celebration of his or her life. The soul then leaves for our sanctuary world and the body is simply dematerialized. It is not uncommon for two or more souls to choose to leave together. Knowing that at soul level we are One and love bonds are eternal, there is no mourning within the family and friends, but rather rejoicing for the lifetime shared so abundantly.

We don't have the range of departure acknowledgements as on Earth, where there are days of honoring primary government figures or other notables and burials in pauper graves of souls who had neither fame nor fortune but may have been far more spiritually evolved than most.

Our sanctuary realm differs from yours in this major respect: There is no need for Nirvana's tender personal care-tending of souls who died in trauma, such as a war or by murder, to heal their severely troubled psyches. So we feel that is certainly a "plus" for our "after-world," but more so it attests to the level of spirituality our civilization has achieved.

But in the exquisite beauty of Nirvana, we also differ. Matthew is right – the higher layers of Nirvana are more beautiful than most other realms serving the afterlife purpose, and we have not achieved that range of wondrous glories as have the residents there. No doubt that is why we don't have the multitude of visitors that Nirvana has!

Nor do we have layers in our realm with their varying energy registrations, as there is no need for more than one, and although it is indeed a serene and pleasing environment, the residents do not remain long. Their only purpose there is the life review process that determines the next level of experiencing, and this is our only similarity with Nirvana.

The residents carefully deliberate what experiencing still is needed on their pathway to God and Creator, and what they are capable of taking on next. Karma, the balancing of all experiencing, still plays a part in our evolution, but it is without the extremes of third density beings. Rather we ascertain which souls wish to share in our next lifetime adventure to the benefit of all and where in the universe that will take place.

Growth means leaving a familiar situation, whether civilization or placement, so it is not often at this point of our evolution that we embody back on our planet. When we do, it is to complete partial learning rather than another effort to learn the same lesson that was totally failed the previous physical lifetime.

This does bear explanation as it is natural to wonder why anyone would choose to leave a physical lifetime unless all chosen learning was complete. It is because the fresh start is beneficial. Usually advanced souls agree to return with weaker souls in a service aspect, which benefits all as the weaker spirits are reinforced with determination to evolve and the stronger souls gain more light through this willingness to return rather than seek new adventures.

S: If you don't reincarnate on your planet, where do all your babies' souls come from? My understanding is that our babies are souls who have reincarnated over and over.

AESCHYLES: Well, since God is limitless in essence, "new" souls can be considered limitless also. However, in the evolutionary process, the free will choices in the light of souls in lower densities affords them the option of placements for "higher" experiencing, and our civilization has attracted many who find living on our planet most appealing. And I don't believe I made it clear that it is fairly recently that souls in our civilization have chosen to find other homelands for their next embodiment.

You are right about the many reincarnations of souls on Earth, and there is good reason for this. So long ago as to be unimaginable in your idea of the planet's history, your civilization was deliberately deprived of both spiritual and cognitive awareness by the influences of the dark forces. It became necessary for the souls to spend hundreds, maybe many more lifetimes of experiencing to complete their chosen lessons, and it is to their benefit to do so in the familiar emotional spectrum, often with the same souls playing different relationship roles as they strive for karmic balancing.

Suzanne, I see no more questions in your mind, so I believe this covers everything. I am most grateful for your many questions that gave me the opportunity to tell you so much about my homeland and my people.

S: Asechyles, thank you so much for coming again today! It's wonderful that I reached you simply by wishing I had asked you those questions before.

AESCHYLES: Suzanne, you are but a breath away from me in *every* moment! The same is true of all of those vast powers with whom you spoke at length long ago. As you well know, it is true of your connection with Hatonn – yes, I surely know of him and his influence – and equally true with any soul at any height within the light whom you wish to contact.

I must clarify that this is not possible from all locations within the universe, but from Earth and your energetic reach, it is. You may not have total ease in adjusting to the reception insofar as instant understanding. Settling into an energy level compatible with both you and your desired source may be necessary, but as I said, this is possible, and no, your understanding the means whereby this happens is not required for the contact.

S: I'm sure you know that I have no idea at all about the "means." I'm glad you know of Hatonn. Actually, what do you know about him and his work?

AESCHYLES: As one of his many ongoing responsibilities, Hatonn is particularly involved now in the communications between Earth and all points beyond. He does not forget you, Suzanne, and if you wished at any moment to speak with him, he would respond. However, if that is not necessary, then I would not advise calling upon him for casual chatting at this time.

He is in serious negotiations on a universal scale to curtail the negativity resulting from the untruthful information that is being dispersed by the darkness. With particular reference to Earth, this is clearing the telepathic channels between any source and your planet so that disinformation and misinformation will cease and only truth from the light is passed on. This is of utmost importance for your people as the light carried by the truth is essential for the planetary cleansing.

It is lamentable that an Earth source of vitriolic and untruthful information is attributing this to Hatonn and has been doing so for a decade or more despite his many requests that this be stopped. While he is making inroads on his universal service, he cannot deny the free will aspect of that dishonest source.

Now I feel your mind and your heart are peaceful, so I take my leave with warmest feelings of loving and bonding with you again on this day and the hope that there will be other occasions when we can communicate. And so, my friend, for now, *adios!*

That bit of the frivolous was to see you smile once again, my friend. But now I willingly say goodbye and thank you most joyously for your abundant service.

S: Goodbye, Aeschyles. Thank you!

SAMINTEN

April 30, 2002

S: Matthew, hello, dear! Here I am to meet the somebody you wanted to introduce. Is he – she? – available now?

MATTHEW: Mother, welcome! Yes, he is. I say "he" but this is another of the collective energies who goes back and forth between "I" and "we." The name is Saminten, with "Sam" getting the emphasis, and he is waiting for you to greet him.

S: Saminten, do I greet you with only "Hello"?

SAMINTEN: It is glorious to be in your company, Madame Suzanne. I am joking with you because of your asking if merely "Hello" is sufficient! Indeed it is more than sufficient as "Hi" would serve as well. I am delighted to be in your midst this evening.

It is my understanding that this is only to introduce us and that perhaps tomorrow or soon after, you will have time for the prepared announcement that I have been requested to give for Book Number Three. Is that still amenable to you, Mistress?

S: Yes, that's fine, and I'm sorry we can't continue tonight. Saminten, wouldn't you feel more comfortable calling me Suzy? I would!

SAMINTEN: Then Suzy it is. And Sam, if you please. Now I shall delay your other interests no longer. That was the pledge from your son to you, and I honor it. I am delighted to see you smiling! I am eager to pursue our acquaintance in the morning or whenever you please.

S: Thank you for coming just for our introduction, Sam, and for understanding my lack of time now.

SAMINTEN: Absolutely. You will facilitate things if you simply say "Goodbye, Sam I am!"

S: Then I shall do that. Goodbye, Sam I am!

May 7, 2002

S: Good afternoon, sweetheart!

MATTHEW: Mother, dear soul, thank you for the sweetheart name! That always makes me feel "right at home," just like my sister and brothers in your affection and thoughts. Now then, we've had Saminten on tap for several of your days, not waiting unproductively, but eager to resume your conversation.

S: OK! Sam, hello!

SAMINTEN: Hello, Suzy!

S: Are you going to tell me about yourself or your people or your mission?

SAMINTEN: All of the above, I'd like to do. I am here most specifically with a message for the upcoming book, but would you like me to tell you about myself first?

S: Yes, please. I'm more comfortable knowing who I'm talking with.

SAMINTEN: Yes, of course! I am not a transitioning soul from Earth, but my residence for the time being is Nirvana. I am here in collective energy form but not as a mass of amorphous souls rather sliding around. Yes, I am an embodied "fog person" of whom Matthew has spoken and I am visiting here as an emissary from my people.

We are indeed a civilization, but I believe you would not think of us as "people." Matthew described us well as a mist or vapor, dense above the ground and increasingly less dense as it rises into wisps, always moving in a rosy golden glow and with charming fragrances that meander as we do ourselves.

The vapors, shall we say, gather into shapes so there is some form to us, but no weight or clear demarcations. The cloud formations, let us call them, are gleaming silver with undertones of pale crystalline blue, like a fine diamond refracting countless tiny sparkles. Not everything about us sparkles or our world would be too brilliant to behold, but the larger configurations do have an exquisite luminescence.

Farthest into our atmosphere, where the strength of the mist is least, is our haven that is equivalent to your Nirvana. You may remember that Matthew said that we have no DNA programming for aging or death and our sanctuary realm is for rejuvenation only. We go voluntarily for restoration of strength to better perform our service of beaming light into the universe for civilizations in need of it. After ages of this beaming, the strength of our souls diminishes and the formations gradually become only wisps that naturally rise into our highest atmosphere. This area is of a more gentle glowing essence, somewhat like a florescent pastel painting in slow and gentle continuous gliding motion. Never is the light dulled, but it is dimmed, if you can see my difference. Always there is the glowing essence of the souls as they waft in delicate fragrances and the subtle colors, as even our palest tones always are of iridescent nature. This reflects our soul evolution, and our auras are just as intense as our "body" essence.

It is rare that part of our selves embodies for any purpose, but to visit here in Nirvana at the invitation of Matthew and the Council is a glorious opportunity to see this beauty so we can add to the natural beauty of our own sanctuary realm. With our level of intelligence and technology development, we could embody in a twinkling, but that would be such a backward step for us that we would not be interested. However, for me to come here and fully experience the many glories of Nirvana, it seems appropriate and very gratifying to have this body that I am now showing you to describe for the book.

S: I see the torso of a tall, dark-skinned muscular man with shoulder length blond hair and soft blue-gray eyes. Sam, you could be Adonis, but I'm not sure you want to be thought of as the Greek god.

SAMINTEN: That is a delightful comparison, Suzy, but this body I manifested is not out of keeping with the beauty and radiance of the others in Nirvana.

S: Thank you for sending me your image, Sam, but why only a torso above clouds instead of a full figure?

SAMINTEN: Because it is all I can muster, Suzy! No, that is not the case, of course, but it is enough for you to recognize that

I have both fairness like your Nordic peoples and brown skin like your peoples whom you sometimes call black. It is somewhat the chest I have seen in your development of centaurs, their human chests that give way to the rest of the body form of a horse. Do you see that similarity?

S: The handsome man, yes, the horse, no. Are you in full body in Nirvana? Actually, I'd think so, but I don't know what all the beings there do about forms.

SAMINTEN: Yes, I am in full stature here. It allows me to touch and feel, to drink liquids and to feel the many animals brush by me with friendship and to touch the flowers that are incredibly sweet in their aromas. So, yes, I'd say that here just as on Earth a full body is what most are accustomed to.

S: How long have you been there, and is Matthew there now in body or only spirit?

SAMINTEN: He is "fully" here now, yes, but he is not here as often as he used to be, as you know. I have been here approximately four months of your calendar time. I arrived after the celebrations of your Earth festivals of Christmas and other party times, and it was most enjoyable for me to witness those.

S: Can you see me, Sam?

SAMINTEN: Oh, Suzy, of course I see you, and I feel your energy, which is lovely to be in the midst of. It is flowing back and forth between you and Matthew, between you and numerous other points of entry and reciprocity. Suzy, I am aware of the discomfort in your back. Would you like a little break to ease that stress?

S: Thank you, Sam. .... This is much better, and I greatly appreciate your thoughtfulness.

SAMINTEN: You are most welcome for that very small service, Suzy. Now then, before I begin my message to your people, I must tell you that being as frivolous as "Sam I Am" is not my major ingredient as a personality goes. I am usually a bit more shy, a bit reluctant to be in the forefront and noticed above others. That trait also is very evident in your nature–Suzy, I can see and *feel* your nature just as Matthew does–yet there is that very gleeful part of me that on occasion leaps out with flippancies like "Sam I Am." I am explaining only because you are wondering where my "boyishness has disappeared."

S: It was just a very quick thought, Sam. Are you really comfortable with my calling you Sam, or did you tell me to do that because I asked you to call me Suzy?

SAMINTEN: Oh no, not at all. It's because Sam is a fine name and a more personal way for you to regard me.

S: Yes, it is. OK, then, any time you would like to start your message, I'm ready.

SAMINTEN: Thank you, Suzy. Hundreds of millennia past my people were not in this "vapor" or "fog" essence, and the spiritual aspect of ourselves was miniscule compared to today's grand volume of God-connection awareness. Our connection is no greater, please understand, but our *awareness* of it is. That is a most important difference, and it is a similarity that we share with you in this time of your growth of spirit.

We merely existed then. We had no purpose for growing and frankly, we had no interest in helping either ourselves or any others. It was a time of recovery for us, but we were unaware of that as the reason for it was not in our memory. Our minds had been somewhat destroyed, and the memory aspects of our mental abilities had been taken, actually lifted right off our DNA by thieves of the highest dark order in the universe.

Interfering with the growth of a soul is the only infraction that constitutes what you call "sin," and altering the DNA of a soul is the ultimate interference with its growth. It has such major damaging repercussions for the affected souls and it incurs such heavy karmic pressures for expiation for the causing souls that nothing in the universe compares with it.

We languished for eons while our strength of knowledge and spiritual sparks were rejuvenated through the efforts of volunteer physicians of the universe's highest light capabilities. They rejoiced as they saw the beginning of our memory returning, and our signs of intelligence and stimulation coming through the "fog."

It is not by chance that you have expressions like "seeing the light" and "being in a fog," as these are manifestations of a depth of understanding–remembrance, actually–that you do not associate at all with your idiomatic expressions. But in many instances these go back to eras way before your civilization of today, even before life of any beautiful nature came in the first seeding program of Earth. *(NOTE: The beginning of the planetary population is explained in "Origin of Earth Humankind" in* Revelations For A New Era.*)*

Now then, Suzy, would you like to read what I have given you in this dictation? You may want to ask me questions and correct many of those red underlined words I see. I was told they are nothing for me to feel concern over, that they are merely your computer's indications of wrong keys being tapped and you will correct them.

S: Sam, I'll definitely do that later. I'm really sorry that I must leave now to keep an appointment, but we'll chat again as soon as I can, OK? Thank you for that fascinating story of your civilization!

SAMINTEN: You are most welcome indeed, Suzy, and I thank you for conversing with me. Until later, then, goodbye.

September 6, 2002

S: Good morning, Sam! It has been ages and I apologize, but I guess you know how things have been going.

SAMINTEN: My dear Suzy, I greet you with open mind and heart to your energy. It has been a long time in your counting of days and weeks since we last talked, but to me, the time has flashed by without any interruption in my delight at our communion. Shall I start with my presentation where we left off? Yes? Then, I shall.

In antiquity, even before universes and their god rulers came into being, Creator gave forth Its gift of free will with the intent that it always would be the province of each soul. However, when the darkest of the dark forces emerged, it used its own free will to claim the collective free will of souls who became curious about the dark and then became entrapped by it. This subverted Creator's intent. After eons of light constantly being beamed at those darkest souls so that of their own free will they would release their captives, Creator acted. A few years ago in your counting, It withdrew the collective captured free will from the topmost stations of darkness and restored it to the individual souls.

Thus the original intent of Creator's gift once again prevails, but Creator also decreed that there will be one exception to honoring all free will choices. This unique exception will curtail any choices that would damage innumerable other souls by means of nuclear detonations anywhere in the universe. In many times prior to your recorded history, some civilizations were intensely destructive to many places in the universe. Worlds were destroyed and widespread damage was done to souls' DNA, the ingredient that you understand as imparting distinct individuality to each. Creator has decreed that never again will that happen, therefore Earth will not be destroyed nor any more souls damaged by that means.

However, the health of your planet had become precarious otherwise.

God, the ruler of this universe, which is one within the Cosmos over which Creator rules supreme, is authorizing all civilizations who so choose to answer the cry of Earth for preservation and restoration.

Without help, your precious planet would perish from the predominance of negativity that was strangling her breath and dismembering her body. Thus many of us fairly close by, even though usually from galaxies "light years" distant in your term, have heeded this call. Many diverse areas of assistance are being given by civilizations whose advanced spirituality and technology are helping to rid your planet of the negativity as well as help her stabilize and recover from its effects.

These waning days before total release from negativity are the most exciting and uplifting for Earth since her beginning, when gods and goddesses reduced their high energy registrations to adapt to living in human form in your planet's environment. Retaining their original multidimensional capacity would not permit the fully human experiencing they wished, and so the souls downloaded into heavier density. Over time their desired spectrum of flourishing and reproducing in totally incarnate forms became possible.

Sometimes benevolently and sometimes not, those god and goddess souls reigned over the seeding programs of a variety of civilizations and the introduction and evolution of the human root stock. As conflict grew and former spiritual awareness diminished, the density of the planet's atmosphere was lowered by the resultant negativity. Twice all life was lost and the planet revived to start anew. A third time was not God's intent, and Earth's own soul did not want that, and now we have reached that point whereof I spoke, when she cried out for help and many of us willingly answered.

Suzy, I digressed into that sketchy outline history of your planet to assist in the remembrance of that era. Many souls on the planet today were embodied then and time and time and time again during successive eras.

And now I shall tell you the part my civilization has been playing as a collective group of souls in Earth's revival to her former health and glory. We are strengthening the resolve of each life in the kingdoms of animal or plant or mineral that wishes to rise into the higher density with remembrance, clarity and evolutionary soul status. Cellular changes have been in process for several decades, and assimilation of what is happening with the fuller light now beaming can be greatly assisted by the leveling process or leavening agent we can provide.

You decry the loss of time that seems to be zipping by and

another loss you lament is memory. Neither of these aspects of third dimensional awareness is being lost, dear ones. "Time" never has been as you devised it with 24 hours each day and 12 months in a year and so forth. This has served you well, but no longer is this happening. Your time structure is collapsing as energy is moving at its lighter density speed, and your periods of light and dark are coming with more velocity. So rather than time being lost, it is speeding up.

The memories that many of you speak of as "gone," are not. With the acceleration of everything within the universe, it is natural that the cells of your body are reacting to being lifted into a higher survival mode. Most of all, this is affecting your brains – the computers that turn on your thinking and reasoning processes – and this is necessary! The light being absorbed by your cells is allowing your brains to slough the layers of forgetfulness and programming that have denied them full functioning ability.

If you are not experiencing any memory loss or a sense of scattered thinking, then you are stuck in the third density that not much longer will be the status of Earth's being. So it is desirable for you to feel not quite firmly in touch with the reality of the day or the environment.

All of Nature, which is everything with a soul, is evolving. Earth's soul – her own inviolate soul and the collective of all souls living on the planet – is evolving. Only if you speak with animals and trees and hear their response can you appreciate that you and they – every life form that is receptive to the light – are moving into the lighter essence of all existence.

Third density has served you for good and for not so good insofar as your mastering chosen lessons for so many millennia that even those of you who are becoming aware of that "past" cannot remember. There are no divisions of past, now, and what is coming. It is more accurate to think in terms of learning and knowing what next needs to be learned. And even this is not altogether correct, as peeling away the layers of forgetfulness is not a learning process, but a remembering and allowing process.

Suzy, I know your need to be on your way. I feel that we have had a lovely time together today and I hope that soon, whenever you wish that is peaceful for you, we can speak more. I do have other things to add and I hope you will have questions that will give rise to areas of interest that I have not thought of.

S: Sam, I have time for one question. What did Matthew do for your sanctuary realm?

SAMINTEN: He recommended to the main "keepers of the doorways" the incorporation of the various rejuvenation levels so that the weaker beings were not segregated, but instead integrated with the strongest. As you can imagine, being surrounded by weaklings like yourself provides the comfort of "misery loves company," and there's little incentive to leave your niche. By putting together all but the very weakest, who will be integrated after the initial most tender nurturing, the weaker beings are restored much more rapidly by being part of the vigor and joyousness of the stronger.

Yes, that does seem plainly sensible and simple, so, as you're thinking, why didn't we think of that ourselves? I have no answer that satisfies me now that Matthew's recommendation is within our essence, so I shall answer by telling you why we invited him. You see, in our awareness there was no omission in our sanctuary realm, but hearing of Matthew's service and frequent travels gave us the thought to invite him for the joy of sharing his energy, and he accepted with much favor.

Since he is the expert in the field of sanctuaries, to him an area of improvement was identifiable. He assisted in his plan's execution, and the new arrangement is so successful in achieving its purpose that I can tell you we are enduringly respectful and grateful to your son.

S: Sam, thank you for telling me that – thank you for your whole wonderful message today. Goodbye for now.

January 3, 2003

S: Sam, it has been so long since we talked that my embarrassment must equal your patience. But I know from Matthew that you are here, and I welcome you back.

SAMINTEN: Indeed I am, and it is as I told you before, your time lapse exists only there and not with me. I am delighted to be in your energy again, Suzy. Each time we talk, I feel more at ease and I feel that you do as well. Now shall I continue my presentation?

S: Sam, you are a dear! Just one question before you start, please. Are you still in Nirvana?

SAMINTEN: No longer am I in that beauteous, wondrous place of such activity, Suzy. I have shared with my people the glories I witnessed and participated in, so you could say that we now have a spot of your Heaven within us all.

S: Thank you, Sam – that seems lovely. Now please continue with your message.

SAMINTEN: The light on Earth has been accelerating in sustained amount for the past year of your timing. It was necessary for this sustained situation to occur so that more souls could awaken to their godselves and rise along with your planet into fourth density. My people have been assisting joyfully in this process.

The importance of this ascension cannot be overstated. The souls who rise with Earth will be living in the paradise that once flourished there so gloriously. The souls who do not reach the level of light required for this journey with Earth will be removed to placements for remedial lessons in consonance with their lower energy registration.

It is lamentable that your science sees little connection between the power of the spirit and their developments. There is no separation of spirituality and science. There cannot be! The ingredient of souls is light from Creator Source, and light is the scientific expression of the love that is the parent, or manufacturer, you may say, of light. Your science recognizes only the directional use of light without understanding its true property or origin. So this division in belief needs additional resolving, and my people have been strengthening the assimilation process.

What is occurring there is an amazing sight from here or anywhere else in the universe! The new sparks continuously evident are the souls lighting up with the connections between their souls and their minds. You will appreciate this spectacular necessity as you rise into the lighter density, but for this moment, let me say that it is fireworks of the most magnificence in power and the same in the rejoicing of all light beings.

Suzy, I did intend to say more, but it has been so adequately covered by the others whose messages will be included in the book that I shall not repeat any more than I may have already.

Yes, I am well aware of all that is to be in this book that is of such importance that God Himself has ordained its soaring to His children who so greatly need this information.

So now, I would welcome those questions in your mind.

S: Thank you, Sam. This is the first time I've heard of the kind of help you're giving Earth, what you called the "leavening" process. Thank you for caring and for helping! Can you describe your civilization in numbers of souls?

SAMINTEN: Not nearly as easily as you can, with a body for each. However, in our collective essence we could be considered as having about 100 million souls, although that seems rather few. It has been so long since we considered ourselves as individuals that no doubt that figure is a poor estimate, much too low. You see, each wafting "part" may be the essence of one or a million souls as there is no mental or emotional division.

S: I see. Does your civilization increase by any means?

SAMINTEN: Well, surely not by any reproductive methods you might be familiar with, but we welcome any and all wandering souls or free spirits who find us and would like to enter into our essence. Since we are not limited by space, the newcomers never are crowding in. Because there is limitless freedom at this height of evolution, any soul who wishes to leave for additional growth may do so, and in our collective awareness that there is no separation, those souls enrich us with their self-discoveries anywhere in the universe.

S: Do you consider any souls young or old?

SAMINTEN: Suzy, you heard me laughing and I'm delighted to see you joining with me in amusement. I am aware that you speak of "old souls" there, but nothing could be further from an accurate description of a soul than anything ascribed to "age." What *is* different is the learning, or remembering, status of each soul. Every one of us started with Creator's first sharing of Itself insofar as the elements for all creations, which are love and light. So we, like all other souls, are as old as those elements, which literally are age-less.

S: As you can tell, Sam, that's a brand new perspective for me. So then, you have no infants, children and adults?

SAMINTEN: No. We are truly ageless. The souls who join us totally meld into our essence and bring no age into it.

S: Are there any kinds of groupings, like family units or souls who share the same interests?

SAMINTEN: No, not as you perceive family relatives, or organizations or a division of any sort where "outsiders" may have no personal knowledge of the "insiders." Without compromising the inviolate essence of each of us, we truly are One in love, thought, philosophy, desire, aspiration, discovery, inspiration, pathway back to God and Creator.

S: Do you have any form of governing?

SAMINTEN: Nothing that could begin to compare with anything you would recognize as a structural hierarchy, no. We have a sense of self, we are One. That is all there is to it. Suzy, I know that is meaningless to you, but it is the best I can do to describe how we "operate."

S: I think we have a long ways to go before we reach that ideal-sounding arrangement. Do you speak telepathically or in language, or is there no need for either because the same single thought is shared by all?

SAMINTEN: I must smile at your question of whether we might be sharing a single thought because it is more like sharing the whole universe of thoughts. And yes indeed we communicate, but any sound would be tones, not speech. In keeping with the gentleness of our movement, the tones are like your most charming lullabies, but barely audible. Telepathy is such a natural way for us to communicate that when toning is done, it holds the awe and joy for us that hearing symphonic music does for you.

S: Then how did you learn such articulate English?

SAMINTEN: And so we laugh together again, Suzy! I knew your question before you typed it and felt your embarrassment as well as amusement as soon as you did yourself. Yes, at our height of awareness we know all languages of the universe, including those without speech, such as ours.

S: Sam, I should have been thinking faster, but it does feel good to laugh with you! Where is your homeland?

SAMINTEN: In a galaxy "near" your own. This is a return to the distance scheme you have devised that doesn't exist beyond Earth, so "near" and "far" are not suitable ways to give you our location relative to yours. However, we are not as close to you in *energy* as many other civilizations are. I realize you cannot conceive of this type of relativity, Suzy, and it isn't necessary.

I see your question about whether this is a solid type of "residential area," which is a much more accurate term than I had thought to use. In my efforts to describe my "people" and "homeland," I have had to use many of your words that are not accurate, such as our densest parts being nearest the "ground." We have no ground as we are not on a celestial body, but rather in a protected space. It automatically is protected because of our high energy registration that no entity of darkness could approach.

S: Just space! Well, do you have any scenery or does space not accommodate that kind of environment?

SAMINTEN: We have marvelous scenery! Just as in Nirvana, we manifest our scenery as we wish, and obviously with no zoning laws or neighbors to consider. We have glorious vistas in keeping with our very light density, both in mass and spirit, and it can be wafting with ourselves or stationery, whichever is desired.

Our collective thought forms provide this uniformity of desire, and with all the scenery in the universe to envision, whatever images we choose are manifested in a twinkling. Our scenery is delicate and usually in proportion to the largest wafting essence, so there are no mountains, just molehills.

My boyishness is back, Suzy! And, we really *do* have mountains, but I couldn't resist that bit of levity that I knew you would appreciate.

S: Sam, you're terrific! May I take a break to think of more questions, please?

SAMINTEN: You know you may with my delight in your wishing to know about us.

S: .... OK, thank you. It seems from what you said that you have no music, only communication toning. Or am I assuming too much?

SAMINTEN: From what I told you, no, not at all is that an assumption. But in the larger picture, oh yes it is. I see you are picking up my full thought without my expressing it in words, and that is splendid! Yes, we are immersed in the music of the spheres, which is the province of the angelic realms, and since much of your most refined music has come from there, you can imagine what surrounds us. No, it doesn't "drown out" our toning. Actually, our communication is a merging of the occasional toning with telepathy, and I didn't make that clear.

S: I see. Do you have any animals, Sam?

SAMINTEN: Perhaps not what you would consider animals, Suzy, as you see them as individual forms and temperaments just as your human population. But indeed animal soul energy is very much within our total essence and is recognized as having experienced in form in various worlds before rising to this level of light. The bonding of any civilization with animal energy is an aspect of the higher light dimensions. In fact, respecting and nurturing animal lives is required of civilizations or individual souls before ascendance in energy registration is possible.

S: All animal lovers will be happy to know this! Sam, now that you have experienced life in Nirvana, do you miss all that you enjoyed in a body?

SAMINTEN: Suzy, I don't think of it as something that I relinquished by returning home, but rather as a dimension I have shared with my people. With rare exceptions they have not had the experience of embodying because their souls never were in lower densities. And none have shared life with a multitude of various civilizations such as I met in Nirvana, but through the essence of our collective selves, they, too, share the sensations I had in body.

There is no division in our awareness of each other and our collective knowledge and experiencing, so even while I was in Nirvana, my people were sharing my visit. You have noticed my use of "I" and "we" interchangeably, and both were suitable in my speaking. You have no word for the individual yet composite experiencing of the "I" in Nirvana and the "we" of my entire civilization.

As we waft in search for more of the universal all-knowledge, which is to say self-discovery, when we connect with more remembrance of our beginnings in Creator, there is an enormous burst of light as that is assimilated into our essence. I do not mean that my visit reached that height of discovery, but it did add welcome light through our "newly" remembered level of connection.

Another aspect of this is, I did not leave Nirvana when I came home. It still is my experience in the continuum, and in that respect, I am there even as I am home. This is not only a province of memory, it is actual continued experiencing.

Suzy, I see that you have no more questions and are feeling quiet joy in our communion. This elates me, and it is a good stopping place for material for the book. But just as I came today and we talked before you reached the computer, always and evermore we are that close. So I bid you not goodbye in departure, but "Hasta luego."

*S: Sam, I don't quite know what to say. I feel love for you –
that's the sensation flowing through me.*

SAMINTEN: Yes, my very dear friend, I know, as I feel the
same. We *are* love, it is our *connection.* And with that, we never
are more than a thought apart.

When Matthew told me the name of Sam's civilization is *Hy-a-nita* and
their home space is *Co-stray-na*, he added: "That is an embarrassingly
feeble facsimile of the sound of those names, which are lilting music with
slight gradations of beautiful soft tones. Mother, this is like describing
color to a person who was blind at birth, I want you to know!"

PART V

MATTHEW: AN UPDATE

Christmas Day 1997

S: Merry Christmas, sweetheart! What did you do today?

MATTHEW: It touches me deeply that you ask, Mother. You are curious about Michael's day because you haven't heard yet from him, you are picturing Eric and his little family at the seaside, and you have talked with Betsy at length, and with your grandchildren, too, about how they have been spending this day. *Thank you* for thinking of me in this same way!

And now to weep a bit! Mother, Mother! Let me brighten your spirits and tell you that today was a *glorious* celebration of the highest hosts in residence here and the visits of Jesus and others from the archangelic realm's energy. Jesus looks just as he does in the picture beside mine on your windowsill, so you can picture us chatting and embracing in the light.

We all wore white robes today, even those in medical transition service, and it was a spectacular sight—a *really* white Christmas, just NOT "like the ones I used to know." I was not on duty today because I have been appointed to a task force, I guess it could be called, for improving the transitional pathway that is being adversely affected by negative entities. They are intensifying their efforts everywhere they possibly can to the detriment of all that we have established for comforting arrivals *prior* to their leaving physical bodies.

The dark forces are on their last legs of holding forth with such power on Earth, and they had made some inroads on this pathway. Their purpose is to capture souls about to transition by promising a lighted route to Heaven, but actually it is toward their forces. The obvious difference in the pathways leading to their negative outposts or to our realm is the vibrations and light. Our light is brilliant and pulsating with a warmth and security that you can know only by experiencing, not by hearing about it. That is the major distinction, but also there is a visible difference in the sentries, which isn't exactly the right term, who guard the entrance to the final moment of physical life.

It is a "life exchange" doorway, which again is not the best term, that serves only those souls coming directly to Nirvana from an Earth lifetime and none of the others who are continuously arriving here for other reasons. It is the lightning moment of energy registration placement for each soul and it is in consonance with the free will choices throughout the Earth lifetime. That departure and arrival placement situation also is true of other sanctuary realms serving the same density level of Earth.

This recent service is in line with my higher responsibilities that I told you about in connection with being considered for a master teacher role.

S: You didn't tell me what it entails, though.

MATTHEW: Well, in this case it's more than just what the words convey. For me it means that not only would I be teaching medical transition assistance at the level where I have been helping the most severely traumatized souls, but also I'll be expanding my own knowledge by the association with other master teachers. They are not the same as the "masters" associated with higher planes than here, but master teachers are on many levels of existence and residence.

I would be a master teacher for this realm as well as a visiting teacher to other realms, just as we have those masters who come here as visiting professors. That's a good comparison, a visiting professor, and my specialty is how best and quickest to repair the psyches of traumatized transitioning souls.

S: Congratulations, dear! That promotion seems to be the logical progression for you. Have you been with me at all today?

MATTHEW: Mother, how can you doubt that I was with you! How would that be for us if I refrained from spending time with you on Christmas day? When you felt that rare sensation that you needed a nap, it was not fatigue, but a time that I wished for you not to be elsewhere, doing other things, as it was my first opportunity to leave here and visit Earth. I didn't stay there, though— both of us came here and we had a most joyful time together during your hour of sleeping.

It is not that being with you early this afternoon was the first that I saw any of my Earth family in their various celebrations, but the first time that I could visit in body. There is quite a difference in my spirit being with you and my traveling there in body, as you will understand once you're making astral trips. I've told you that I am with you much more than you are aware, more often than previously. Partly I can do this because my regular service has been pretty much curtailed in favor of preparation for master teacher responsibilities.

You are wondering about the sleigh. Yes, of course it was I! You were feeling rather sad and needed a loving jolt, and that image of a beautiful crystal sleigh was my little gift to brighten your spirits in that moment.

S: I adore you, Mash. Thank you for being my son!

MATTHEW: Mother, *we chose each other.* Our bonding began so long ago in your counting that you cannot begin to think of such antiquity. Yes, even before dinosaurs! I love to see you smiling and laughing! Thank you for this beautiful shared feeling.

S: Yes, sweetheart, it is a beautiful feeling!   It is a merry Christmas, isn't it, a holy day for us all.

MATTHEW: A holier-than-thou day for some, though, but that is another topic for another day. Thank you, dearest soul, for this communion – it is my holiday present from you.

April 17, 1998

S: Happy Nirvana birthday, darling!

MATTHEW: Mother, dear heart, thank you for thinking of it as my birth-day and not my death day – this is so important to me. I know it has been a long time since you were lovingly told by dear Margaret to regard this anniversary with joy on my behalf. But she didn't tell you that this day is just as significant for you, in your connection with me, as it is to me in my connection with you. The understanding we have, the intensity of our closeness as if I am within you, is far more glorious for me than an "external" relationship.

But I know you can't regard it that way, the way I can greet you with all the love in the universe flowing between us and feel it is more sublime than my living there as before.

…. Say ye, what?

S: What? What's with the "say ye"?

MATTHEW: Playfulness, only that and nothing more, and it is to raise your spirits that are starting to sink as you're remembering this date years ago.

So, then, Mother! I see that today you have a lot on your plate, as Bob might say, and to you, getting my flowers is the most important. No, definitely I'm not telling you that it isn't important to me – I'm meaning that it always should be for *us,* never for *just* me. So, when I suggest this or that as you are flower shopping, it's only my preference – you get equal billing on the decision making. I think we usually wind up approving of whatever we choose, don't you?

S: Yes, I think so, Mash.

MATTHEW: Dearest one, in all those years before our connection when you bought flowers for both my Earth and Nirvana birthdays, always I was with you. You did that as a ritual and felt sorrowful each time. Think how different that would have been had you just allowed me to lift your spirits and let you know of my presence as I so wanted to do! Now our shopping trips are a delight to both of us.

S: Yes, sweetheart, they are. I'm wondering why just today you're telling me the significance to you of "our" day? Why didn't you tell me long ago?

MATTHEW: Well, first of all, it hasn't been all that long that I could tell you *anything* directly! But you are right, I could have told you this before. There is no significance to my not telling you before, and if you ever doubt how human I still am, you can think of my just plain forgetfulness. But now that we both realize this is a joint celebration, what do you think?

S: It's fine for us because we have our connection, but despite what Margaret said, I never could regard this anniversary as a celebration before we had this closeness. I doubt that very many people here could regard such an occasion as a happy celebration.

MATTHEW: No doubt that is so, Mother. Only one essential purpose of the books is to provide information such as this to people who are grieving. Not everyone does it in the measure you did, and that is most fortunate for those people there and their beloved souls here. *Bond with us in love,* don't bind us with your grief!

Anyway, dear soul, we are unique and not only because we can talk whenever we want to. There are many such unions of soul mates such as we are, but not many have our energy beginnings or our history of total love. We have not experienced together an adversarial relationship in any lifetime, and *that* is unique!

S: By adversarial, do you mean we were never mortal enemies, like in one lifetime one of us killed the other and in another, vice versa? Were we ever in darkness in our shared lives?

MATTHEW: You are looking more deeply into this than I was thinking when I mentioned it. No, that's not exactly it, Mother. We have been on opposing sides, but ALWAYS that was made within the light. Never have we lived in darkness – ignorance in personage, yes, but never as captive of the dark forces. Always we have emerged from a shared lifetime with a higher appreciation of the light, so our journey back has not been as rocky and thorny as many journeys have been or are in this moment.

We fell from the pinnacle of light within which we originated because our common root soul was among those experimenting with the newly given free will. Only when the experimentations became so grotesque and so painful for the manifested entities was it realized by all of the experimenters that indeed the inexperience had become a curiosity and a game, and the horrible creatures being made were not of God's light any longer.

Some entities realized this before others, and they were the first to reach into their origin and ask for the forgiveness they knew was required to enable them to reach the light sources through a long journey "home." We are of a root soul that was among the first to retreat from the horror and start the return journey. Some never did.

You are accepting this well, Mother. Almost to my surprise, there is no doubt in your mind of what I'm telling you. Yes, this is quite a distinctive beginning and middle and continuance of our journey.

S: Matthew, I'm accepting this almost without any sensation at all. Is this because I'm aligned with the truth of it or am I in shock?

MATTHEW: Very likely you're hearing what your soul is letting you know, that it is the truth. You are flowing within the light that is offered for your journey. That is so *snazzy!* Mother, I love to see and hear you laughing! That definitely was not from the "professor," you know!

September 11, 1998

S: Happy Earth birthday, sweetheart! Have you been with me a lot today or was I imagining it?

MATTHEW: Mother, dearest soul, no, you have not been imagining any of those times when you thought I was with you. Of course you know we chose together the flowering plant, which delights me more than it does you, I know, but that dear little plant was struggling from lack of water and food and needed the nurturing you have given it. In this case, you did give into just my choice, and I thank you for that.

And when the little dog came to you, just as you thought, I knew the little soul could fit very nicely into your fur family. So, yes, I have been with you a lot today, and I have known your heart ever since you wakened with the thought that 36 years ago this date I came into your life this time around.

Now you say "Happy Earth Birthday, sweetheart," and I say to you, *Thank you for being my mother on Earth those several years.* I was about to say "many" years and I realized that in your counting, there were not many at all. However, my missions were accomplished thoroughly and I was ready to leave.

But my natal day was something neither of us ever will forget in this lifetime as Mother and Matthew. The instant love and bonding we felt was soul level remembering of what you didn't consciously know, but I was so close to my godself that I did know. I suspect that in all lifetimes we share, there will be subliminal memories of that bonding that no one else could feel or understand. We are soul mates from the first being of our oversoul's parenting.

Now let's talk about whatever you wish.

S: Mash, I cherish this bonding above all. And what I wish most is to see you and Ithaca and Esmeralda, if you can arrange that, please. (NOTE: The unique relationship between Matthew and Ithaca and their joy with Esmeralda, who arrived in Nirvana as a toddler about four years prior to this sitting, is described in "Divine Love, Children" in *Matthew, Tell Me About Heaven.*)

MATTHEW: Mother dear, that is a most touching request for this birthday celebration. One moment, please.

....

The three of us are here but unable to transmit an image. Perhaps if we simply stay in this pattern of light we can make the connection.

....

Mother, I'm so sorry about the lack of success we're having in this transmission. Your emotional scrapbook is incomplete without "pictures" of my 36th year birthday, Earth timing.

S: Matthew, I'm trying to hold my energy steady, but whatever you're trying to send is just a blur fading in and out.

ITHACA: Dear Miss Suzy, I greet you with sensitivity and regret for our disappointing you in this sense of sending our image. I can attest that the weak energy is solidly in the light so that you need worry not at all about a lessening of your connection or your ability to receive.

It is a joy for me to tell you that Matthew is such a fine representative of our world to those other worlds similar to ours. He is away much of the time, as he has told you, but Esmeralda and I see each other very often even when Matthew is not here. We are a family in total love and respect but not in commitment to remain always together, as Matthew has explained to you. However, you may always think of us as your heavenly children, your darlings in Nirvana, for we are that indeed in spirit, even in the essence of closeness at geographic partings.

S: Ithaca dear, thank you so much for your message. I wish I could see you clearly, but at least I am seeing you a bit now. Are you wearing an orange brocade kimono and white sox and black sandals? Your face is white, as if you are in costume makeup. Is that a correct image?

ITHACA: Yes, it is indeed! It is not exactly how I look in this world, as most of the time I am in white robe with gold sash and I am barefoot, but I wished to dress more formally for this family gathering and portrait to send you.

And now can you see Esmeralda also? I am projecting more energy to assist her and now I allow her to take over and wish you good evening. In great love and respect and all haste for your perfection, dear soul, I say now, good night.

S: Ithaca, thank you for your words that are so heart-warming for me. Esmeralda, I am so very happy to see you! I hope I'm seeing you correctly. Are you smiling a lot and sometimes laughing? Is your dark hair short and curly and is your skin brown and glowing? Are you wearing a green and blue plaid outfit and skipping around?

ESMERALDA: Yes, Grandma Suzy! You are seeing me as I am! I know my skin is darker brown than when you last saw me, but I am sunning a great deal and I am a very nut brown color now. I could be this color without the sun, you know, but it delights me to rest or play in sunshine.

You see Tango is with me. We sent you a little dog today because it is my godfather Matthew's Earth birthday. Did you think that could be why you found that little dog?

S: Esmeralda dear, he is a wonderful little dog, and what a beautiful gift for me! But since it is your godfather's birthday, wouldn't you give a present to him rather than to me?

ESMERALDA: Oh no, Grandma Suzy! The present is for *you,* the mother of the infant Matthew. It is a policy – no, tradition is a better word for this – it is a tradition here that we honor the mother on the day of the birth and remember the mother always on the successive birthday celebrations. Gifts are given to the child *and* to the mother.

We gave my dear godfather a present as well, but not a kitten, which was my idea but it didn't work out so well in that sense of his many travels. He is not at home as much as I wish he were and I do miss him a great deal because we have such very good times, all three of us. But Ithaca is my dearest godmother of all. She is great fun and also a source of much comfort and help to me in my singing.

I wish you could hear me sing! Godfather says that someday you will be able to hear me really singing. I am blessed very much with a lovely soprano voice and I also am blessed with loving to sing.

They are telling me this is enough chattering with you this time. But I don't often have this chance to talk with you or anyone else on Earth, so I really did talk a lot. I love you and I love the way I see you in the shimmering lights.

Goodbye for this time. Please come more often to talk with

us. I am Esmeralda saying good evening and much love and also good respecting of your station on Earth. Goodbye.

S: Esmeralda, thank you SO MUCH! You are a beautiful and wonderful little girl. Actually, you are so much taller than I was expecting – you look to be about 10 or 11. How old are you?

MATTHEW: Mother, Esmeralda and Ithaca have left, but you are right in estimating that age in correspondence to an Earth child. Esmeralda is almost six in Earth years, but closer to 12 in growth of body and mind and spirit. She is not aging as rapidly in some physical ways as others because her voice needs to mature gradually and not leapfrog into maturity. That's why she looks older than you would expect in some ways but younger in others, according to what you know about the faster aging and de-aging here.

So, dear one, she told you about the little dog. Now, seriously, can you really believe that just "coincidence" put that little fellow in the road in front of your car in an isolated area on the way to the vet with your fur kids?

I think Bob will understand this exceptional situation and not object to a seventh dog when you tell him it is Esmeralda's gift to you, which I could not refuse her. However, Tango had more to do with this than you can imagine, because you can't imagine at all a former Earth pet doing anything of influence in this realm, and Salty was in on it, too.

And now surely you can see the connection of that little black and white fellow with black Salty and white Tango. But first I shall tell you that the little dog did not have a caring or happy home life during all those years before he came to you. He wasn't abused by beating, but he was terribly neglected and left to himself always, tied by a chain to a tree. Salty and Tango were aware of his sadness and they remember with gratitude their happy lives with you.

They felt they could combine a happy life for the little dog with a gift for you, so they were the instigators, but Esmeralda thought it was a most special arrangement and she blessed it as well. With some energy maneuvering, the little dog was untied from his mooring and off he went. We guided him in safety until you reached him, and you noticed that without hesitation he went right into your arms. We were with him then, too.

So, you were right in wondering if I had a hand in it. A faint hand, but nevertheless, the knowledge, some energy and a bit of grace for the little dog. Considering his filthy matted fur and the army of fleas and his eye infections, you won't be surprised to know that there wasn't a second of regret or concern in that home when he was nowhere to be found.

Lucky is a fine name – true, as you have thought, not unusual or imaginative, but certainly appropriate – and you now know that it is as you felt, a most special treat that he came to you on this particular day.

S: Matthew, thank you and the others for this very, very special gift! Please tell Esmeralda and Tango and Salty that I love little Lucky.

MATTHEW: Mother, they *know!* Your feelings and thoughts that include them reach them just as yours about me reach me. Your prayer before this sitting—"to God or the universe or whoever can guarantee sanctity of connection"—was touching. We are touched in loving sentiments at the same time we are sad that you still are not certain that your telepathic connection is *sacred.* It can no more leave you than you can leave Earth by simply willing it to be!

That wasn't a good analogy. Maybe I'm all out of analogies and don't need one for this moment anyway. Shall we simply say goodnight for this 36th event and understand that never will there be any separation in our love or our talking. No matter where I am in my service, I shall never fail to know when I am in your thoughts or "on call." Always I am within you, so how could I not respond to your calling?

S: I miss you, Mash.

MATTHEW: Mother, I miss you, too. I have never said that before, but I could have many times. I miss what we did not have, more years together there, and I miss it because I am so much within your feelings and thoughts and know the suffering you have felt. I have mourned more than you can imagine. For myself, too, just as you do for yourself.

But this is a *happy* day, Mother, with little Lucky brightening your heart and your lovely chats with Ithaca and Esmeralda. Now then, I say goodnight, dearest soul, with my love embracing you.

S: I love you with all my heart. Good night on your happy 36th birthday.

March 2, 1999

S: Mash, dear, I know it's been ages since our last sitting, but you know why. I'm in a better frame of mind now and don't even want to touch on any of that stuff today. So, what have you been up to?

M: Mother, dear soul, I welcome you back, and yes, I'm aware of all you've been dealing with and I'll say no more about that. Now then, I'm busier than you can imagine and my new service is *fascinating!* I'm just not home as often as I would like. Most of all I miss Esmeralda and Ithaca, of course, but my work is so immensely gratifying that the missing part means that our time together is even more precious and fulfilling and meaningful.

Usually I travel out of [*etheric*] body because of the distances and the highways in space that are needed to reach all the destinations. Most of my trips, which are by invitation only, are in the nature of adviser or consultant, I guess is the most appropriate way to define my role, because it's a progression from master teacher. My service is to assist in upgrading the spirit life sanctuaries of alien civilizations – not all of them are human as you know human, so I'm referring to them as alien only to make that distinction.

Some of these sanctuaries are greatly in need of spiritual alignment, as the souls' embodied lives – on planets, usually, but not always – are so different from what you would think of as doing benevolent works. Therefore their discarnate realms also are considerably imbalanced, and that is why I am invited to evaluate, advise and give hands-on assistance to get these realms into balance so true learning and restorative surroundings can be achieved.

The side benefit of this, which holds equal importance, is that once these imbalanced civilizations see how much grander and more effective their sanctuary realms are with improvements, their physical realms follow suit. That is, the civilizations become more open to the light always available to them and choose to uplift their lives through loftier thoughts and motives and deeds. I don't mean that they were immersed in negativity, only that they had lacked the impetus to activity pursue evolvement spiritually into more beautiful beings in all aspects of their lives.

This is something that I have only now thought to tell you – when civilizations are highly evolved spiritually, their forms can *only* be beautiful. They may not look like the human forms you're familiar with and call beautiful, but they are indeed exceedingly lovely, perfect creations in their own sense of beauty and in God's eyes as well.

Mother, I want to tell you about the beings I've met who have so captured my heart and my interest. These people are of the most gentle persuasion I have ever met! As you are seeing from the image I'm sending, this being could fit into illustrations in your comics or animated films, and I'd like you to type my description "for the record."

The body is like a tall cylinder – no curves like shoulders or breasts and no indentations like a waist – and there are no feet because these beings don't walk, they glide over surfaces like hydroplanes. They are not really glowing, as you're thinking, but there is a radiation that is not a regular light but rather an energy surrounding them. That is what propels them also. They are much less dense in form than you, but not as light as I am – if they were on Earth in their homeland bodies, you could catch glimpses of them in the right light.

The men and women don't have the variations in features or forms as do Earth and other human civilizations, but there is

enough visible difference between the sexes so that I never confused one for the other. They speak with their mouths, just as
we do, but they have no ears – they hear with their small anten-
nas, which also help them control their direction when they
travel in body – and the hair is smooth and tight to the perfectly round head.

You can see that their eyes are huge by your standards and so
deeply gentle that they are almost without expression, but they did-
n't start out that way. They grew into this due to their evolved
vision into what you call future and what they call growth. They
see distances that you cannot even imagine, nor can I, because their
vision extends throughout this universe into other universes.

They give live birth, which you might think is rather primitive
for such an exalted spiritual and intellectual station that this means
of reproduction is not necessary. However, their nature is such that
they wish this intensity of bonding and closeness both as a union
and as the birth process, and so by choice they reproduce biologically rather than by cloning or any other process for creating progeny. The nurturing of their children is with such love that no child
on Earth has ever known this constant gentleness, guidance and
devotion. That height of emotions and sensitivity simply isn't possible in Earth's lower density.

Spiritually these people have attained a beauty that is pure joy
to be near. The energy created by their loving nature is as radiant
as ever I've seen in Nirvana at its most glorious. These people do
not live quiet lives as in dwelling only in thoughts and feelings, but
they don't hustle and bustle about as you do. Their assistance to
other civilizations is beaming love and light wherever they see a
void and hear a cry for help to fill that void. This is what they have
been doing for Earth in response to her cry for light so she would-
n't perish.

They do not impose themselves upon any civilization without invitation, you can be sure of that, and when they respond to a request for help, they can be trusted completely to do only what they have been asked to do. I don't mean that they never would extend themselves beyond the request, but rather that they can be fully trusted never to do anything self-serving or sly along with the help, and always their assistance is to the great benefit of the requesting civilization.

S: These are amazing beings! Sweetheart, what an honor for you to be invited there! Where do they live, and how large is their population? Would they be called suprahuman?

M: They could be called suprahuman as a generic term, but that doesn't describe their spirituality aspect. A lot of suprahuman civilizations insofar as evolved intelligence and technology have no spirituality whatsoever, or such a minute amount that it's barely perceptible. Maybe *ultrahuman* would be a good term for these people, because they are a highly advanced human civilization.

These souls are about 40 million in number, perhaps a few million more – it's a very, very small population – and they live in a tiny planet that revolves around a number of suns. This is a strange part of their homeland planet, with the gravity situation so different from Earth's where there is interaction with only one sun. There is no gravitational in-fighting or tugging among the energy layers at that height of light, and all is in such harmony that these beings can almost be considered as taking a leisurely trip with little side jaunts and stopping now and then to smell the roses in their revolutions.

Yes, Mother, I know you would like names for these exquisite beings and their world. It's the same "word," but I don't know how to give you this even phonetically as I've been able to do before because their language – communication is better – is in soft lilting musical tones and not word-sound syllables. Nevertheless, I'll try. Think of *la la tra la la* in beat, or rhythm, and a parallel sound of *do re me me re do* over and over. Those sounds in tandem resonate to something close in vibration to the name of these people and their world.

S: Thank you, dear, for going to that extent to describe the name. What does their planet look like—the environment?

MATTHEW: Absolutely magnificent, simple beauty in keeping with their purity, gentleness and vision. By "simple" I mean it is not cluttered or very uneven in elevation, nothing is harsh or jagged, such as mountain peaks or canyons, and everything is immaculate but definitely not with a "sterile" look. The bodies of water are shallow and crystalline pure and the different pastel shades of fine sand are visible.

The range of colors in everything from flowers to the sky is beyond description! The sky is ever-changing in tones ranging from the slightest tinge of pink or coral and gold to myriad shades of blue that sparkle like sunlight on rippling water. Your aurora borealis is not a good comparison by any means, but its changing colors is about as close as I can come to explaining the difference between that sky and those of Nirvana and Earth.

S: But you do make it sound "indescribably" beautiful. Are there any animals?

MATTHEW: They wouldn't be recognized as such on Earth as their forms are in keeping with the peoples' forms – sleek, radiant, and little variation in size or configuration. They have no fur at all and they also have disproportionately large eyes. Their soul energy, too, has evolved to the extent of "supravision," and their intelligence is astounding. There is total telepathic communication between them and the people. Actually, at this light density, their energy is worthy of human experiencing at a high level, but the animals' choice is to experience as they are within this culture where they are respected in keeping with their soul evolvement.

S: Matthew, that is amazing – and wonderful! Have any of the people ever embodied on Earth?

MATTHEW: Some have made visitations only to bring light and higher level energy to you, but being there is not necessary for serving Earth in that same way. However, at their high energy station, embodying as a handsome human on your planet is as quick as a wink if that is what they choose to do.

S: Where is their planet in relation to us?

MATTHEW: It's about the farthest from you it can be and still be within this galaxy. But then again, Mother, you know that what you call distance doesn't exist "out there" – it's all a matter of energy alignment. Actually, it's realignment, alignment, realignment when I travel both within the Milky Way and to other galaxies.

I have an open invitation to visit these people whenever I can, and because I am enthalled with their essence and their homeland, I would love to do that. Only the extent of my new responsibilities has prevented my returning to the joyousness of being in that height of sentience and service. But I shall indeed return when I can.

S: With their level of evolvement, I'm surprised that they needed changes in their sanctuary realm.

MATTHEW: They invited me only to visit, not to assist, as their nature would not allow them to freely seek assistance from others but rather defer to others' desire to visit, and they were pleased when I gave their sanctuary the high compliments it so well deserves. But their modest nature almost required them to beseech me for an improvement idea, otherwise they could appear to consider that realm in perfection and their humility would not allow that. Considering my advisory service capacity, I had to think of something so they would know the extent of my caring about that realm. I was graced with remembering your enchantment with Rachmaninoff's Second Symphony, so I mentioned that perhaps adding that to the realm's repertoire or choosing it more often would hold that same pleasure for the residents as it does for you.

S: Matthew, that delights me!

MATTHEW: I *feel* your delight, Mother! And when they extended their invitation, *I* was delighted, I can tell you, because it is rather rare that someone from a fourth density station like Nirvana's is invited to visit that far up the light ladder to seventh-come-eighth spiritual density.

Here again is the possibility of confusion between density of mass, as in form, and density, or light frequency, of spiritual evolvement. These can differ vastly in the same civilization – that is, often but not always are the very spiritually advanced people in extremely light density of form or are discarnate. In this case, although these people's spiritual density is of that very high station I mentioned, their body mass is fairly heavy in comparison with discarnate beings. Because they wish to experience intimate union and reproduce biologically, there has to be sufficient density mass to permit those functions.

S: Yes, I see. How long do they live?

MATTHEW: There is no limit. At that spiritual level aging doesn't exist in the cellular structure because it no longer exists in the thought patterns. I think you would consider the purpose of their sanctuary haven more in the nature of a spiritual retreat or a solitary vacation in a setting of unsurpassed beauty, as leaving embodiment for them is voluntary and done on a respite, not a permanent, basis.

S: If no one leaves for good, then is there reincarnation or just continual increase in population?

MATTHEW: Now I know I must return to get an answer for you! No, of course I wasn't serious there, Mother, I was just surprised by your question as I didn't see it coming, and yes, if I didn't already know, I could ask from wherever I was. There is both, and the choice as you may imagine, is each individual's and is based upon the good of the entire population.

Being among these souls in their surroundings would be the greatest inspiration I can imagine for everyone on Earth to "live the good life," spiritually speaking!

April 17, 2002

S: Happy heavenly birthday, Mash! What do you think about this hailstorm to distinguish your celebration?

MATTHEW: Dear soul, a blessed day to you! I thought I'd remind you of our special joint occasion by hurling down those big hailstones outside your window. No, of course I didn't really arrange that wild occasion, but it was rather spectacular, wasn't it?

I'm glad you came to the computer early because I could hardly wait to tell you about the unique fiesta that Ithaca and Esmeralda planned for my return! They arranged for a huge banner to be fluttered across treetops in that static part of our scenery announcing that I would be back for my birthday celebration and all are welcome. It is absolutely amazing to me, the huge crowd of well-wishers who have come or sent good wishes.

Mother, you were with us last night and I do so wish you had clear memories of this. I see that you're trying to remember your dream, and with good reason, because it actually was a smattering of your memories of being here. You were agape for most of your visit because everything was so unusual even for here.

Yes, Grandma and Grandpa and Annie and Lyle were with us, and all the dear dogs including your little Lucky, who arrived so recently. Ithaca and Esmeralda did not leave out anyone on a personal invitation basis – the banner is to let the realm know that all are welcome to enjoy the festivities.

Many come mostly out of courtesy, but some out of love – family and friends from this and other lifetimes, colleagues in the medical assistance field from my days of leadership there, and the masters and other high souls living here. But it seems that the call went out to other civilizations, too – sanctuary realms as well as the incarnate realms where I've been invited as consultant, and they have sent good wishes and some even sent representatives.

My two most beloved souls here did an enormous amount of planning and arranging so this would be the rousing party it is. It has been a several-day affair in your 24-hour days, and many have said it is the most elaborate and enjoyable party ever in this world.

The abundance of flowers and blooming trees that were created for the main arena, you could say, is magnificent in scope and beauty. That area is where the main greeting doorway and refreshments are, although the doorway is so spacious and tables so numerous that it's like a mile-long stretch of entryways and banquet settings. Think how Jesus fed the multitudes and you'll know how Ithaca and Esmeralda and their helpers keep providing delicacies of marvelous flavors for thousands at a time.

And the entertainment! Musicians abound from every music specialty imaginable that is harmonious or peppy and uplifting – classical, rock and roll, ballads and instrumental compositions representative of all cultures on Earth. But the many varieties are isolated so that all can listen to their favorite genre or join in the songfests without intrusion from the others. And of course the styles designed for dancing, from waltzes to ethnic dances and line dancing, draw thousands of guests to their favorites.

Storytellers are here, both for the children's amusement and a higher level of tales for adults. There are puppet shows and a "circus" of animals performing as *they* desire – they arranged that with Esmeralda. There are aerialists like your Cirque Soleil but without the gravity – can you imagine how spectacular *these* performers are! And the fireworks are phenomenal! These are announced realm-wide each time so that people who can't be on the party scene can "tune in" from wherever they are. Although not announced, the same arrangement is available with all the types of music.

Mother, it has been an *incredible* celebration that not only thrills me a million percent, but really stuns me in its scope of thought and love. There is such love here that you cannot imagine the joy that has prevailed! The party will go on for a few more days of your counting because people from a distance are having such a grand time in the vibrations of this top layer of the realm.

S: Sweetheart, this celebration is absolutely amazing! Is the large attendance because you were asked to be on the Council?

MATTHEW: Well, that could be part of it since the realm knows of that offer because of the open means whereby Council members are chosen, and my declining was greeted with the understanding that my service in other solar systems and galaxies also is important. So yes, I'd think that might have some bearing on the attendance. But mainly it's the thought and effort that Ithaca and Esmeralda have put into this that has made it the overwhelming success and ongoing festivity that so many are enjoying.

It's not as if all are here the whole time – it's like your open house entertaining, where guests come and go during the party. So it's possible that even millions have enjoyed some of these special offerings as well as meeting up with family and friends and colleagues. Those reunions are a paramount and joyous attraction of this entire affair, and no doubt that's why it is being heralded as a truly wondrous occasion even by Heaven's standards.

S: But still, dear, I think you must be very well liked and respected for so many people to come. I haven't talked with Esmeralda for a long time—she's a young woman now, isn't she?

MATTHEW: Yes, Mother, she's a stunningly beautiful young woman in spirit, mind and body. Her radiance is not only goodness and in beauty of appearance, but in her music. The quality of her voice is beyond description as it surpasses the brilliance on Earth, where third density captures the higher tones. Would you like to speak with her yourself?

S: I'd love to! It's been ages since we last talked.

(NOTE: Esmeralda talked with me a long time, but briefly, she still is in the large home where she lived when she arrived in Nirvana. Possessing the nurturing qualities the realm requires for care of babies and younger children, she has been offered one of these respected roles. She hasn't decided whether to choose care-taking, *"which I love with all my heart,"* or go into medical service *"following the steps of my godfather Matthew,"* both of which are full-time services.)

S: Esmeralda, I'm so happy about our long talk. Again, my heartfelt thanks for that magnificent birthday celebration you and Ithaca planned for Matthew. I'm more than impressed with EVERYTHING—I'm in awe of all you did!

ESMERALDA: It was such a great joy for us to do this! We just put our ideas together and refined the most outrageous into a workable plan that could encompass all the aspects of this world and the others my godfather knows. We put these into an atmosphere that he could enjoy along with people he loves and the many others who know of him, but don't know him personally.

Grandma Suzy, godfather Matthew is very humble about his distinction in this realm and way beyond. If he were less than modest about it, he would not hold his high station. Humility and honesty are his character, and those qualities are infused with a light of spirit that is not known on Earth.

January 6, 2003

MATTHEW: Mother, you know perfectly well that it is *God's* choice, not mine, that not only the words about my station remain in place, but also those that show your light status, too. So in this, your "be in the background" nature must give way to God's intent that those parts you still want to remove stay right where they are. You've already cut some, so this can be the compromise, that the rest you wanted to cut but didn't because you were firmly told "No, no no!" remain as they are.

GOD: Matthew, excuse me, please. Suzy, listen to your son, whose humility is even greater than your own. He must be recognized as the high soul he is so his information is respected as totally trustworthy.

And you, my dear child, please remember that this is MY book, entrusted to you for publishing. You must be known as the clear, pure channel you are so all of these Matthew Books will be heeded as MY truth given to you by Matthew and all other sources therein.

PART VI

WAR

MATTHEW'S MESSAGES

I completed the preceding parts of this book before leaving the country for a month and I was visiting my family in Chile when the war officially started.

In October 2002 Jean Hudon had asked Matthew if the United States government really would declare war on Iraq. Over two months later, when peace rallies, petitions and international disagreement with the US plans were intensifying, Jean asked if the growing opposition would prevent a war.

Knowing that Matthew's replies to both of those questions were to be inserted as Part VI - The War when I returned home, I knew that the last words in this book would be given to me then, too.

October 5, 2002

MATTHEW: Mother, I wish to reply to Jean's request for my take on this potential war situation. Jean, I shall address you personally now, and ask that you honor my request that you NOT publish my message until a time later when you will know it is appropriate to do so.

My mother is thinking that what I am about to say is not what you would like to hear as I have told her there *will be* the war that President Bush is determined to wage with Iraq. It will not be a protracted war, as were World Wars I and II, nor will it be as short as the so-called Desert Storm. And it will **NOT** be a nuclear war! You already know this cannot be as Creator has decreed it cannot, and the technologies of civilizations far advanced of yours are at the ready with power to prevent nuclear detonations should any be attempted.

Why cannot the sustained light on Earth prevent a war that most people on Earth do *not* want? Because individuals' free will still reigns, and those who are determined to start a war are exercising their free will to do so. It is not that there is insufficient light being directed toward peace, but rather that the determination of the few with positions powerful enough to initiate a war, as well as troops and weaponry to proceed, is within their free will choices.

These souls operating in total darkness are either members of the non-human civilization incarnated into human bodies or those humans captivated by the power they believe that dark force has given them. They are in total refusal of the light continuously being beamed at them and thus are proceeding without conscience to further their control of the planet.

How I wish that I could tell you otherwise! But I am telling you what cannot be prevented, and it is for *that* reason – it *can't* be prevented – that I wish you not to release this message. It is gratifying, of course, that many people you reach with your illuminating reports believe my words. Always my messages are in truth from my vantage point, and I don't wish ever to discourage ones from feeling hope and love and sending forth those vibrations to the universe. This *must continue* even after war is started as those vibrations will assist in bringing in the era of peace that will follow.

That is all I have to say unless my mother has questions. I can't tell – do you, Mother?

S: Give me a minute, please, Matthew. ... Thank you. Will biological or chemical weapons be employed? I mean, will God or Creator allow that?

MATTHEW: That kind of warfare is not *intended* by God or Creator, certainly! But there is this free will determination that must be recognized and honored, so I must tell you that the warmongers' intention is to wage this kind of unholy war themselves but officially ascribe it to the defenders. *If* this happens, the "silver lining" is that the same benevolent civilizations whose technologies can prevent nuclear detonations also have the technology to counteract the worst effects of the toxin- and virus-laden weapons.

S: Do you see many deaths?

MATTHEW: Here again I wish I didn't have to tell you *Yes*, but that's what we see at this juncture in the field of potential.

S: Is all of this karmic? Are the "dark minds" determined for war only playing out the karmic roles they agreed to, and are all the "innocents" who will die or be wounded only playing out their roles?

MATTHEW: Now I can say *No*, but again I wish my reply could be different because then it would follow what you have heard from other sources and find more acceptable – that everything is in divine order, and everything that is happening is what all souls on Earth agreed to eons ago. This is not necessarily so, Mother. While it definitely *is* so that ULTIMATELY in the universal continuum divine order is prevailing, the universe itself is in enormous upheaval, and translated into your linear time, "divine order" is not prevailing.

While it definitely also is true that the souls who have embodied on Earth during this unprecedented time of planetary changes willingly did so, their soul level agreements have been severely compromised by the dark minds' relentless tyranny and deception that is in far more dire measure than these "innocents" agreed to experience.

Millions have made new soul-level agreements after being born into their agreed-upon families and experiences because the circumstances went so far beyond the provisions of their original agreements. These souls have left or will be leaving their physical lifetimes via the obvious means of disease and starvation and slaughter in wars, but it is actually renegotiated soul-level contracts that is the reason. Their misery was only adding negativity on your planet, which was the opposite of their purpose for embodiment in this time of great transition – their purpose was to achieve balance for themselves and Earth. By dying physically these souls now are reducing that negativity by joining the ranks of countless other lightworkers off-planet who are serving to bring about the new era of peace, love and harmony on Earth.

So you can see that the karmic roles of souls who agreed to be "oppressor" have extended way beyond those agreements as well, and they do not intend to aid the light in any way! And of course, the darkness that exists as a force field in the universe does not agree to anything responsive to the light and is fighting more fiercely than ever in its desperate attempts to not let the light extinguish it.

S: Are souls still willingly embodying in areas where many souls are opting to leave?

MATTHEW: Yes, and their soul-level agreements call for only enough experiencing to complete karmic lessons before they leave. And please understand that many souls living in those areas where disease, starvation and wars are rampant *are* living out their chosen karma.

S: I see. Will the imminent war be the turnaround for us, the last major hurdle before the era of peace, love and harmony?

MATTHEW: *YES!* The combat of the war and its life and land destruction will so profoundly affect your world that souls who have been thinking war will lead to peace or "fence-straddling" will be forced to clearly see that only peaceful means of settling any dispute will ever result in peace on Earth. *And feeling love is the way to peace.* Those who resist this will not continue in positions of power and their physical lives will end as the ascension of the planet and her light-filled life forms hastens into the higher frequencies of fourth density.

S: Will that process definitely be completed by 2012? If the war will have those profound effects, can't that decade between now and then be reduced?

MATTHEW: As I explained before about that year, which I know has been heralded as having great significance for Earth, aside from being a part of your linear time in third density and thus not applicable elsewhere in the universe, it is not a firm date even for Earth. Free will shall continue to determine individuals' energy direction in thoughts, words, actions and motives, and 2012 as a pivotal date can be speeded or deterred by the amount of "new" light added as people consciously connect with their souls. What IS a constant is the continuing ascension of the planet and her light-filled beings, so evidence of the results of efforts toward peace and harmony among peoples of all nations will be growing.

S: Matthew, do you know if God wishes He could throw out some peoples' free will and prevent the war and suddenly change Earth into the paradise it once was?

MATTHEW: Mother, you amuse me, and this bit of light-heartedness uplifts my spirits at having had to tell you what I did.

You know I'm not ever intending to be God's spokes-soul and further, you know you can ask Him yourself. But since I'm into your thoughts and know you're not going to do that, and since you think I have a vantage point of talking with God that is more "normal" than you consider yours – never mind that this is NOT the case! – I will tell you that God weeps for every one of His creations who suffers as well as for those who cause the suffering.

December 18, 2002

MATTHEW: I ask that my message today, like the prior one regarding war, also not be released until the appropriate time. That message stating that war is inevitable was dire indeed, and so it must be again. It is intended that free will be continued on Earth, and despite all the light being poured forth to cleanse all areas of human despotism and the situations this has created, it is not the will of Creator to withdraw individual free will choices EXCEPT in the case of nuclear detonations.

The mind-set for war, which is within the free will of those few who are determined to proceed with their plans, cannot be bent. But with more and more souls focusing FOR peace, love, alleviation of suffering and pain, the war's consequences will be reduced in corresponding response to this focus. That is why I requested in my previous message that you not release it – the continued intense fervor focused for peace is *imperative!* If you knew that averting war could *not* happen, that optimistic fervor of focus could be turned into the negativity of fear and despair, and that must NOT happen! When it is finally seen that war is unavoidable, that same positive focus for peace STILL must be continued so the aftermath of the war's onset is lessened in duration, death, destruction and misery!

The mind-set for war does not end with the invasion of Iraq—it is a mind-set for complete control of the Mideast because of its oil resources. The intention of the darkness is to establish puppet regimes controlled by the cabal, only a few of whose members are publicly acting, so clearly the conquest of one country is not their intended end but rather another step toward that further aim, which would require more invasions, more death, more suffering.

And the mind-set doesn't stop there. Total domination of all the planet's peoples either as willing or slave labor after the populations are "adequately thinned" is the furthest goal. That is, until Earth herself is so devastated that she cannot live with the intense negativity, and then the on- and off-planet dark forces will simply abandon the dead planet along with their human puppets. That is their *plan* – but it will *not* happen! Except for the invasion of Iraq, all of that intended conquest is what will be thwarted by continued intense focus FOR peace, love, harmony, justice, fairness, equity of resources allocation and the like. THAT is what your collective focusing will manifest on Earth!

Clear channels have been relaying messages that for several decades the light forces have been defusing situations of their negativity. Ameliorating the effects of depleted uranium is one such situation – one of the most vital because it's one of the most destructive – wherein these forces are assisting. So it is not that this is a bargaining chip, as some have said: *Have no war and we'll clean up the uranium.* It is rather that your focusing on peace, love and so forth will have the same imperative need after the war begins that it has at this moment, and the elimination of that hazardous situation will be a result of your collective focusing along with the extraterrestrial help.

April 13, 2003

MATTHEW: The war and all of its undercurrents are proceeding as both the light and the dark forces are intending, but the latter is only because of the energy momentum that must be played out. The light is beaming in such brilliance that you cannot imagine it, otherwise the death toll and injuries and the land and property destruction would be far, far greater than it is.

While we weep with those who are in sorrow, pain and fear on Earth, we rejoice in this massive light effort that has prevented greater suffering and loss of physical life. The souls who have left have been welcomed into Nirvana and are being treated with utmost gentleness and constant personalized care.

What will happen with the further aims of the darkness no longer is a matter of their free will. That will remain along with their plans for further conquest and global control, but their intentions will not come to fruition. The world is crying in unison for a permanent end to slaughter and domination. Although this outpouring of energy is fractured due to the grief, fear, continuing combat and the urgency and fervency in prayers, the light in the souls who are awakening spiritually and the steadying influence of extraterrestrial light forces is balancing the energy flow.

The tribulations that will continue in the short term is a sad endurance for Earth, but the evidence of change will become increasingly apparent with the ever-expanding light intensity. So do not bow to despair and hopelessness, thinking that your world is heading into devastation or oblivion. Even if the playing out of this phase doesn't cease as quickly as you desire, know that beyond what is visible, the glorious new era of peace, love, and health in mind, body and spirit is underway!

GOD'S MESSAGE

GOD: Yes, my child, as I had told you, it is appropriate that I shall have the last word in this book that I have mandated to be published.

As is clear through the parts of our many conversations that I chose to include herein, I am each and all souls everywhere in this universe. Yes, even those who are being despised in this time for causing the outrage as it is seen by all who are abhorring war's death and brutality and destruction even as I speak.

You are wondering what I can say that will give comfort and sustained hope for the peace that has been promised for my very own Eden to begin. My child, yes, of course I *wish* I could stop the carnage this instant, but I cannot. Yes, I *wish* I could instantly ease the grief of families already suffering and prevent that which others will be feeling all too soon, but I cannot. Yes, I *wish* I could instantly end the fear that is so pervasive, but I cannot. And *yes*, I wish I could instantly instill love and harmony among all my children, among all peoples and all in the kingdoms of animals and plants as it once was on Earth, but I cannot.

So then, what *can* I say that you will consider acceptable to all who pray to me for peace to come soon, for peace and justness and love to reign on Earth? I can say this: *I hear your prayers – they are my very own prayers! – and they shall be answered as we who desire this wish!*

The days at hand are the final chapter of violence, hatred, grief, destruction, tyranny, and death as you know it on Earth. Even as the war rages, as death claims physical bodies and beloved souls are greeted in Nirvana, the promised new era is being ushered in. Sources most of you don't know are helping you and your planet with abundant and profound aid – the light, love and technology of my children of civilizations who at the right moment will introduce themselves to you.

These are the long, sad, dark days before the universal brotherhood can make known their presence among you and be your helpers in restoring your planet. The darkest of souls, wherein lies the free will that I cannot control, curtail or even touch by my own love because they refuse it, will be leaving Earth as their energy cannot withstand the higher energy of the light arriving in your atmosphere by the moment.

Know that this entity you call God or other equally suitable names is "taking sides" with Goodness, the godliness you associate with love, mercy, compassion, justness, caring for one another. I cannot intervene in or circumvent the laws of Creator that have allowed desecration of that Goodness by the free will of dark souls who equally are a part of me, but I can speak my piece for my children of Earth and its sanctuary realm Nirvana whose godliness remains:

The radiance of Spirit, your planet restored to her former glory, and the abiding love of All is One is what you came into this lifetime to experience. And you SHALL, on Earth as it is in Heaven! Know that this is so!

THE MATTHEW BOOKS

The first book in the series is
Matthew, Tell Me About Heaven.

Matthew Ward
1962-1980

"The dialog between Matthew and his mother is nothing less than an instruction manual that can rescue the human race—just in time. It should be printed in every language and read by—or to—everyone from the age of seven upwards. It is probably the most complete picture the world has ever had of the Universe we all came from and to which we will all return when our lives here have run their course."

— **Michael Joseph**, author; London

The second book is *Revelations for a New Era.*

"*Revelations for a New Era* embodies the very essence of being. It has simultaneously given me reassurance of self and opened a doorway into a universe of grand design. Thank you again for your efforts in enabling this material to be available for the benefit of all spirits."

— **David Leas**, New York

The Matthew Books can be ordered through
www.matthewbooks.com or your favorite local or
on-line bookstore.

GLOSSARY

Akashic records. Universal recording and storage system
of all souls' experiencing in all lifetimes

Angelic realms. Placements of love and light closest to Creator

Angels. Collective beings of light manifested by archangels
in co-creation with Creator

Archangels. First beings created by Creator

Aspect. Individuated part of a cumulative soul; also called
personage, soul fragment, God spark

Balance. Goal and epitome of all experiencing

Christ. State of being one with God

Christed light. Manifestation of Creator's love, constantly
available to all beings for soul evolvement and protection
from dark forces

Co-creation. Process or product of souls manifesting in
conjunction with Creator

Cosmos. The total of creation

Creator. Supreme Being of the cosmos; also referred to as
Totality, Oneness, All That Is, I AM, etc.; sometimes
used interchangeably with God to denote supreme
being of our universe

Cumulative soul. Ever-expanding composite of all experiencing in all lifetimes of its individual personages

Dark forces, darkness. Powers originating in deepest
antiquity whose experiencing choices eliminated all
light except a connective spark to Creator; foes of light
beings and of the light itself

Density. In accordance with universal laws, dimensions of
soul experiencing and spiritual evolvement descending
from the pure light and love of Creator into total spiritual darkness

Energy. Basis of all life throughout the cosmos

Energy attachment. Positive or negative interpretation given the effects of any energy motion

Etheric body. Body used in spirit realms

Extraterrestrial. Anywhere beyond planet Earth; non-Earth civilizations

Free will. Each soul's ability to choose and manifest lifetime experiencing

God. One name given the supreme being of our universe, and as such, possessing the power, wisdom and knowledge of Creator to rule this universe

Godself. Each person's inseparable and constant link with God; also known as higher self, inner self, soul-self

Guardian angel. Primary celestial helper assigned to each person for spiritual guidance and physical protection

Karma. Cause and effect of a soul exercising free will; basis for selecting subsequent lifetime experiencing

Light. Creator's wisdom, love and the power of love manifested in energy form

Lost souls. Souls whose free will choices led to entrenchment in the basest density placement

Manifestation. Process or product of co-creating with Creator or God; the inherent ability and indivisible aspect of free will

Mission. Primary purpose of each Earth lifetime, selected for spiritual growth by the soul prior to birth of its personage; the selection by souls regardless of form throughout the universe

Negativity. Destructive forces initiated and expanded by dark thought forms

Personage. Independent and inviolate essence of a soul experiencing an incarnate lifetime

Placement. Realm composed of various related areas for
   specific experiencing
Prayer. Direct communion with God through thoughts and
   feelings
Pre-birth agreement. Soul level agreement made prior to
   incarnation by all primary souls participating in a
   shared lifetime
Reincarnation. Return to a physical life after a discarnate life
Soul. Spiritual life force; inviolate essence of each individual's inextricable connection with Creator, God and all
   other life forms throughout the universe
Spirit guides. Discarnate beings other than angels who are
   our unseen helpers
Thought forms. Indelible and eternal energy substances
   produced by mental processes of all souls from the
   Beginning; the stuff of universal knowledge
Transition. After death of the physical body, the soul's
   lightning-fast passage in etheric body to Nirvana
Universal laws. Parameters within which all souls experi-
   ence and to which all are subject; also called laws of
   God, laws of nature
Universe. One of several such placements manifested by Creator
   and the angelic realms